Table of Contents

Numbers **2**
These pages help improve the child's number skills. They include practice activities for number recognition and counting from 1-100, printing numerals to 20, skip counting, and number sequence. This section also reinforces the child's understanding of *more* and *less*, *larger* and *smaller*, and *before*, *after*, and *between*.

Addition **36**
Develop and sharpen the child's math skills with this section, which includes activities for learning addition facts to 18, place value, and 1- and 2-digit number addition.

Subtraction **67**
In this section, the child practices subtraction facts from 18 and below, learns the inverse relationship between addition and subtraction, and begins subtracting 1-digit numbers from 2-digit numbers.

Math Concepts **98**
A variety of early math concepts are presented in these pages, including bar graphs, shapes, patterns, standard and non-standard units of measurement, and first fractions.

Time & Money **126**
This section teaches time to the hour and half-hour for both analog and digital clocks. It also presents the value of coins and helps the child learn to count and add them.

Phonics I **152**
These pages teach and reinforce consonant sounds, consonant blends, and short vowel sounds.

Phonics II **187**
In addition to teaching long vowel sounds and the variety of spelling patterns that represent them, these pages teach the sounds of diphthongs, digraphs, *r*-controlled vowels, and *a*/consonant combinations.

Grammar & Writing Skills I **224**
This fun-filled section teaches noun and verb identification and usage, subject-verb agreement, and the present tense forms of commonly used irregular verbs.

Grammar & Writing Skills II **256**
The variety of language skills presented in this section includes adjective identification, punctuation and capitalization usage, writing short letters and book titles, and forming compound words.

Reading Comprehension **286**
These pages introduce commonly used words, develop skills in reading and completing sentences and stories, and teach comprehension skills such as identifying the main idea and details of a story, making inferences, drawing conclusions, and understanding cause and effect.

Garden Counting Fun

 1    2    3    4    5

Count. Trace and circle the right number.

   Counting objects and tracing numerals 1–5

How Many Friends?

Count. Write how many.

9

Have a Ball

Count. Write how many.

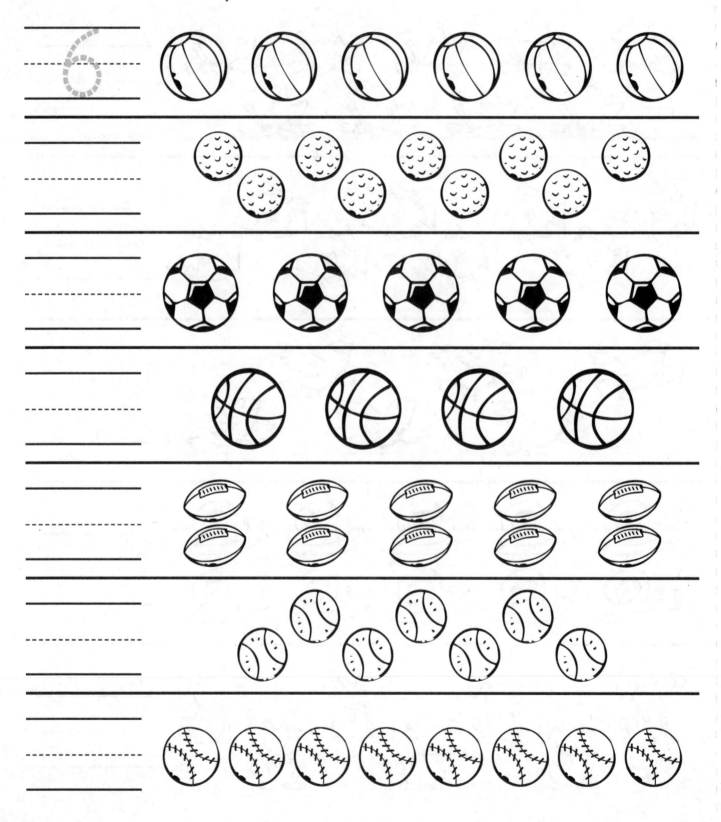

Counting objects and writing numerals to 10

1 to 10, Then 10 to 1

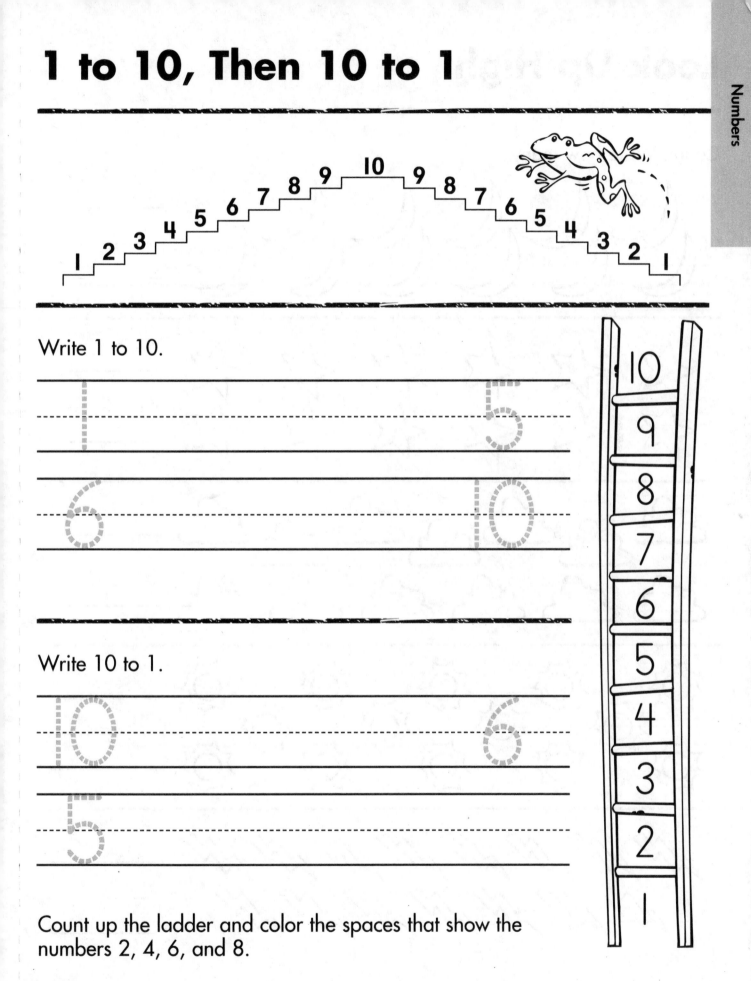

Write 1 to 10.

Write 10 to 1.

Count up the ladder and color the spaces that show the numbers 2, 4, 6, and 8.

Look Up High

Count. Write how many.

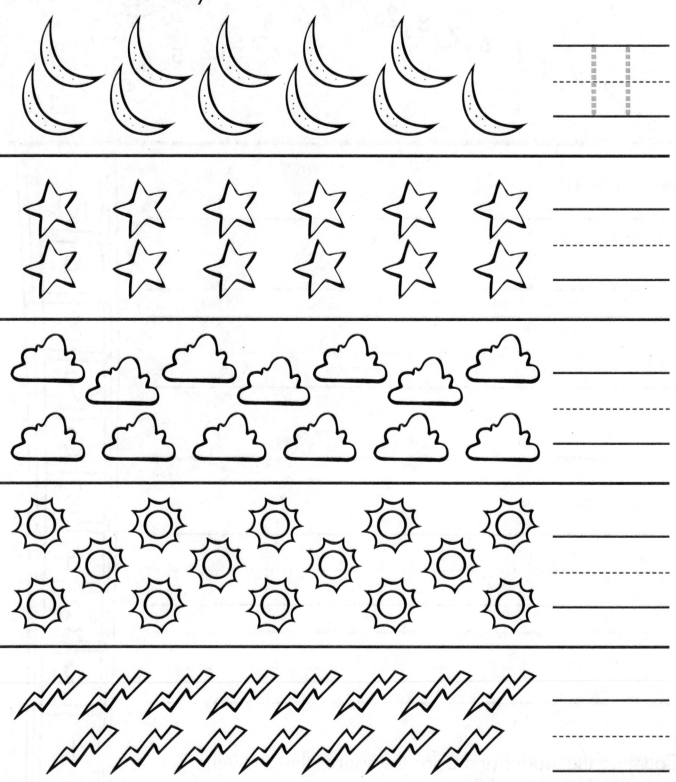

Counting objects and writing numerals 11–15

Fruity Snacks

Trace the number in each box. Draw lines to match.

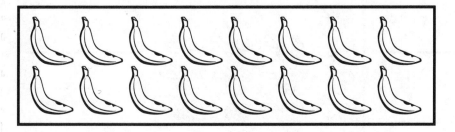 

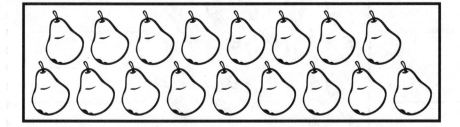 

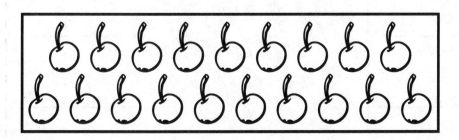 

Counting objects and tracing numerals 16–20

7

School Supplies

Count. Write how many.

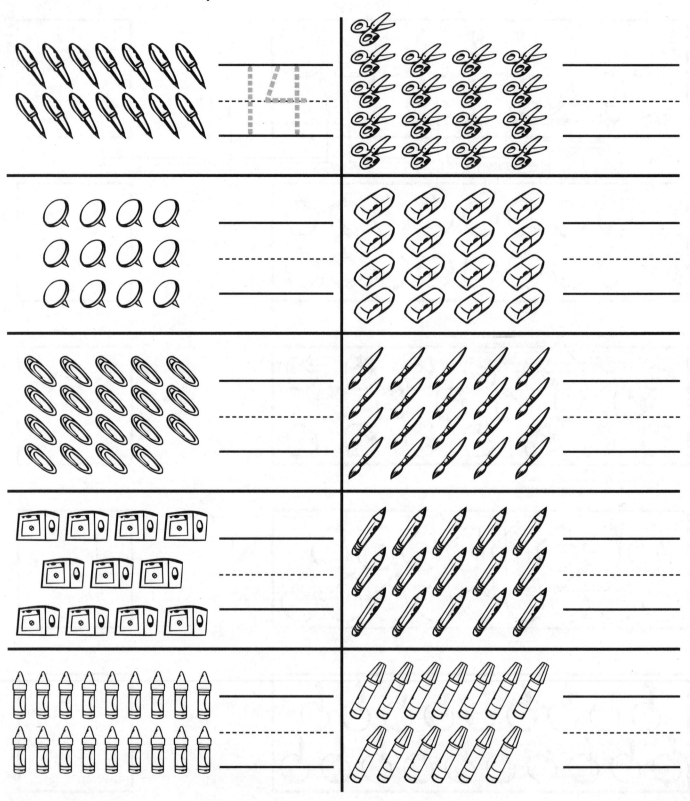

Counting and writing numerals to 20

All Numbers Aboard!

Write 1 to 20.

Dot's Great!

Connect the dots from 1 to 20. Color the picture.

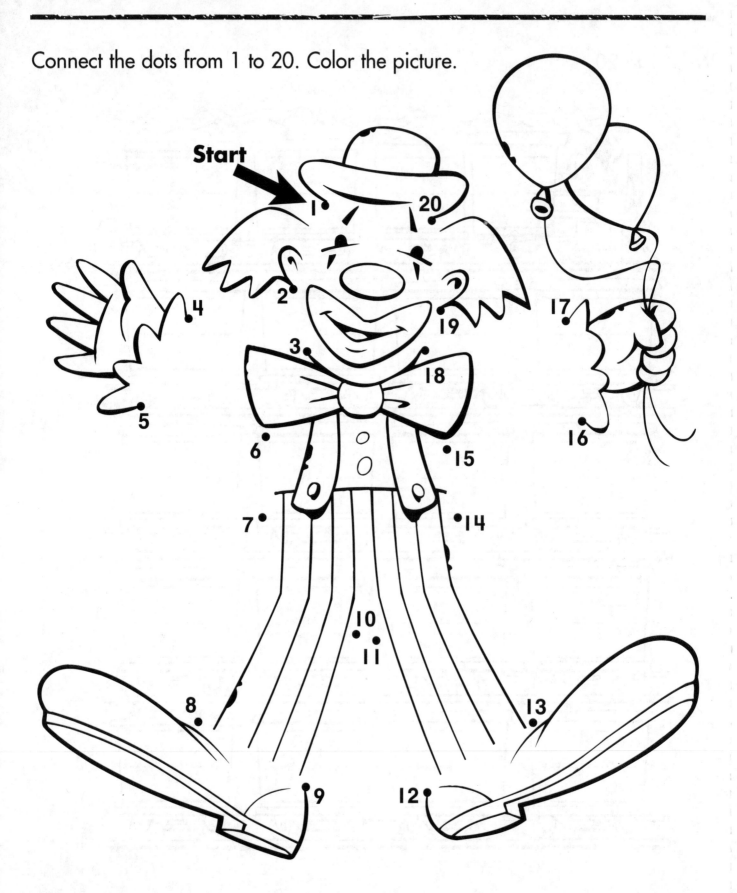

Start

Counting and sequencing numbers 1–20

Counting by 2's

Eight big cats walk two by two.

Count by 2's. Write the numbers.

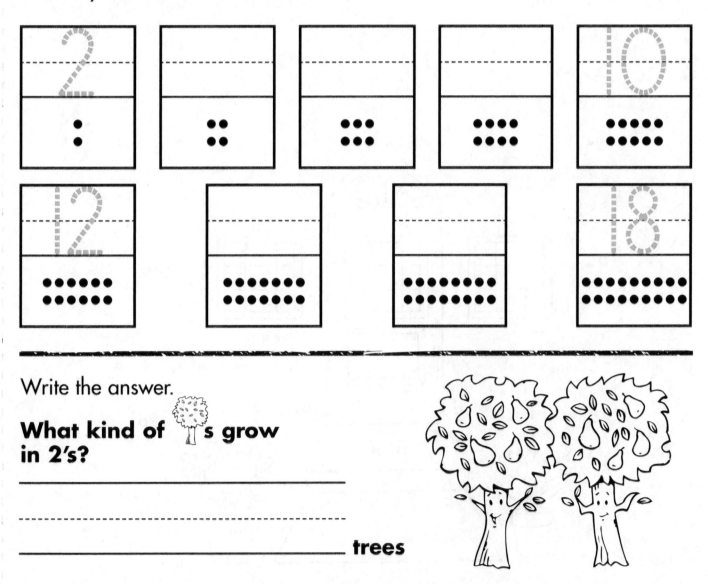

Write the answer.

What kind of 🌳's grow in 2's?

_____

_____ **trees**

Home for Twos

2 4 6 8 10 12 14 16 18 20 22 24 26 28 30

Count by 2's to connect the dots.
Color the picture.

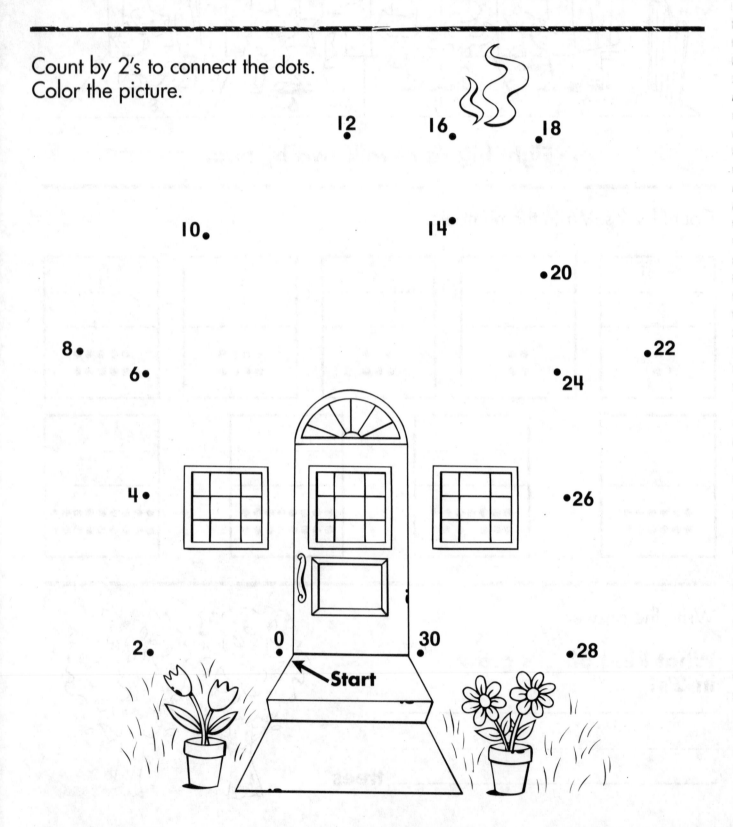

Counting and sequencing numbers by 2's

How Many Shoes?

Count by 2's. Write the number.

Counting by 5's

Count by 5's to 50. Say the numbers.

5 10 15 20 25 30 35 40 45 50
55 60 65 70 75 80 85 90 95 100

Count by 5's. Write the missing numbers.

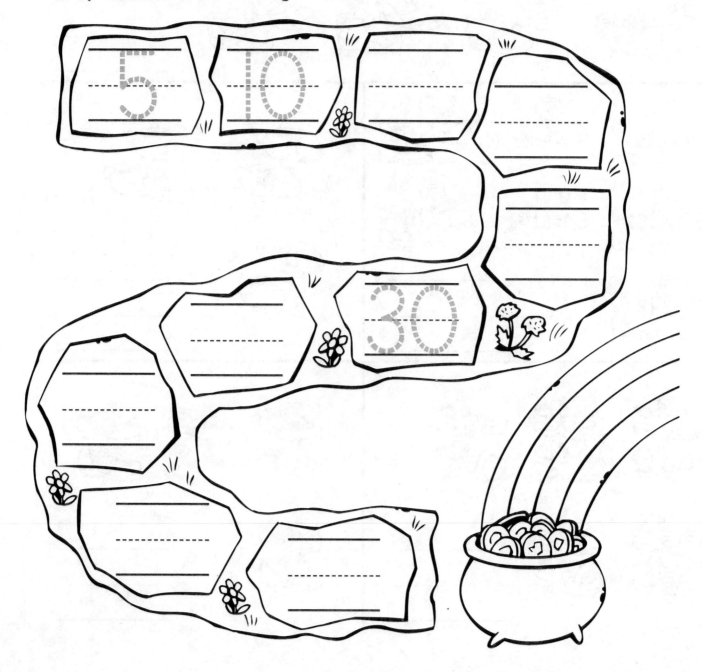

Counting and writing numbers by 5's

Give Me Five

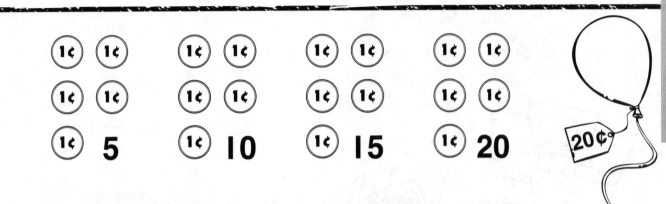

Count by 5's to 50. Write the numbers.

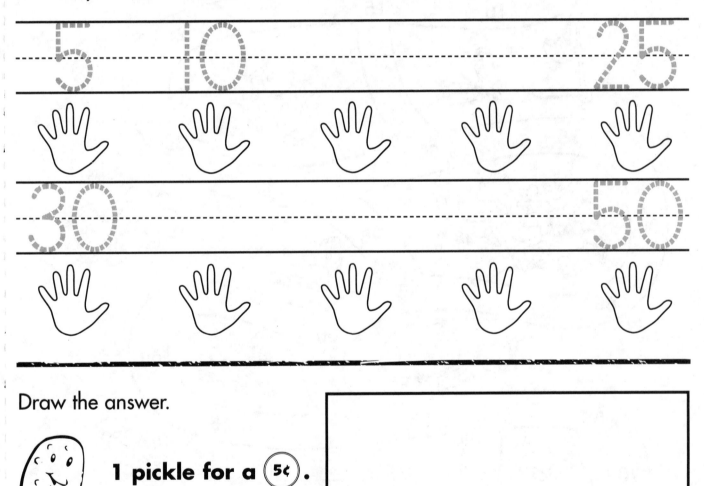

Draw the answer.

1 pickle for a 5¢ .

How many 1¢ s?

A-maze-ing Fives

Count by 5's to draw a path through the maze.

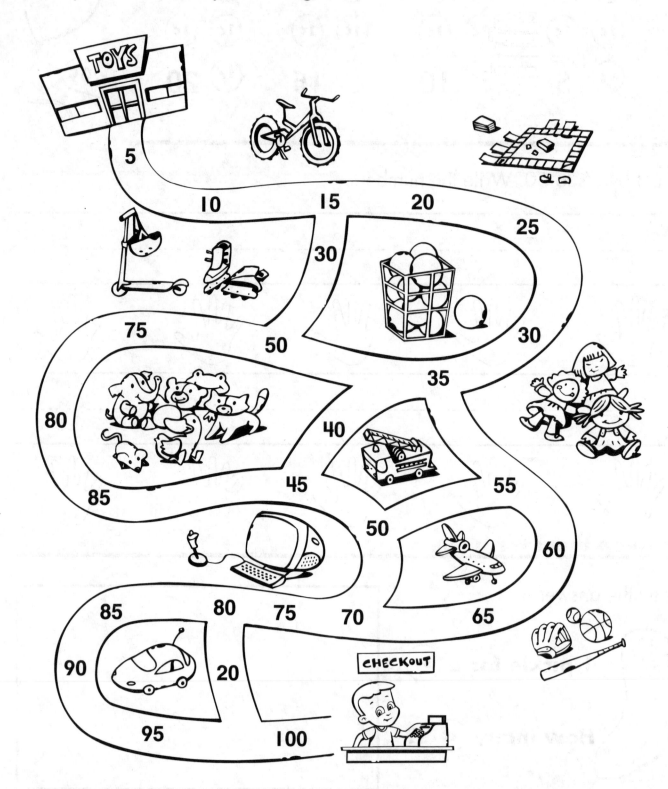

Counting and sequencing numbers by 5's

Counting by 10's

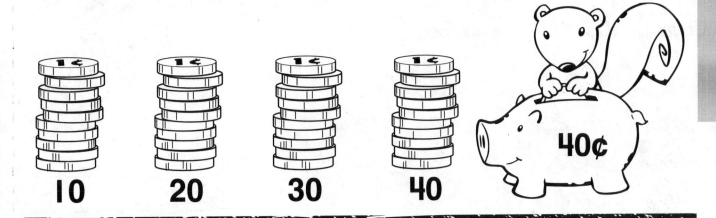

10   20   30   40   40¢

Count by 10's to 100. Write the numbers.

10 20   50

60   100

Count 10 (1¢) s at a time,

or swap them for a (10¢).

How many (10¢) s equal

these stacks of (1¢) s?

_____

- - - - - - - - - -

Write the number. _____

Counting and writing numbers by 10's

Counting Marbles

Count by 10's. Write the number.

_____

- - - - - - - - - - - -

_____

_____

- - - - - - - - - - - -

_____

_____

- - - - - - - - - - - -

_____

_____

- - - - - - - - - - - -

_____

_____

- - - - - - - - - - - -

_____

Counting and writing numbers by 10's

Missing Tens

Count by 10's. Write the missing numbers. Color the caterpillars.

10	20	30	40	50	60	70	80	90	100

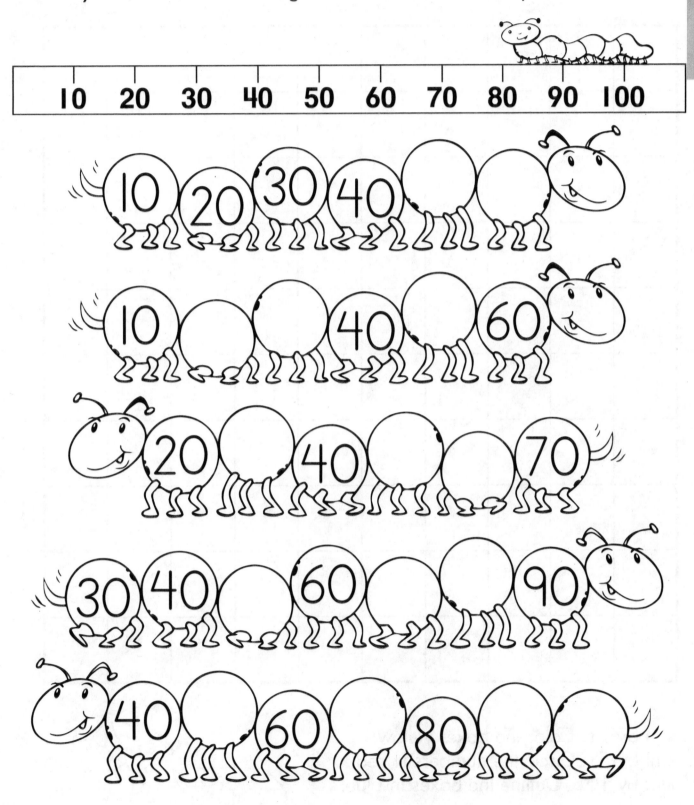

Counting and writing numbers by 10's

19

Chart Your Way

Write the numbers to finish the chart.

1	2			5			8		10
11		13				17		19	20
21			24	25				29	30
31		33			36		38	39	
	42		44			47			50
51				55	56				60
61			64			67		69	
71		73			76				80
	82			85			88		90
91			94		96		98		100

Count by 2's. Color the boxes yellow.
Count by 5's. Circle the numbers in red.
Count by 10's. Outline the boxes in blue.

20 Counting and writing numbers from 1–100

Zoo Detective

Look at the pictures in the chart. What numbers belong there?
Write the number beside each picture below.

1	2	3	4	5	6		8	9	10
11	12	13	14	15		17	18	19	20
21	22		24	25	26	27	28		30
31	32	33	34	35	36		38	39	40
	42	43	44	45	46	47	48	49	50
51	52	53		55	56	57	58	59	
61	62	63	64	65		67	68	69	70
71		73	74	75	76	77	78	79	80
81	82	83	84		86	87	88	89	90
91	92	93	94	95	96		98	99	100

Counting and writing numbers from 1–100

One More, One Less

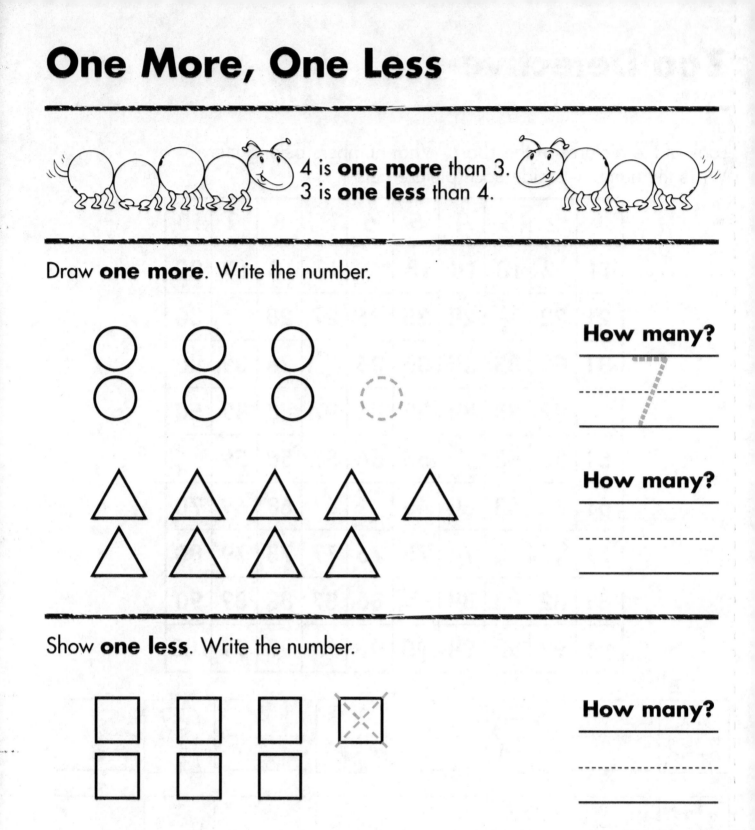

4 is **one more** than 3.
3 is **one less** than 4.

Draw **one more**. Write the number.

How many?

7

How many?

Show **one less**. Write the number.

How many?

How many?

Constructing and recording sets with one more or one less

Counting Bears

5 is **more** than 2.

Circle the number that is **more**.

1	(4)	3	6
6	8	9	11
10	7	15	12

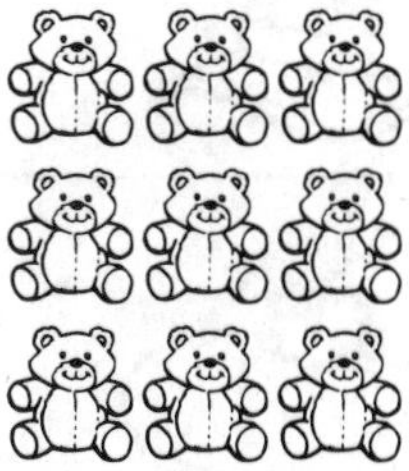

So Many Hats

Color the set in each row that shows **less**.

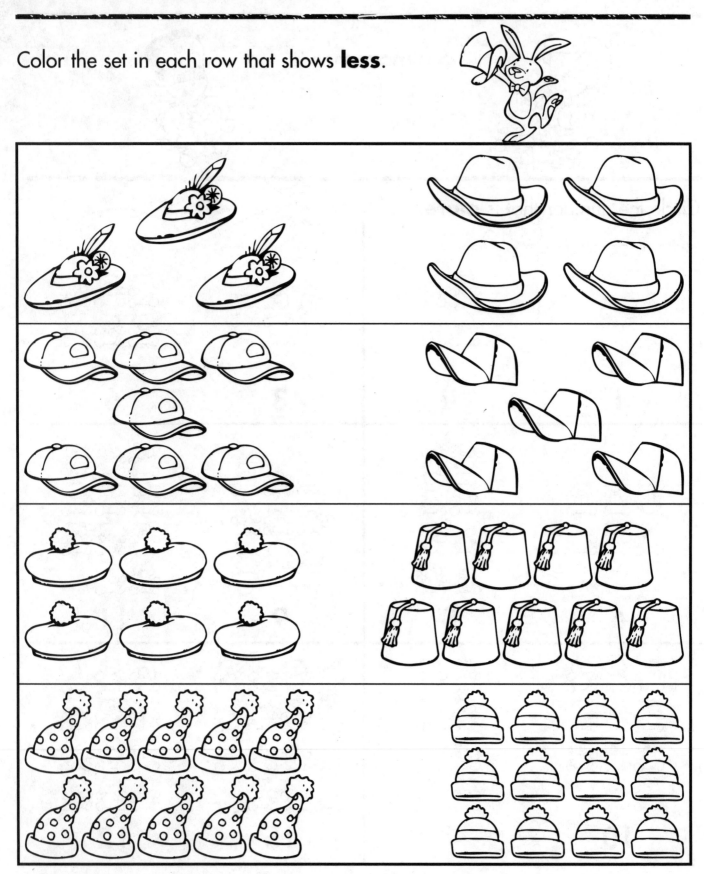

Identifying the set that shows less

Before

3 comes **before** 4.

Write the number that comes **before**.

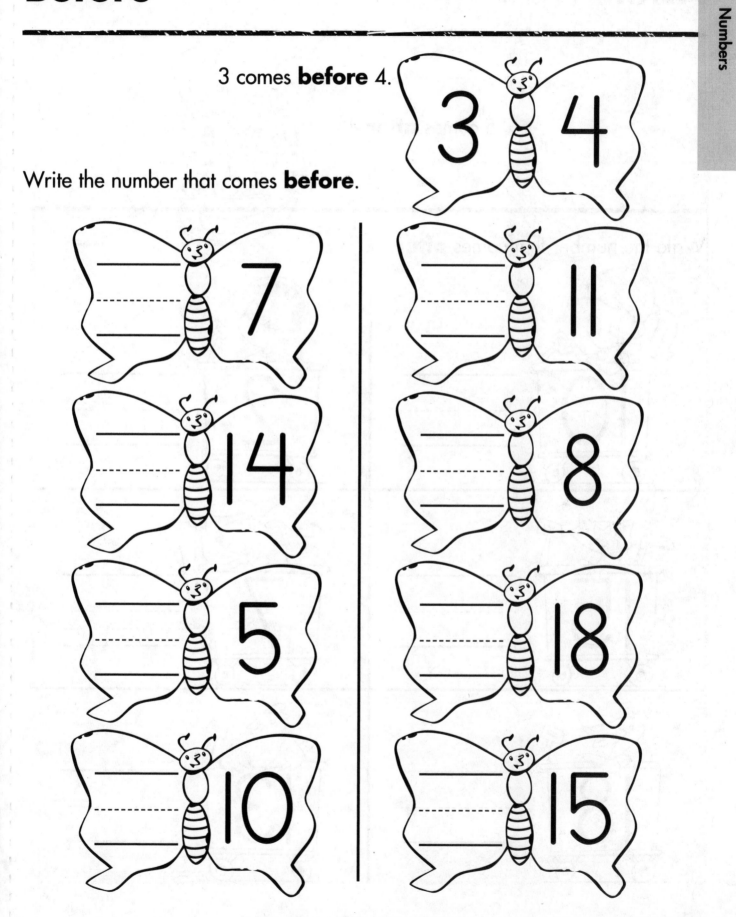

After

5 comes **after** 4.

Write the number that comes **after**.

10 _____

2 _____

15 _____

7 _____

18 _____

13 _____

Writing the number that comes after

Between

4 comes **between** 3 and 5.

Write the number that comes **between**.

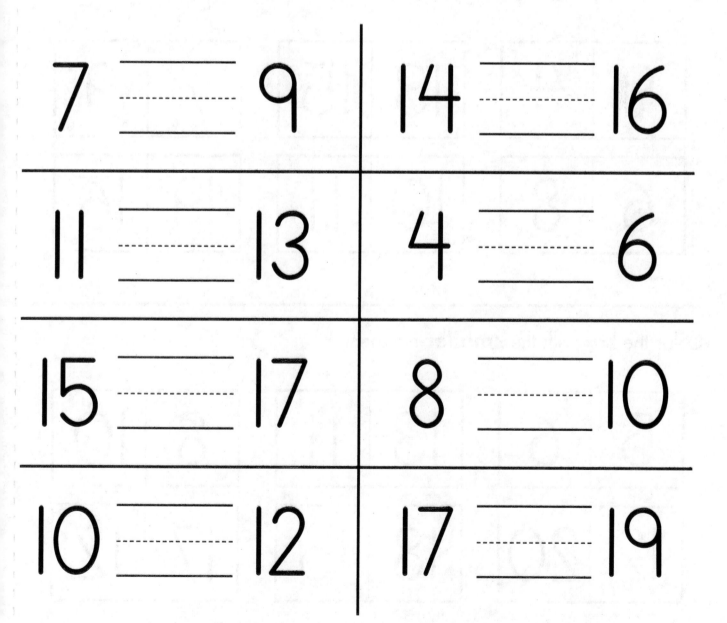

7 ___ 9	14 ___ 16
11 ___ 13	4 ___ 6
15 ___ 17	8 ___ 10
10 ___ 12	17 ___ 19

Larger and Smaller

5 is the **larger** number.
3 is the **smaller** number.

Color the box with the **larger** number.

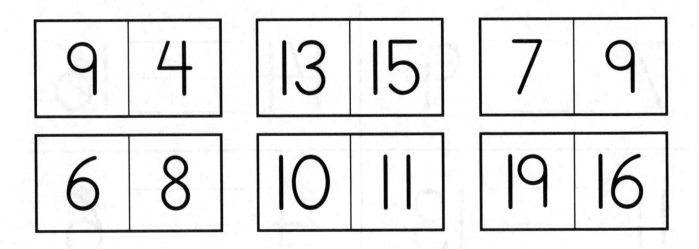

Color the box with the **smaller** number.

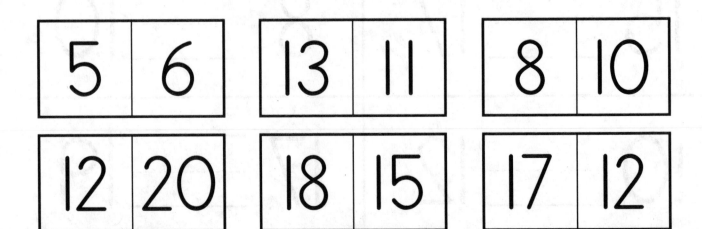

Identifying larger and smaller numbers

Largest and Smallest

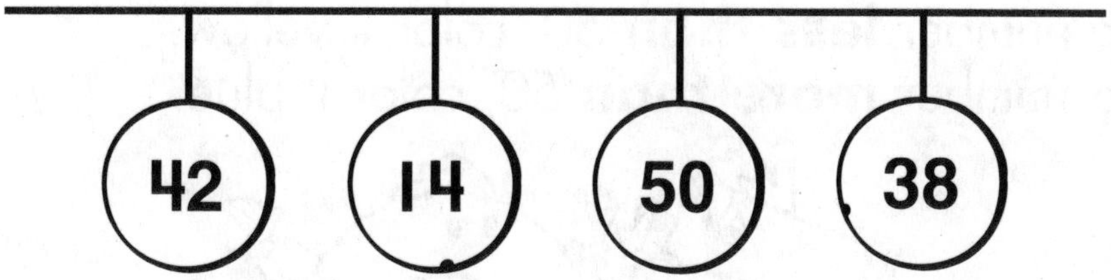

42 14 50 38

50 is the **largest** number.
14 is the **smallest** number.

Circle the **largest** number. Draw a square around the **smallest** number.

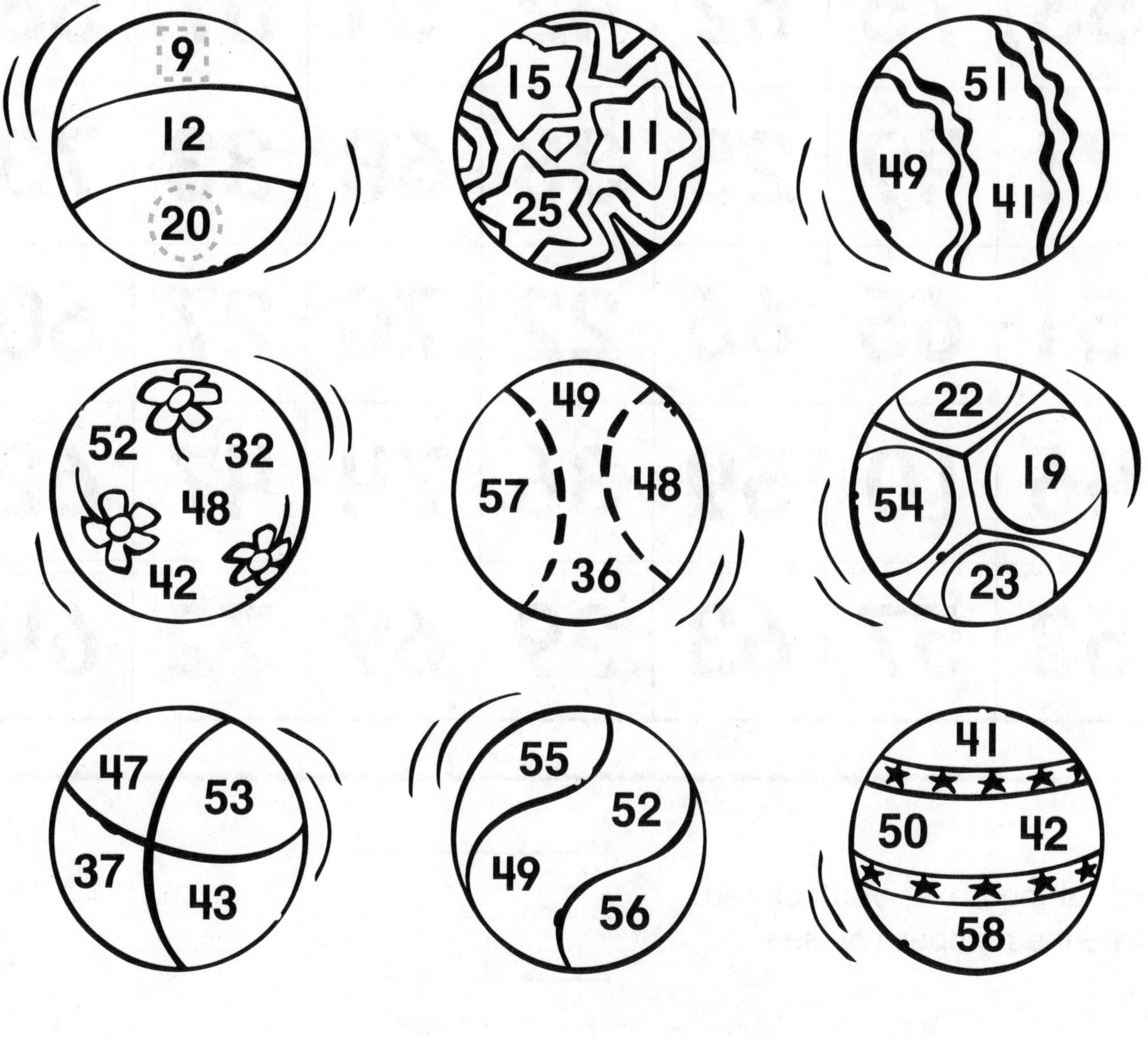

9
12
20

15
11
25

51
49
41

52 32
48
42

49
57 48
36

22
54 19
23

47
53
37
43

55
52
49
56

41
50 42
58

Comparing 2-digit numbers   **29**

50 More or Less

If a box shows a number **less than** 50, color it yellow.
If a box shows a number **more than** 50, color it blue.

53	75	62	42	61	67	58
71	49	25	38	68	33	73
51	65	66	22	70	27	60
46	10	59	36	74	47	62
53	57	63	29	69	72	64

Look at the boxes you colored.
Write the number you see.

_____
- - - - - - - - - - - - - - - - -
_____

Comparing 2-digit numbers

Roller Coaster

Write the missing numbers.

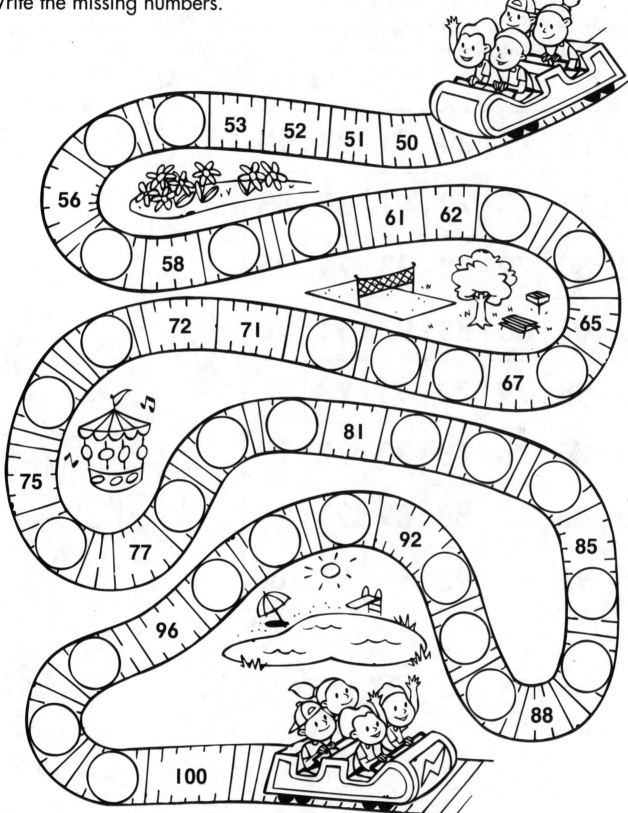

Garden Path

Color the boxes from 75 to 100, in order, to make a path from Start to Finish. Then color the rest of the picture.

Start

75	76	77	80	81	93	94
78	71	78	79	91	80	83
72	89	79	83	93	94	95
82	81	80	88	92	91	96
83	88	79	72	91	98	97
84	76	75	78	90	92	98
85	86	87	88	89	93	99
88	92	94	93	91	87	100

Finish

Answer Key

As the child completes the pages in this section, review his or her answers. When you take the time to correct the work and explain mistakes, you're showing your child that you feel learning is important.

page 2

Garden Counting Fun

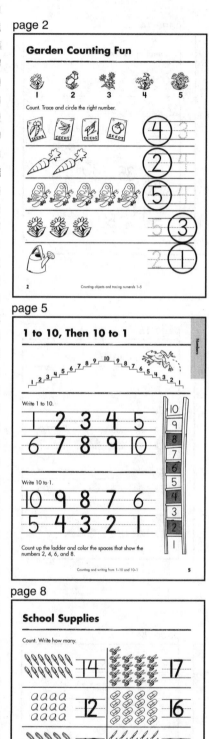

page 3

How Many Friends?

page 4

Have a Ball

page 5

1 to 10, Then 10 to 1

page 6

Look Up High

page 7

Fruity Snacks

page 8

School Supplies

page 9

All Numbers Aboard!

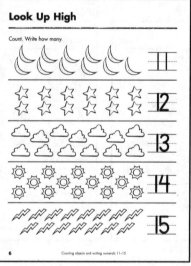

page 10

Dot's Great!

page 11

Counting by 2's

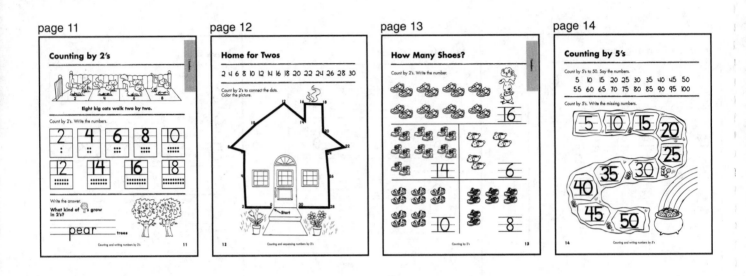

Eight big cats walk two by two.

Count by 2's. Write the numbers.

2	4	6	8	10

12	14	16	18

Write the answer.

What kind of 🍐's grow in 2's?

__pear__ trees

Counting and writing numbers by 2's   11

page 12

Home for Twos

2 4 6 8 10 12 14 16 18 20 22 24 26 28 30

Count by 2's to connect the dots.
Color the picture.

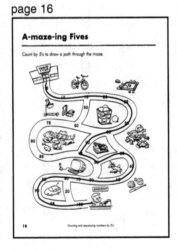

Start

12   Counting and sequencing numbers by 2's

page 13

How Many Shoes?

Count by 2's. Write the number.

16

14   6

10   8

Counting by 2's   13

page 14

Counting by 5's

Count by 5's to 50. Say the numbers.

5 10 15 20 25 30 35 40 45 50
55 60 65 70 75 80 85 90 95 100

Count by 5's. Write the missing numbers.

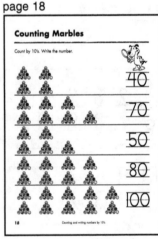

5 10 15 20 25 35 30 40 45 50

14   Counting and writing numbers by 5's

page 15

Give Me Five

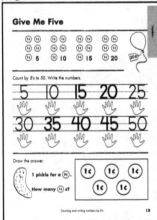

5   10   15   20

Count by 5's to 50. Write the numbers.

5	10	15	20	25

30	35	40	45	50

Draw the answer.

1 pickle for a 🪙.

How many 🪙s?

1¢ 1¢ 1¢
1¢ 1¢

Counting and writing numbers by 5's   15

page 16

A-maze-ing Fives

Count by 5's to draw a path through the maze.

16   Counting and sequencing numbers by 5's

page 17

Counting by 10's

10 20 30 40   40¢

Count by 10's to 100. Write the numbers.

10 20 30 40 50
60 70 80 90 100

Count 10's at a time,
or swap them for a 🪙.

How many 🪙s equal
these stacks of 10's?

Write the number.   2

Counting and writing numbers by 10's   17

page 18

Counting Marbles

Count by 10's. Write the number.

40

70

50

80

100

18   Counting and writing numbers by 10's

page 19

Missing Tens

Count by 10's. Write the missing numbers. Color the caterpillars.

10 20 30 40 50 60 70 80 90 100

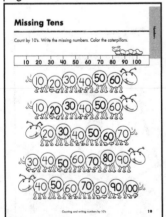

10 20 30 40 50 60

10 20 30 40 50 60

20 30 40 50 60 70

30 40 50 60 70 80 90

40 50 60 70 80 90 100

Counting and writing numbers by 10's   19

page 20

Chart Your Way

Write the numbers to finish the chart.

1	2	3	4	5	6	7	8	9	10
11	12	13	14	15	16	17	18	19	20
21	22	23	24	25	26	27	28	29	30
31	32	33	34	35	36	37	38	39	40
41	42	43	44	45	46	47	48	49	50
51	52	53	54	55	56	57	58	59	60
61	62	63	64	65	66	67	68	69	70
71	72	73	74	75	76	77	78	79	80
81	82	83	84	85	86	87	88	89	90
91	92	93	94	95	96	97	98	99	100

Count by 2's. Color the boxes yellow.
Count by 5's. Circle the numbers in red.
Count by 10's. Outline the boxes in blue.

20   Counting and writing numbers from 1–100

page 21

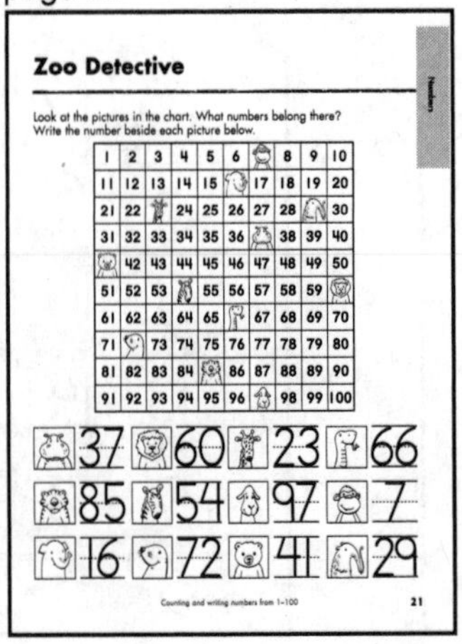

Zoo Detective

Look at the pictures in the chart. What numbers belong there?
Write the number beside each picture below.

1	2	3	4	5	6	7	8	9	10
11	12	13	14	15	16	17	18	19	20
21	22	23	24	25	26	27	28	29	30
31	32	33	34	35	36	37	38	39	40
41	42	43	44	45	46	47	48	49	50
51	52	53	54	55	56	57	58	59	60
61	62	63	64	65	66	67	68	69	70
71	72	73	74	75	76	77	78	79	80
81	82	83	84	85	86	87	88	89	90
91	92	93	94	95	96	97	98	99	100

37 60 23 66

85 54 97 7

16 72 41 29

Counting and writing numbers from 1–100   21

page 22

One More, One Less

4 is **one more** than 3.
3 is **one less** than 4.

Draw **one more**. Write the number.

○ ○ ○ ○ ○   How many? 7

△ △ △ △ △   How many? 10

Show **one less**. Write the number.

□ □ □ ⊠   How many? 6

☆ ☆ ✻ ☆ ☆   How many? 4

22   Constructing and recording sets with one more or one less

34   Answers

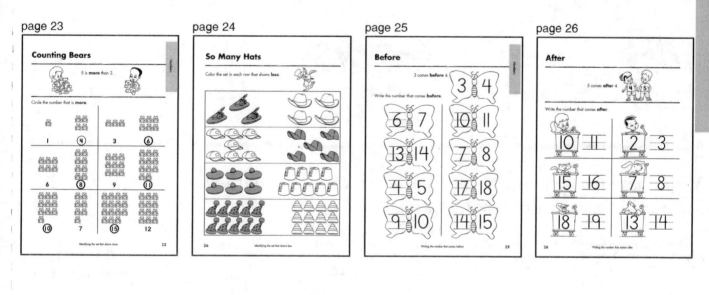

page 23 — Counting Bears

page 24 — So Many Hats

page 25 — Before

page 26 — After

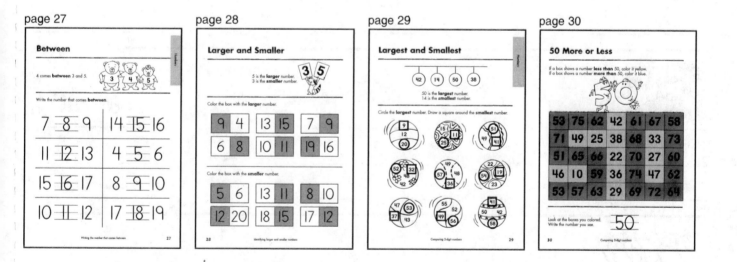

page 27 — Between

page 28 — Larger and Smaller

page 29 — Largest and Smallest

page 30 — 50 More or Less

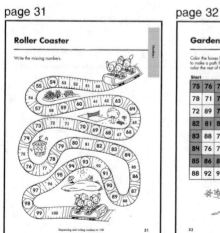

page 31 — Roller Coaster

page 32 — Garden Path

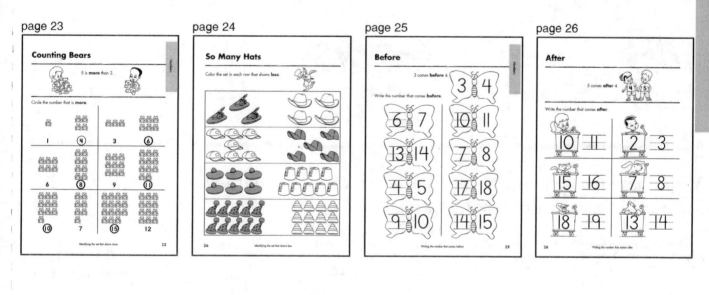

Answers

So Many Flowers

1   +   2   =   **in all**
                                      3

Write how many in each group. If there are none, write **0**.
Then add to show how many in all.

in all

3   +   0   =   3

in all

_____ + _____ = _____

in all

_____ + _____ = _____

in all

_____ + _____ = _____

Adding numbers to 5; using 0 (zero)

Collecting Sums

Add. Write the sum.

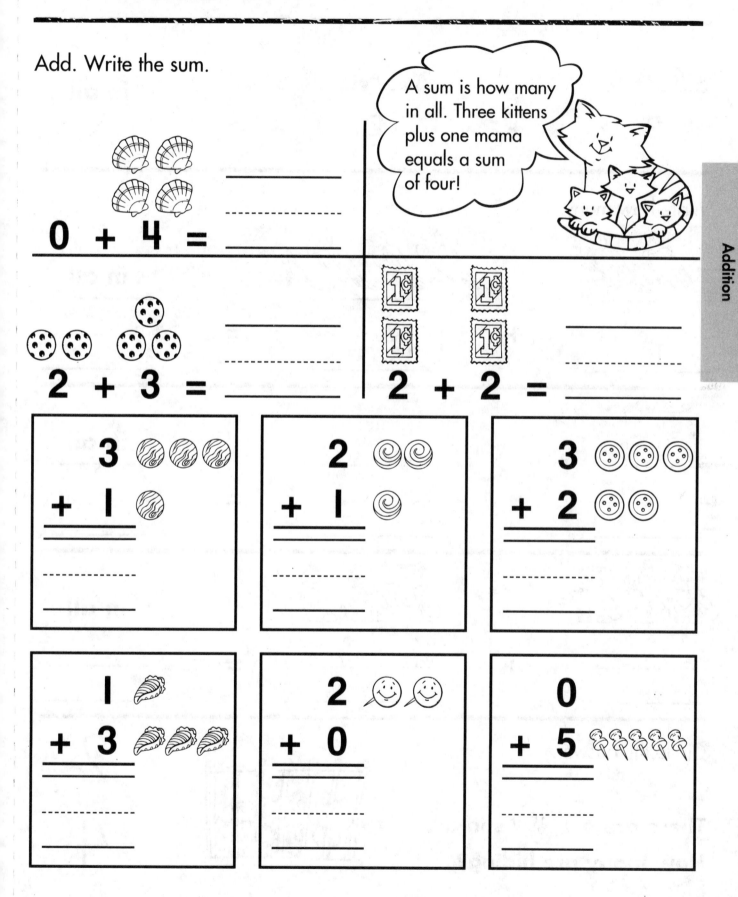

A sum is how many in all. Three kittens plus one mama equals a sum of four!

0 + 4 = _____

2 + 3 = _____

2 + 2 = _____

3
+ 1
_____

2
+ 1
_____

3
+ 2
_____

1
+ 3
_____

2
+ 0
_____

0
+ 5
_____

Animal Math

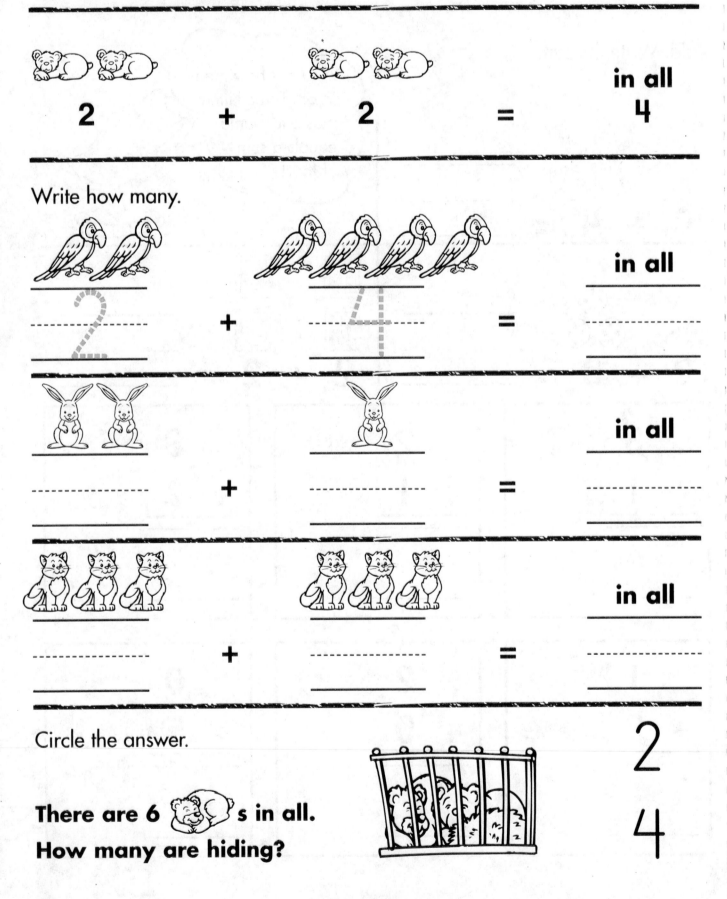

2 + 2 = in all 4

Write how many.

___ in all

2 + 4 =

___ in all

___ + ___ = ___

___ in all

___ + ___ = ___

Circle the answer.

There are 6 🐻's in all.
How many are hiding?

2
4

Adding Treats

$$\begin{array}{r} 3 \\ + 2 \\ \hline 5 \end{array} \text{ in all}$$

Write how many.

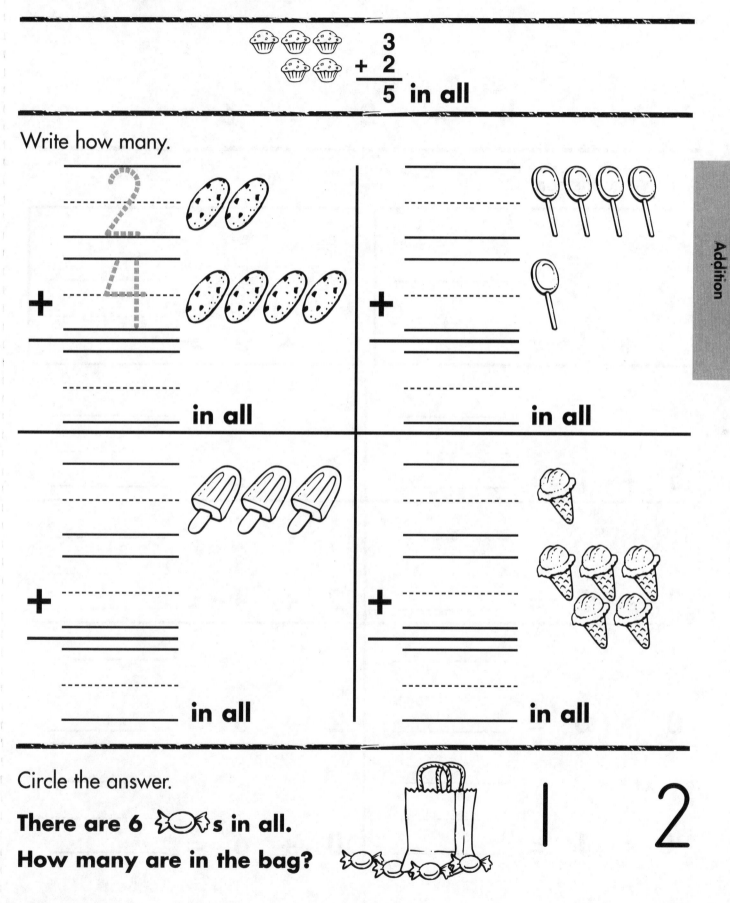

+

_____ in all

+

_____ in all

+

_____ in all

+

_____ in all

Circle the answer.

There are 6 🍬s in all.

How many are in the bag?

1   2

Grocery Store

$$4 + 2 = 6$$

Add. Write the sum.

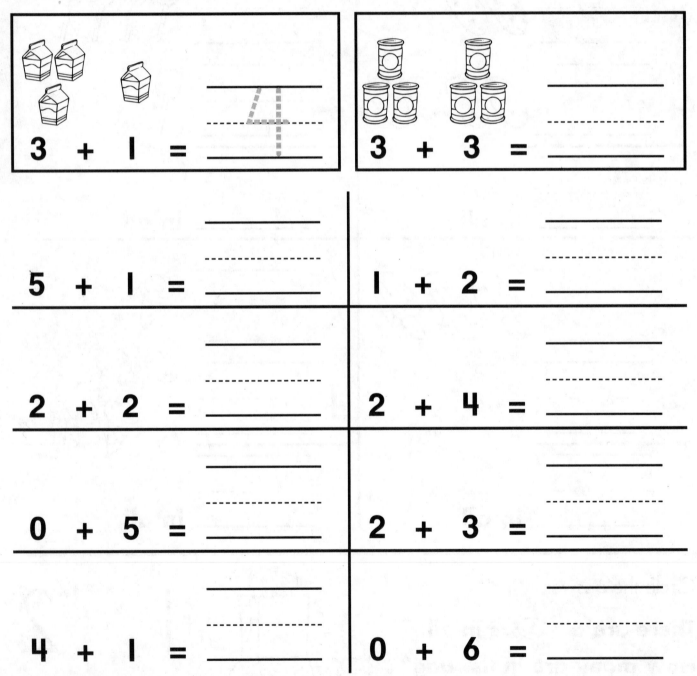

$3 + 1 =$ ____

$3 + 3 =$ ____

$5 + 1 =$ ____

$1 + 2 =$ ____

$2 + 2 =$ ____

$2 + 4 =$ ____

$0 + 5 =$ ____

$2 + 3 =$ ____

$4 + 1 =$ ____

$0 + 6 =$ ____

Finding sums to 6

Frosty Fun

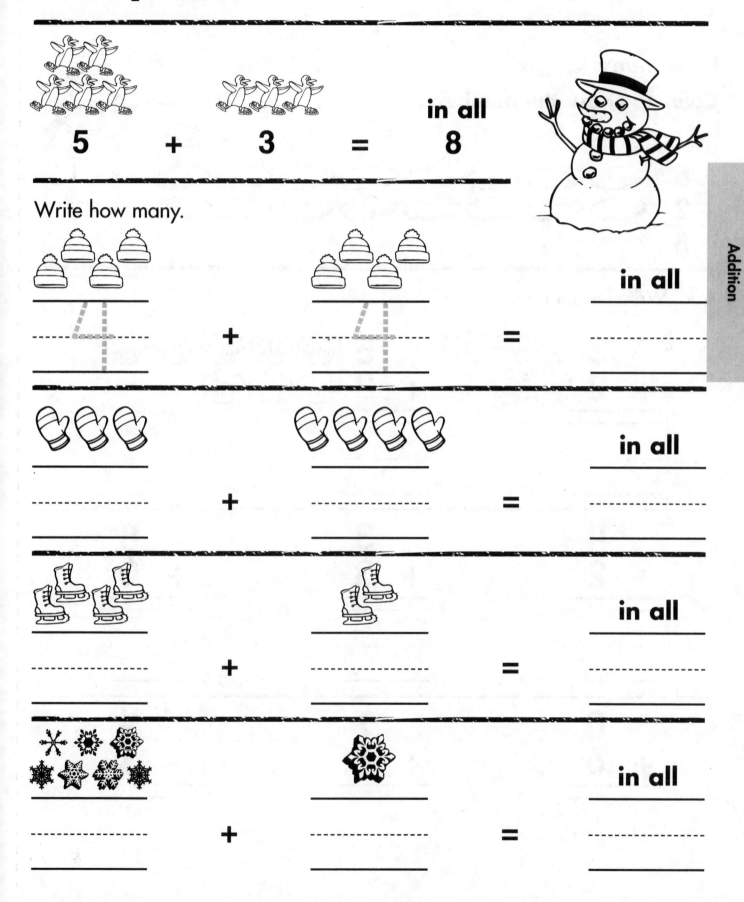

5 + 3 = in all 8

Write how many.

___ + ___ = in all ___

___ + ___ = in all ___

___ + ___ = in all ___

___ + ___ = in all ___

Cooking Up Breakfast Fun

How many 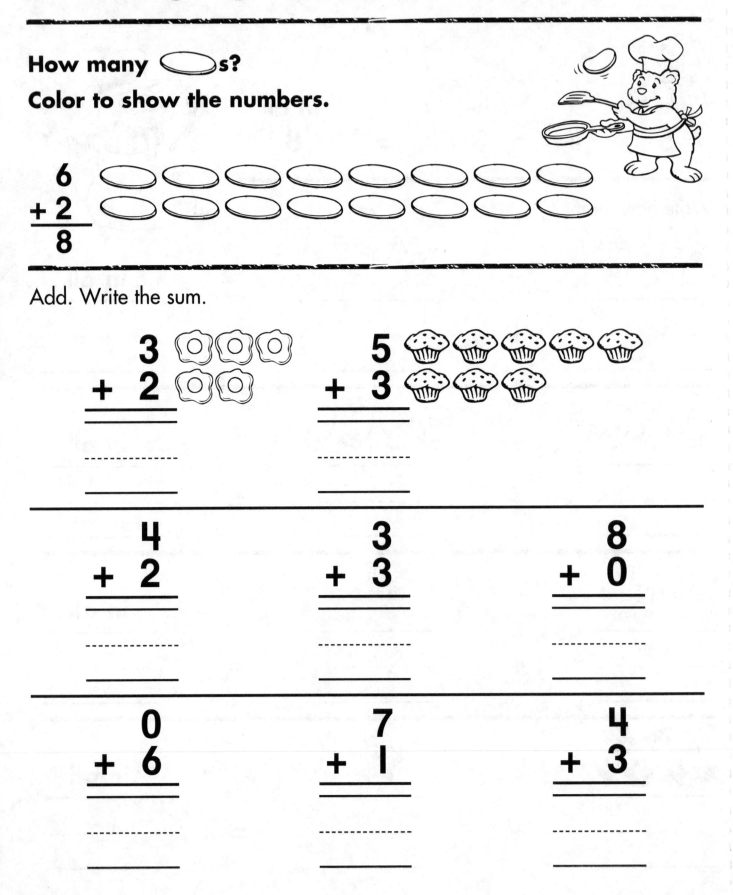s?

Color to show the numbers.

$$
\begin{array}{r}
6 \\
+\,2 \\
\hline
8
\end{array}
$$

Add. Write the sum.

$$
\begin{array}{r}
3 \\
+\,2 \\
\hline
\end{array}
\qquad
\begin{array}{r}
5 \\
+\,3 \\
\hline
\end{array}
$$

$$
\begin{array}{r}
4 \\
+\,2 \\
\hline
\end{array}
\qquad
\begin{array}{r}
3 \\
+\,3 \\
\hline
\end{array}
\qquad
\begin{array}{r}
8 \\
+\,0 \\
\hline
\end{array}
$$

$$
\begin{array}{r}
0 \\
+\,6 \\
\hline
\end{array}
\qquad
\begin{array}{r}
7 \\
+\,1 \\
\hline
\end{array}
\qquad
\begin{array}{r}
4 \\
+\,3 \\
\hline
\end{array}
$$

Finding sums to 8

Tennis, Anyone?

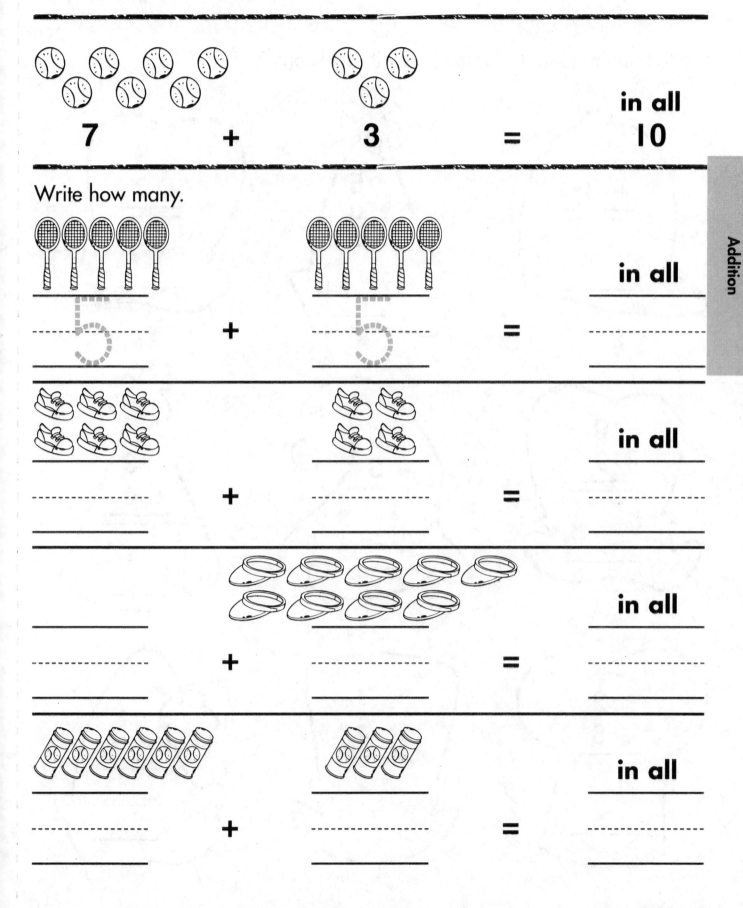

7 + 3 = in all 10

Write how many.

in all
5 + 5 =

in all
+ =

in all
+ =

in all
+ =

Math Hats

Add to find the sums. Color the hats with sums of 10.

7
+ 3
_____

5
+ 4
_____

4
+ 3
_____

0
+ 9
_____

5
+ 5
_____

3
+ 6
_____

2
+ 8
_____

3
+ 5
_____

6
+ 4
_____

Finding sums to 10

Oh, How Colorful!

Color the sections for the sums using the code. Then finish coloring the picture.

10 = red	9 = blue	8 = green
7 = yellow	6 = orange	

Turn-Arounds

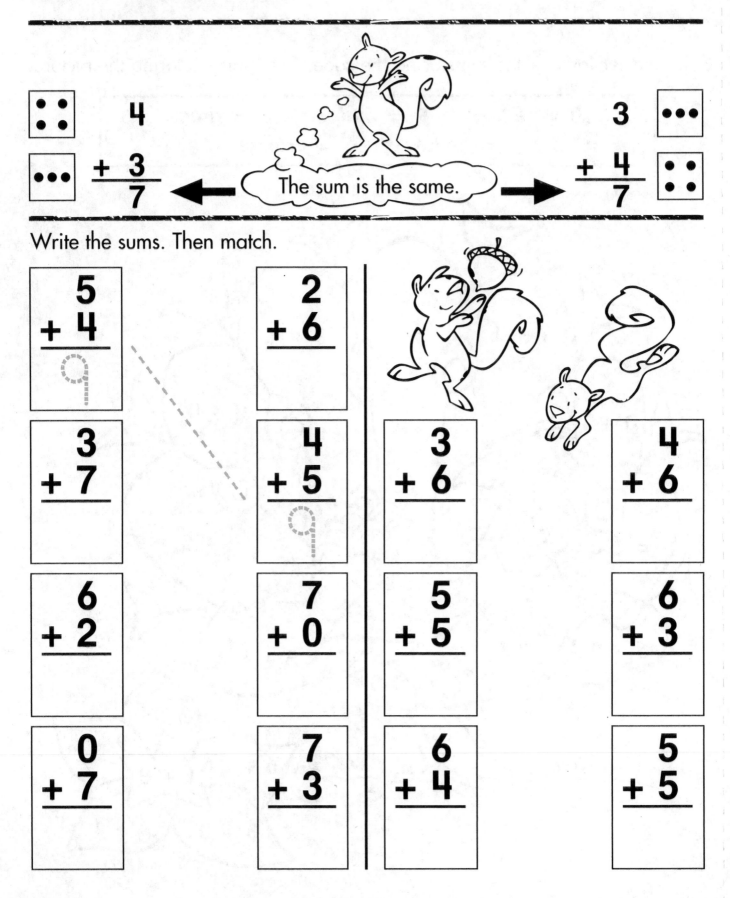

4
••• + 3
      7

The sum is the same.

3
+ 4
  7

Write the sums. Then match.

5
+ 4
  9

2
+ 6

3
+ 7

4
+ 5
  9

3
+ 6

4
+ 6

6
+ 2

7
+ 0

5
+ 5

6
+ 3

0
+ 7

7
+ 3

6
+ 4

5
+ 5

Using turnaround addition facts to find sums

Seashells

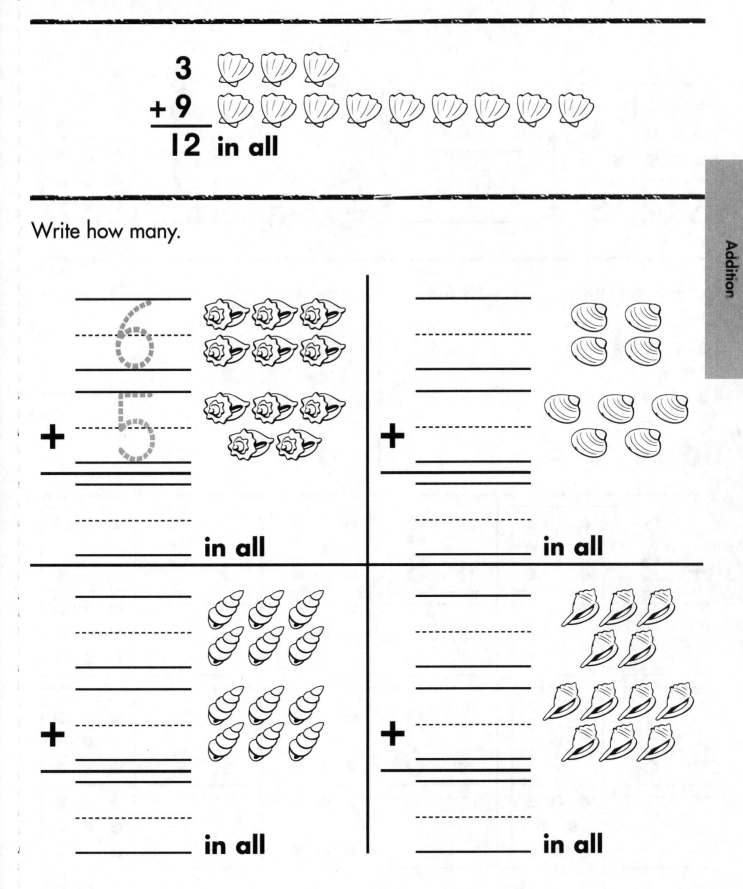

3 🐚🐚🐚
+9 🐚🐚🐚🐚🐚🐚🐚🐚🐚
12 **in all**

Write how many.

6
+ 5
_____ **in all**

_____
+ _____
_____ **in all**

_____
+ _____
_____ **in all**

_____
+ _____
_____ **in all**

Domino Dots

9 + 3 = _12_

$$\begin{array}{r} 3 \\ +\ 9 \\ \hline 12 \end{array}$$

Add. Color the dominos with sums of 10 or more.

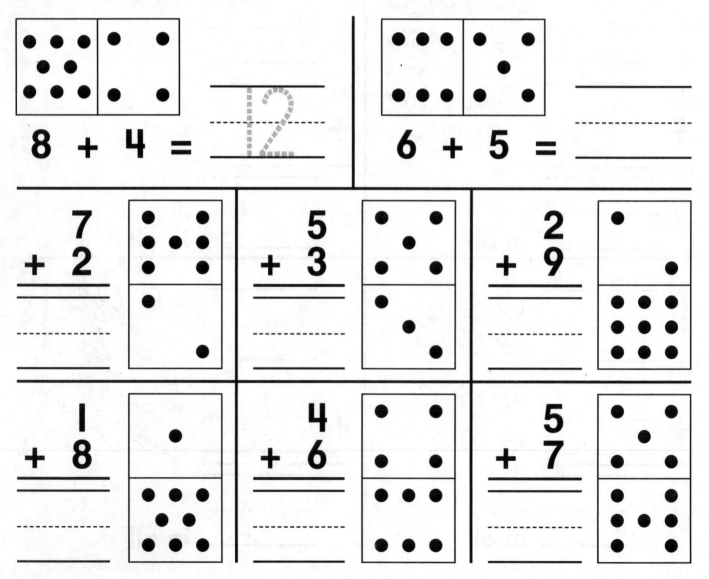

8 + 4 = _12_

6 + 5 = _____

$$\begin{array}{r} 7 \\ +\ 2 \\ \hline \end{array}$$

$$\begin{array}{r} 5 \\ +\ 3 \\ \hline \end{array}$$

$$\begin{array}{r} 2 \\ +\ 9 \\ \hline \end{array}$$

$$\begin{array}{r} 1 \\ +\ 8 \\ \hline \end{array}$$

$$\begin{array}{r} 4 \\ +\ 6 \\ \hline \end{array}$$

$$\begin{array}{r} 5 \\ +\ 7 \\ \hline \end{array}$$

Rainy Day Math

Add. Then color the sections for the sums using the code.

9 = yellow	11 = blue
10 = green	12 = red

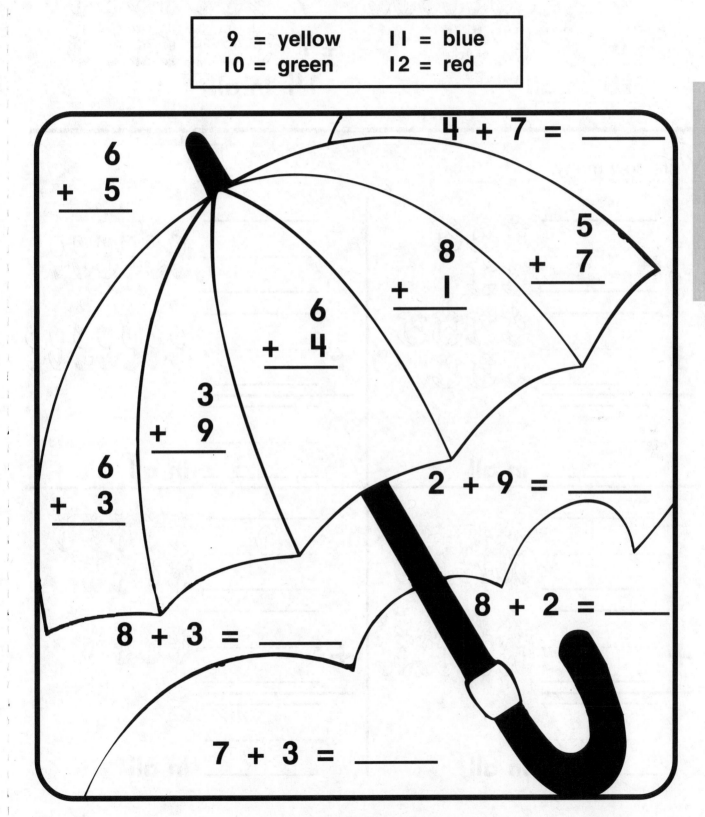

$4 + 7 =$ _____

$\begin{array}{r} 6 \\ + 5 \\ \hline \end{array}$

$\begin{array}{r} 8 \\ + 1 \\ \hline \end{array}$

$\begin{array}{r} 5 \\ + 7 \\ \hline \end{array}$

$\begin{array}{r} 6 \\ + 4 \\ \hline \end{array}$

$\begin{array}{r} 3 \\ + 9 \\ \hline \end{array}$

$\begin{array}{r} 6 \\ + 3 \\ \hline \end{array}$

$2 + 9 =$ _____

$8 + 2 =$ _____

$8 + 3 =$ _____

$7 + 3 =$ _____

Flower Show

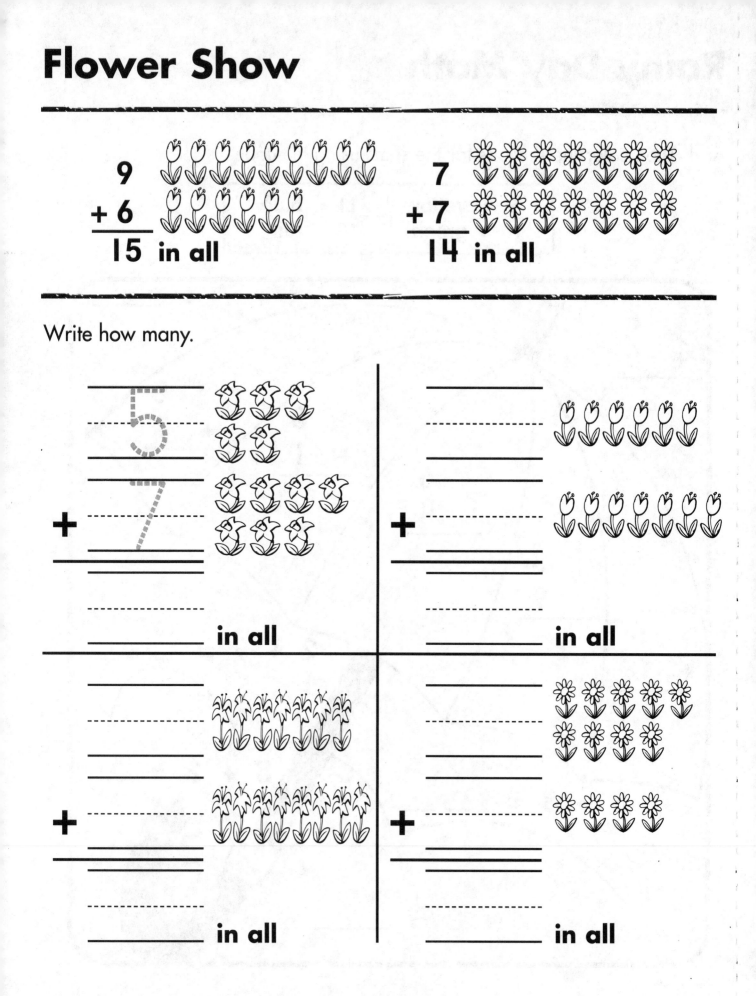

$$9 + 6 = 15 \text{ in all}$$

$$7 + 7 = 14 \text{ in all}$$

Write how many.

5
+ 7
_____ in all

+
_____ in all

+
_____ in all

+
_____ in all

Adding numbers to 15

Cars and Blocks

8   +   7   =   15

Add.

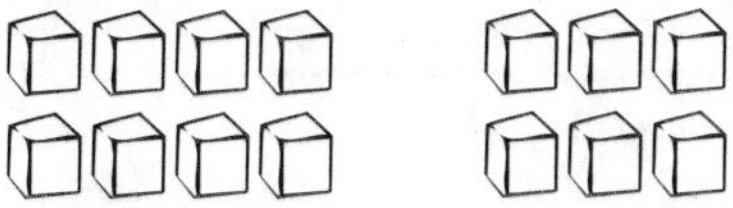

8 + 6 = 14

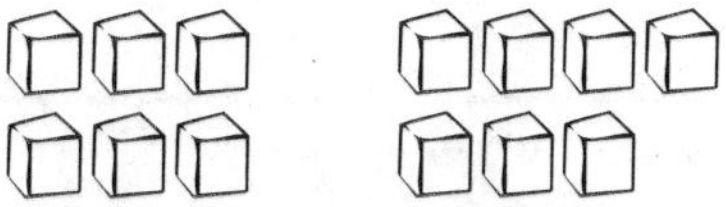

6 + 7 = _____

9 + 5 = _____

8 + 7 = _____

6 + 8 = _____

7 + 4 = _____

7 + 7 = _____

6 + 9 = _____

What's next?

$$\begin{array}{r} 9 \\ + 3 \\ \hline \end{array}$$

$$\begin{array}{r} 9 \\ + 4 \\ \hline \end{array}$$

$$\begin{array}{r} 9 \\ + 5 \\ \hline \end{array}$$

$$\begin{array}{r} 9 \\ + \boxed{} \\ \hline \end{array}$$

Review

Add.

5 + 6	3 + 9	6 + 7	9 + 4

8 + 6	2 + 9	9 + 0	8 + 3	7 + 4

9 + 5	7 + 7	4 + 4	9 + 6	7 + 3

4 + 8	6 + 2	6 + 6	8 + 5	7 + 8

Reviewing addition facts to 15

Kitten Mischief

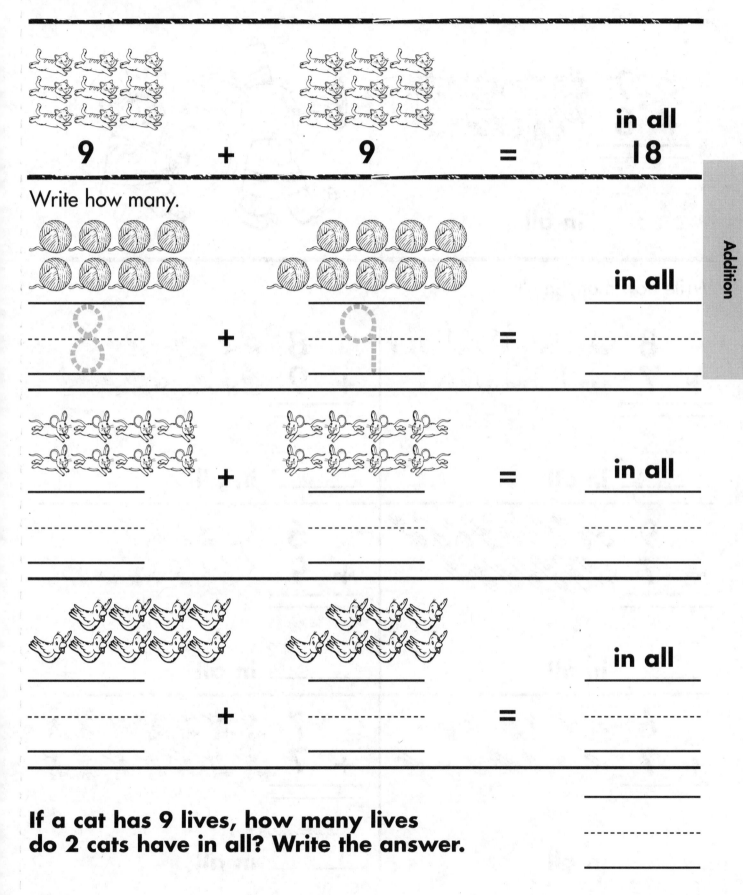

9   +   9   =   **in all**
                                              18

Write how many.

8   +   9   =   **in all**

_____ + _____ = **in all**

_____ + _____ = **in all**

**If a cat has 9 lives, how many lives
do 2 cats have in all? Write the answer.**

Addition

Marching Band

$$\begin{array}{r} 9 \\ + \ 8 \\ \hline 17 \end{array}$$ in all

Write how many in all.

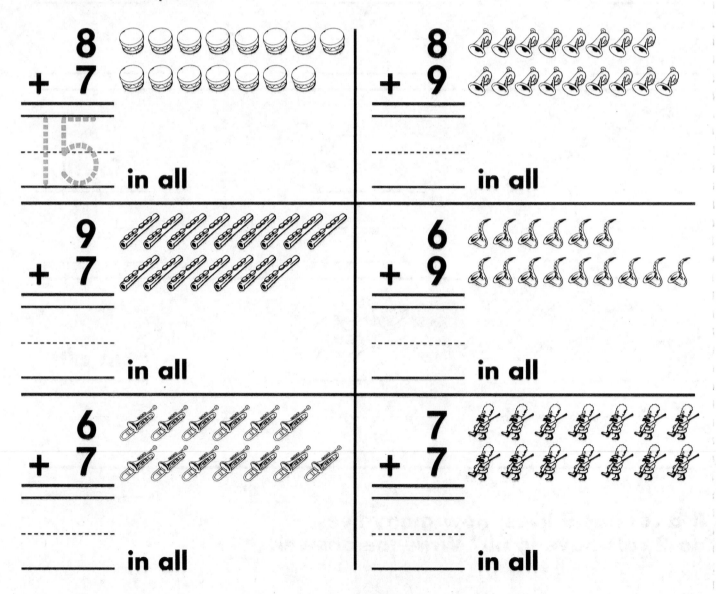

$$\begin{array}{r} 8 \\ + \ 7 \\ \hline 15 \end{array}$$ in all

$$\begin{array}{r} 8 \\ + \ 9 \\ \hline \end{array}$$ _____ in all

$$\begin{array}{r} 9 \\ + \ 7 \\ \hline \end{array}$$ _____ in all

$$\begin{array}{r} 6 \\ + \ 9 \\ \hline \end{array}$$ _____ in all

$$\begin{array}{r} 6 \\ + \ 7 \\ \hline \end{array}$$ _____ in all

$$\begin{array}{r} 7 \\ + \ 7 \\ \hline \end{array}$$ _____ in all

On the Green

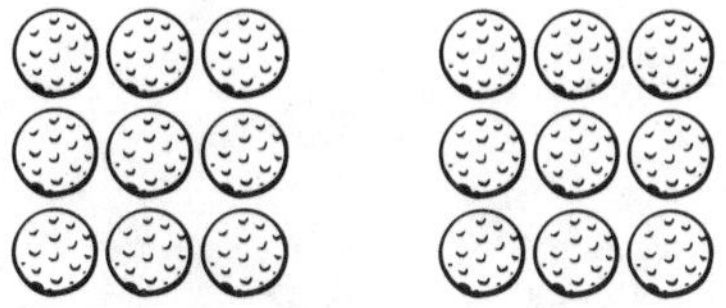

$$9 + 9 = 18$$

Add.

$$9 + 8 = \underline{17}$$

$$9 + 7 = \underline{}$$

$$8+9 = \underline{}$$

$$7+9 = \underline{}$$

$$9+6 = \underline{}$$

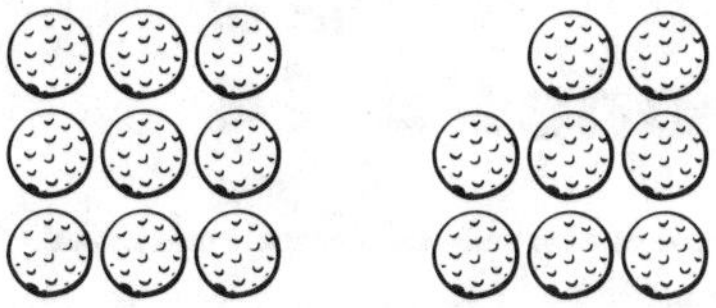

$$8+8 = \underline{}$$

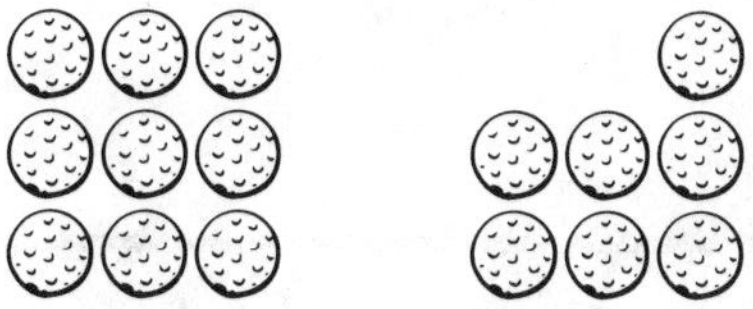

$$7+3 = \underline{}$$

$$0+7 = \underline{}$$

$$2+6 = \underline{}$$

$$8+0 = \underline{}$$

$$6+3 = \underline{}$$

Addition

Fish for Tens and Ones

Circle the groups of ten. Write how many tens and ones.
Then write how many in all.

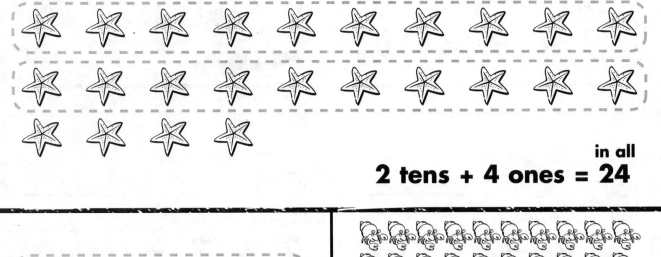

in all

2 tens + 4 ones = 24

____ tens + ____ ones = ____   in all

____ tens + ____ ones = ____   in all

____ tens + ____ ones = ____   in all

____ tens + ____ ones = ____   in all

____ tens + ____ ones = ____   in all

____ tens + ____ ones = ____   in all

Counting groups of tens and ones; adding

Good and Fruity

Write how many tens and ones. Then write how many in all.

Addition

in all

_____ + _____ = _____
tens   ones

in all

_____ + _____ = _____
tens   ones

in all

_____ + _____ = _____
tens   ones

Write how many tens and ones.

35 = ___ tens + ___ ones | 54 = ___ tens + ___ ones

81 = ___ tens + ___ ones | 29 = ___ tens + ___ ones

Write the number.

4 tens + 3 ones = _____   1 ten + 6 ones = _____

6 tens + 0 ones = _____   9 tens + 9 ones = _____

Counting, writing, and naming groups of tens and ones

Lots of Squares

23
+ 4
27 in all

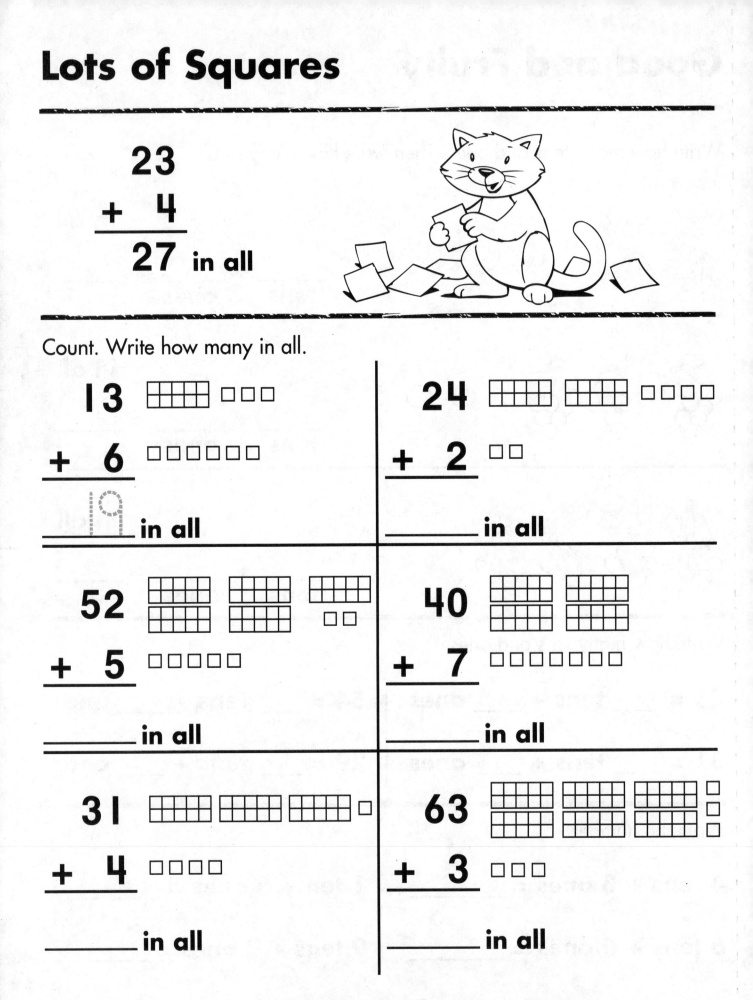

Count. Write how many in all.

13
+ 6
19 in all

24
+ 2
_____ in all

52
+ 5
_____ in all

40
+ 7
_____ in all

31
+ 4
_____ in all

63
+ 3
_____ in all

Counting to add tens and ones

Fun in Tenstown

In Tenstown, everything comes in packs of 10.

tens	ones
3	0
+2	0
5	0

First add the ones. Then add the tens.

tens	ones		tens	ones
4	0		7	0
+1	0		+2	0
5	0			

$$\begin{array}{r} 30 \\ +30 \\ \hline \end{array} \qquad \begin{array}{r} 10 \\ +70 \\ \hline \end{array} \qquad \begin{array}{r} 40 \\ +30 \\ \hline \end{array} \qquad \begin{array}{r} 50 \\ +20 \\ \hline \end{array} \qquad \begin{array}{r} 60 \\ +30 \\ \hline \end{array} \qquad \begin{array}{r} 50 \\ +40 \\ \hline \end{array}$$

$$\begin{array}{r} 60 \\ +20 \\ \hline \end{array} \qquad \begin{array}{r} 50 \\ +30 \\ \hline \end{array} \qquad \begin{array}{r} 80 \\ +10 \\ \hline \end{array} \qquad \begin{array}{r} 40 \\ +20 \\ \hline \end{array} \qquad \begin{array}{r} 10 \\ +40 \\ \hline \end{array} \qquad \begin{array}{r} 40 \\ +40 \\ \hline \end{array}$$

More Fun in Tenstown

Sometimes there are extra ones in Tenstown.

20	trees
+ 3	trees
23	trees

First add the ones. Then add the tens.

tens	ones
3	4
+5	3
8	7

tens	ones
2	7
+3	0
5	7

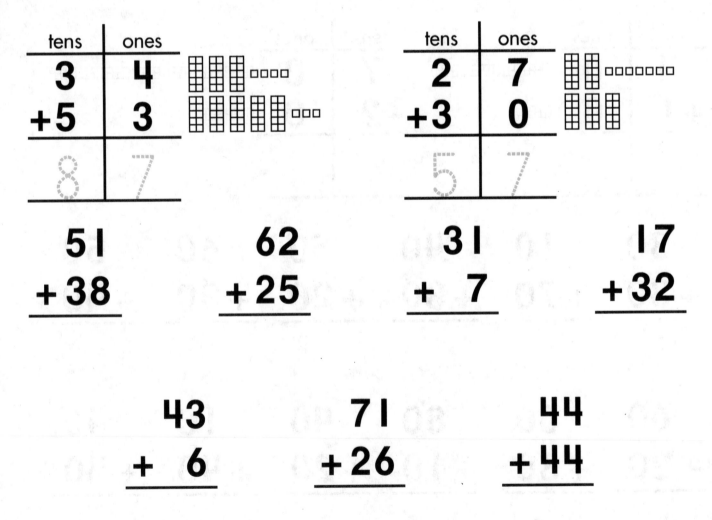

```
 51        62        31        17
+38       +25       + 7       +32
```

```
 43        71        44
+ 6       +26       +44
```

Adding 1- and 2-digit numbers without regrouping

Pop the Balloons

First add the ones. Then add the tens. Write the sum.
Find the balloon with the same number and color it.

$$\begin{array}{r} 34 \\ +\ 5 \\ \hline \end{array}$$
$$\begin{array}{r} 21 \\ +\ 3 \\ \hline \end{array}$$
$$\begin{array}{r} 51 \\ +\ 4 \\ \hline \end{array}$$
$$\begin{array}{r} 81 \\ +\ 2 \\ \hline \end{array}$$

$$\begin{array}{r} 60 \\ +\ 9 \\ \hline \end{array}$$
$$\begin{array}{r} 43 \\ +\ 5 \\ \hline \end{array}$$
$$\begin{array}{r} 70 \\ +\ 7 \\ \hline \end{array}$$
$$\begin{array}{r} 40 \\ +30 \\ \hline \end{array}$$

$$\begin{array}{r} 60 \\ +20 \\ \hline \end{array}$$
$$\begin{array}{r} 33 \\ +23 \\ \hline \end{array}$$
$$\begin{array}{r} 42 \\ +50 \\ \hline \end{array}$$
$$\begin{array}{r} 21 \\ +72 \\ \hline \end{array}$$

$$\begin{array}{r} 53 \\ +26 \\ \hline \end{array}$$
$$\begin{array}{r} 62 \\ +16 \\ \hline \end{array}$$
$$\begin{array}{r} 43 \\ +44 \\ \hline \end{array}$$
$$\begin{array}{r} 91 \\ +\ 7 \\ \hline \end{array}$$

Balloons: 79, 92, 48, 39, 55, 98, 93, 24, 56, 80, 87, 83, 70, 69, 77, 78

Addition

Adding 1- and 2-digit numbers without regrouping

Falling Leaves

First add the ones. Then add the tens. Color the picture.

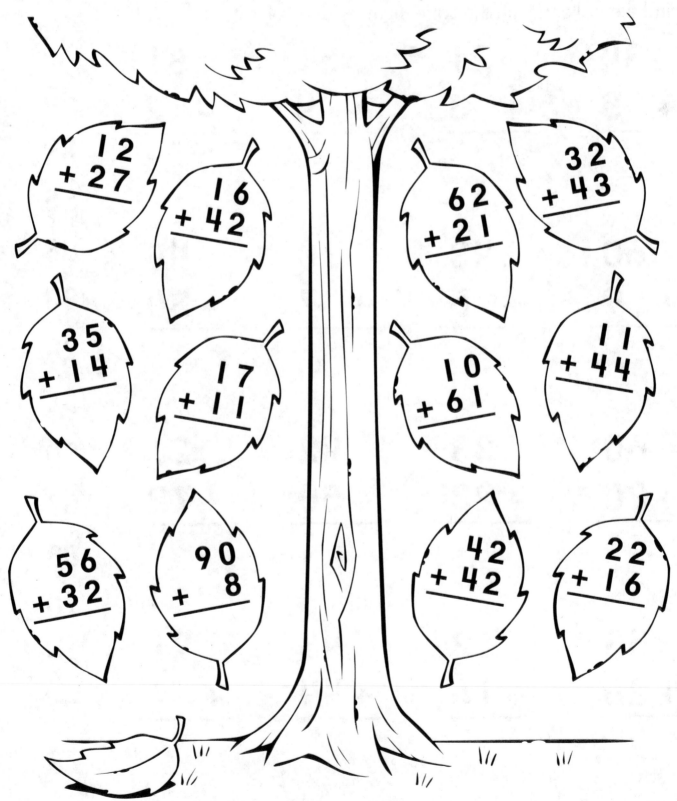

$$\begin{array}{r} 12 \\ +\ 27 \\ \hline \end{array}$$

$$\begin{array}{r} 16 \\ +\ 42 \\ \hline \end{array}$$

$$\begin{array}{r} 62 \\ +\ 21 \\ \hline \end{array}$$

$$\begin{array}{r} 32 \\ +\ 43 \\ \hline \end{array}$$

$$\begin{array}{r} 35 \\ +\ 14 \\ \hline \end{array}$$

$$\begin{array}{r} 17 \\ +\ 11 \\ \hline \end{array}$$

$$\begin{array}{r} 10 \\ +\ 61 \\ \hline \end{array}$$

$$\begin{array}{r} 11 \\ +\ 44 \\ \hline \end{array}$$

$$\begin{array}{r} 56 \\ +\ 32 \\ \hline \end{array}$$

$$\begin{array}{r} 90 \\ +\ \ 8 \\ \hline \end{array}$$

$$\begin{array}{r} 42 \\ +\ 42 \\ \hline \end{array}$$

$$\begin{array}{r} 22 \\ +\ 16 \\ \hline \end{array}$$

Adding 2-digit numbers without regrouping

Practice Test

First add the ones. Then add the tens.

$$\begin{array}{r} 11 \\ +\ 3 \\ \hline 14 \end{array}$$

- ○ 12
- ○ 13
- ● 14

GREAT WORK!

A.
$$\begin{array}{r} 23 \\ +\ 1 \\ \hline \end{array}$$
- ○ 23
- ○ 24
- ○ 25

E.
$$\begin{array}{r} 40 \\ +30 \\ \hline \end{array}$$
- ○ 7
- ○ 70
- ○ 77

B.
$$\begin{array}{r} 65 \\ +\ 2 \\ \hline \end{array}$$
- ○ 60
- ○ 66
- ○ 67

F.
$$\begin{array}{r} 23 \\ +41 \\ \hline \end{array}$$
- ○ 22
- ○ 46
- ○ 64

C.
$$\begin{array}{r} 34 \\ +24 \\ \hline \end{array}$$
- ○ 38
- ○ 58
- ○ 54

G.
$$\begin{array}{r} 82 \\ +16 \\ \hline \end{array}$$
- ○ 98
- ○ 99
- ○ 88

D.
$$\begin{array}{r} 60 \\ +10 \\ \hline \end{array}$$
- ○ 7
- ○ 60
- ○ 70

H.
$$\begin{array}{r} 55 \\ +21 \\ \hline \end{array}$$
- ○ 65
- ○ 76
- ○ 56

Answer Key

As the child completes the pages in this section, review his or her answers. When you take the time to correct the work and explain mistakes, you're showing your child that you feel learning is important.

page 36

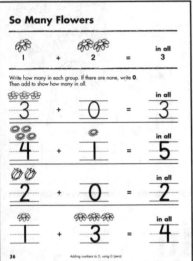

page 37

page 38

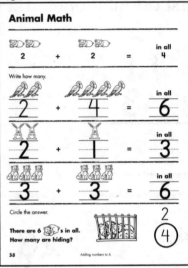

page 39

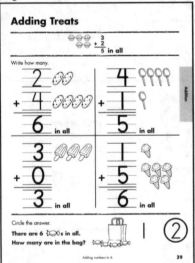

page 40

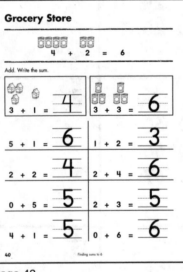

page 41

page 42

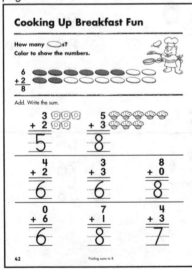

page 43

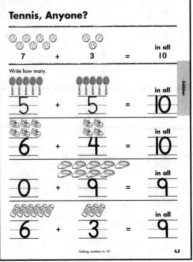

page 44

Answers

Oh, How Colorful!

Color the sections for the sums using the code. Then finish coloring the picture.

| 10 = red | 9 = blue | 8 = green |
| 7 = yellow | 6 = orange | |

6 + 3 blue
7 + 1 green
3 + 4 yellow
0 + 7 yellow
4 + 4 green
5 + 4 blue
2 + 6 red
4 + 5 blue
6 + 0 orange
8 red + 2
7 + 3 red
5 + 1 orange
6 + 2 green
9 + 1 blue
8 red + 8
3 + 3 orange
9 + 7 yellow

Reviewing sums to 10   45

Turn-Arounds

4
+ 3
7
The sum is the same.
3
+ 4
7

Write the sums. Then match.

5 + 4 = 9	2 + 6 = 8
3 + 7 = 10	4 + 5 = 9
3 + 6 = 9	4 + 6 = 10
6 + 2 = 8	7 + 0 = 7
5 + 5 = 10	6 + 3 = 9
0 + 7 = 7	7 + 3 = 10
6 + 4 = 10	5 + 5 = 10

Using turnaround addition facts to find sums   46

Seashells

3
+ 9
12 in all

Write how many.

6 + 5 = 11 in all
4 + 5 = 9 in all
6 + 6 = 12 in all
5 + 7 = 12 in all

Adding numbers to 12   47

Domino Dots

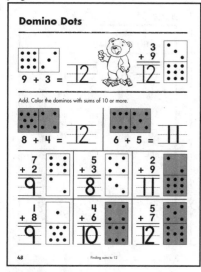

9 + 3 = 12

3
+ 9
12

Add. Color the dominos with sums of 10 or more.

8 + 4 = 12   6 + 5 = 11

7
+ 2
9

5
+ 3
8

2
+ 9
11

1
+ 8
9

4
+ 6
10

5
+ 7
12

48   Finding sums to 12

Rainy Day Math

Add. Then color the sections for the sums using the code.

| 9 = yellow | 11 = blue |
| 10 = green | 12 = red |

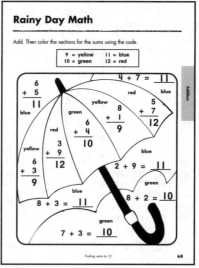

6 + 5 = 11 blue
4 + 7 = 11
5 + 7 = 12
8 + 1 = 9
6 + 4 = 10
3 + 9 = 12
6 + 3 = 9
2 + 9 = 11
8 + 3 = 11
8 + 2 = 10
7 + 3 = 10

Finding sums to 12   49

Flower Show

9
+ 6
15 in all

7
+ 7
14 in all

Write how many.

5 + 7 = 12 in all
6 + 7 = 13 in all
7 + 8 = 15 in all
9 + 4 = 13 in all

50   Adding numbers to 13

Cars and Blocks

8 + 7 = 15

Add.

8 + 6 = 14   6 + 7 = 13
9 + 5 = 14   8 + 7 = 15
6 + 8 = 14   7 + 4 = 11
7 + 7 = 14   6 + 9 = 15

What's next?

9
+ 3
12

9
+ 4
13

9
+ 5
14

9
+ 6
15

Finding sums to 15   51

Review

Add.

5
+ 6
11

3
+ 9
12

6
+ 7
13

9
+ 4
13

8
+ 6
14

2
+ 9
11

9
+ 0
9

8
+ 3
11

7
+ 4
11

9
+ 5
14

7
+ 7
14

4
+ 4
8

9
+ 6
15

7
+ 3
10

4
+ 8
12

6
+ 2
8

6
+ 6
12

8
+ 5
13

7
+ 8
15

52   Reviewing addition facts to 15

Kitten Mischief

9 + 9 = 18 in all

Write how many.

8 + 9 = 17 in all
8 + 8 = 16 in all
9 + 7 = 16 in all

If a cat has 9 lives, how many lives do 2 cats have in all? Write the answer.

18

Adding numbers to 18   53

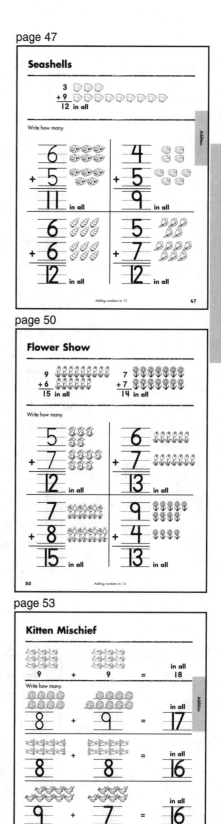

Addition

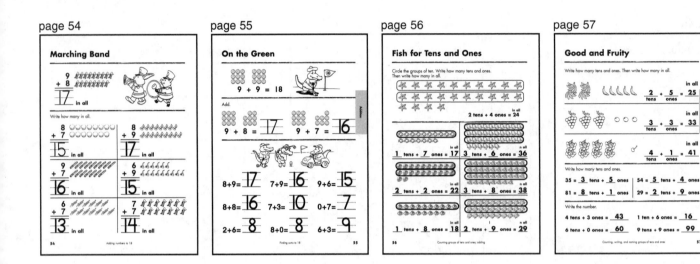

page 54

Marching Band

$$9 + 8 = 17 \text{ in all}$$

Write how many in all.

$8 + 7 = 15$ in all $8 + 9 = 17$ in all

$9 + 7 = 16$ in all $6 + 9 = 15$ in all

$6 + 7 = 13$ in all $7 + 7 = 14$ in all

54   Adding numbers to 18

page 55

On the Green

$$9 + 9 = 18$$

Add.

$9 + 8 = 17$ $9 + 7 = 16$

$8 + 9 = 17$ $7 + 9 = 16$ $9 + 6 = 15$

$8 + 8 = 16$ $7 + 3 = 10$ $0 + 7 = 7$

$2 + 6 = 8$ $8 + 0 = 8$ $6 + 3 = 9$

Finding sums to 18   55

page 56

Fish for Tens and Ones

Circle the groups of ten. Write how many tens and ones. Then write how many in all.

2 tens + 4 ones = 24

1 tens + 7 ones = 17 in all   3 tens + 6 ones = 36 in all

2 tens + 2 ones = 22 in all   3 tens + 8 ones = 38 in all

1 tens + 8 ones = 18 in all   2 tens + 9 ones = 29 in all

56   Counting groups of tens and ones; adding

page 57

Good and Fruity

Write how many tens and ones. Then write how many in all.

2 tens + 5 ones = 25 in all

3 tens + 3 ones = 33 in all

4 tens + 1 ones = 41 in all

Write how many tens and ones.

35 = 3 tens + 5 ones   54 = 5 tens + 4 ones

81 = 8 tens + 1 ones   29 = 2 tens + 9 ones

Write the number.

4 tens + 3 ones = 43   1 ten + 6 ones = 16

6 tens + 0 ones = 60   9 tens + 9 ones = 99

57   Counting, writing, and naming groups of tens and ones

---

page 58

Lots of Squares

$$23 + 4 = 27 \text{ in all}$$

Count. Write how many in all.

$13 + 6 = 19$ in all $24 + 2 = 26$ in all

$52 + 5 = 57$ in all $40 + 7 = 47$ in all

$31 + 4 = 35$ in all $63 + 3 = 66$ in all

58   Counting to add tens and ones

page 59

Fun in Tenstown

In Tenstown, everything comes in packs of 10.

tens	ones
3	0
+2	0
5	0

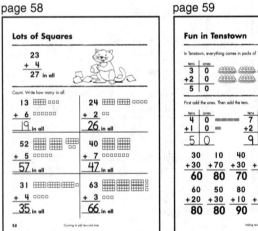

First add the ones. Then add the tens.

tens	ones		tens	ones
4	0		7	0
+1	0		+2	0
5	0		9	0

$30 + 30 = 60$ $10 + 70 = 80$ $40 + 30 = 70$ $50 + 20 = 70$ $60 + 30 = 90$ $50 + 40 = 90$

$60 + 20 = 80$ $50 + 30 = 80$ $80 + 10 = 90$ $40 + 20 = 60$ $10 + 40 = 50$ $40 + 40 = 80$

59   Adding tens

page 60

More Fun in Tenstown

Sometimes there are extra ones in Tenstown.

tens	ones
20	trees
+3	trees
23	trees

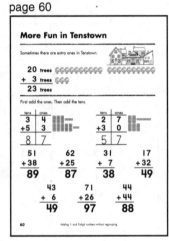

First add the ones. Then add the tens.

tens	ones		tens	ones
3	4		2	7
+5	3		+3	0
8	7		5	7

$51 + 38 = 89$ $62 + 25 = 87$ $31 + 7 = 38$ $17 + 32 = 49$

$43 + 6 = 49$ $71 + 26 = 97$ $44 + 44 = 88$

60   Adding 1- and 2-digit numbers without regrouping

page 61

Pop the Balloons

First add the ones. Then add the tens. Write the sum. Find the balloon with the same number and color it.

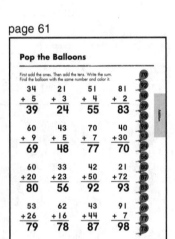

$34 + 5 = 39$ $21 + 4 = 24$ $51 + 4 = 55$ $81 + 2 = 83$

$60 + 9 = 69$ $43 + 5 = 48$ $70 + 7 = 77$ $40 + 30 = 70$

$60 + 20 = 80$ $33 + 23 = 56$ $42 + 50 = 92$ $21 + 72 = 93$

$53 + 26 = 79$ $62 + 16 = 78$ $43 + 44 = 87$ $91 + 7 = 98$

61   Adding 1- and 2-digit numbers without regrouping

---

page 62

Falling Leaves

First add the ones. Then add the tens. Color the picture.

$12 + 27 = 39$

$16 + 42 = 58$

$62 + 21 = 83$

$32 + 43 = 75$

$35 + 14 = 49$

$17 + 11 = 28$

$10 + 61 = 71$

$11 + 44 = 55$

$56 + 32 = 88$

$90 + 8 = 98$

$42 + 42 = 84$

$22 + 16 = 38$

62   Adding 2-digit numbers without regrouping

page 63

Practice Test

First add the ones. Then add the tens.

$11 + 3 = 14$ ○ 12   ○ 13   ● 14

A. $23 + 1 = 24$ ○ 23   ● 24   ○ 25

E. $40 + 30 = 70$ ○ 7   ● 70   ○ 77

B. $65 + 2 = 67$ ○ 60   ○ 66   ● 67

F. $23 + 41 = 64$ ○ 22   ○ 46   ● 64

C. $34 + 24 = 58$ ○ 38   ● 58   ○ 54

G. $82 + 16 = 98$ ● 98   ○ 99   ○ 88

D. $60 + 10 = 70$ ○ 7   ○ 60   ● 70

H. $55 + 21 = 76$ ○ 65   ● 76   ○ 56

63   Adding 1- and 2-digit numbers without regrouping

Hats Off

Subtract.

How many are left? $5 - 3 =$ _____ 2

How many are left? $5 - 4 =$ _____

How many are left? $3 - 1 =$ _____

How many are left? $4 - 3 =$ _____

Color the answer.

What has a head and a foot, but no body?

On Your Feet

Cross out and subtract.

X out 1.

How many are left? $4 - 1 =$ _____

X out 4.

How many are left? $5 - 4 =$ _____

X out 2.

How many are left? $2 - 2 =$ _____

X out 3.

How many are left? $4 - 3 =$ _____

Color the answer.

What has two hands but no feet?

In the Kitchen

Subtract.

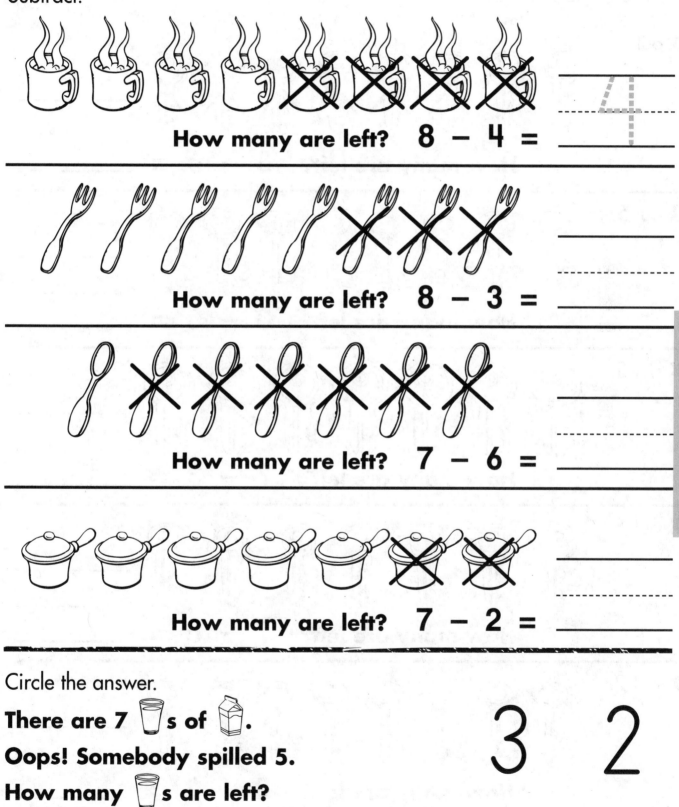

How many are left? 8 − 4 = ____

How many are left? 8 − 3 = ____

How many are left? 7 − 6 = ____

How many are left? 7 − 2 = ____

Circle the answer.

There are 7 ▯s of ▭.

Oops! Somebody spilled 5.

How many ▯s are left?

3   2

Keys, Please

Cross out and subtract.

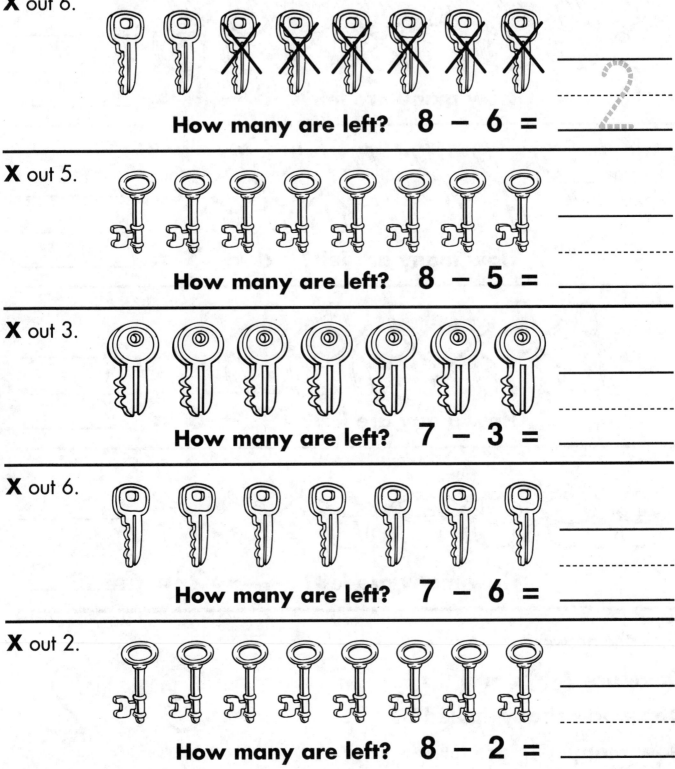

X out 6.

How many are left? **8 – 6 =** _____

X out 5.

How many are left? **8 – 5 =** _____

X out 3.

How many are left? **7 – 3 =** _____

X out 6.

How many are left? **7 – 6 =** _____

X out 2.

How many are left? **8 – 2 =** _____

Subtracting numbers 0-8 from numbers to 8

Top to Bottom

Subtract.

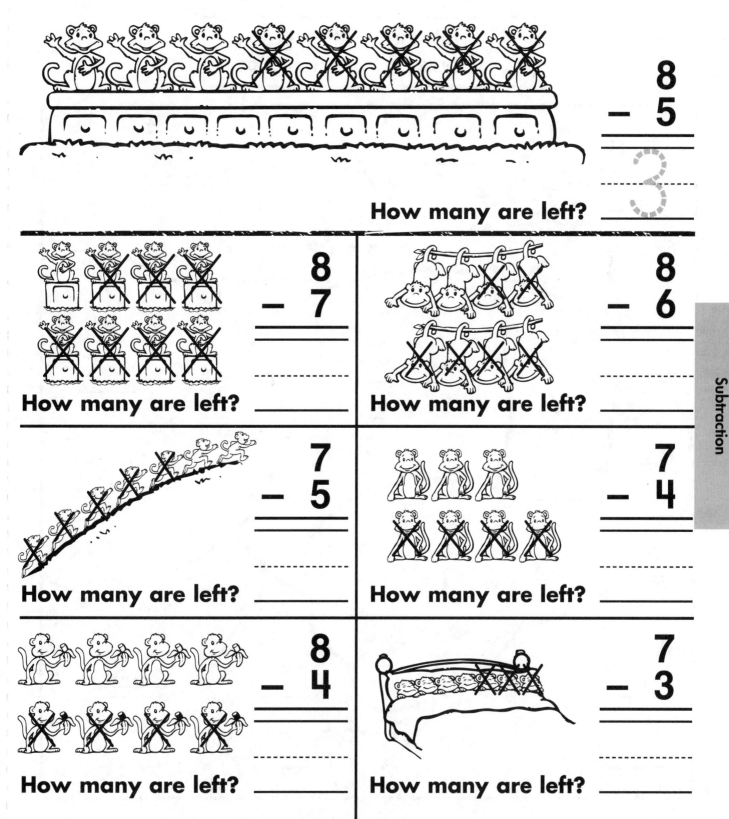

$$\begin{array}{r} 8 \\ -\ 5 \\ \hline \end{array}$$

How many are left? _____

$$\begin{array}{r} 8 \\ -\ 7 \\ \hline \end{array}$$

How many are left? _____

$$\begin{array}{r} 8 \\ -\ 6 \\ \hline \end{array}$$

How many are left? _____

$$\begin{array}{r} 7 \\ -\ 5 \\ \hline \end{array}$$

How many are left? _____

$$\begin{array}{r} 7 \\ -\ 4 \\ \hline \end{array}$$

How many are left? _____

$$\begin{array}{r} 8 \\ -\ 4 \\ \hline \end{array}$$

How many are left? _____

$$\begin{array}{r} 7 \\ -\ 3 \\ \hline \end{array}$$

How many are left? _____

Subtraction

Subtracting numbers through 8 in vertical form

71

Who's There?

Subtract. Color the spaces to match the answers in the code.

2 = orange	4 = green
3 = blue	5 = yellow

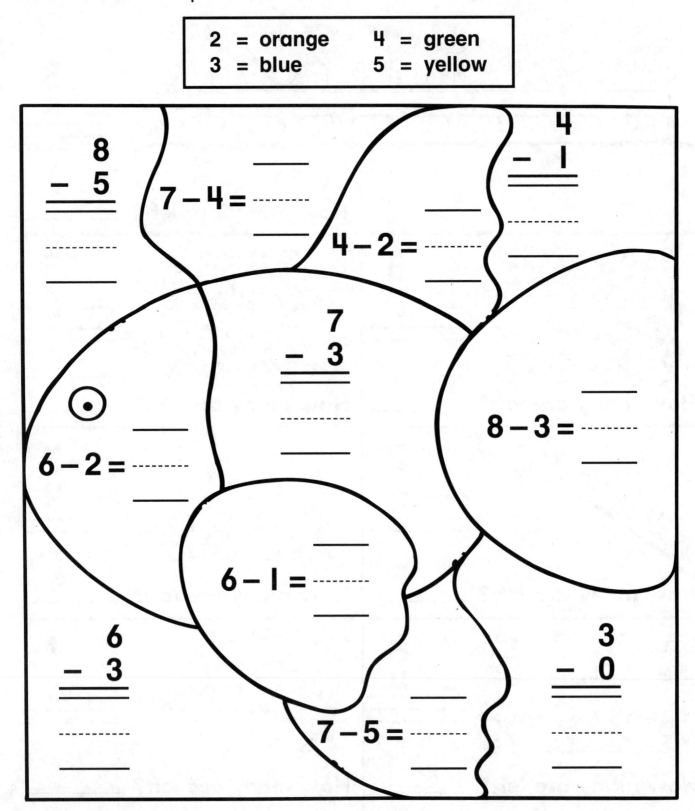

$$\begin{array}{r} 8 \\ -\ 5 \\ \hline \end{array}$$

$7 - 4 =$ _____

$4 - 2 =$ _____

$$\begin{array}{r} 4 \\ -\ 1 \\ \hline \end{array}$$

$$\begin{array}{r} 7 \\ -\ 3 \\ \hline \end{array}$$

$8 - 3 =$ _____

$6 - 2 =$ _____

$6 - 1 =$ _____

$$\begin{array}{r} 6 \\ -\ 3 \\ \hline \end{array}$$

$7 - 5 =$ _____

$$\begin{array}{r} 3 \\ -\ 0 \\ \hline \end{array}$$

Reviewing subtraction facts to 8

Color Away

Subtract.

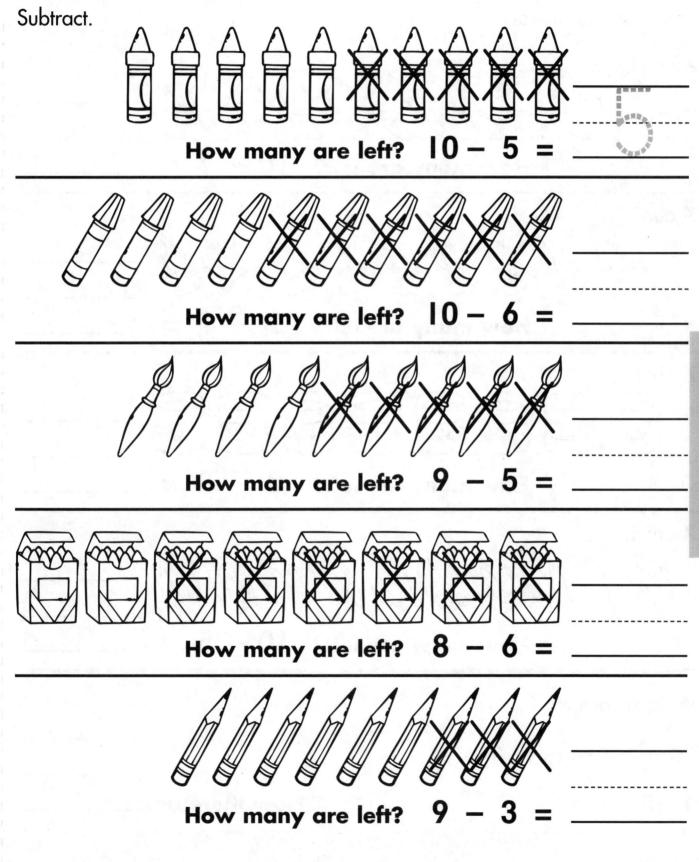

How many are left? $10 - 5 =$ _____

How many are left? $10 - 6 =$ _____

How many are left? $9 - 5 =$ _____

How many are left? $8 - 6 =$ _____

How many are left? $9 - 3 =$ _____

Subtraction

Make Music

Cross out and subtract.

X out 7.

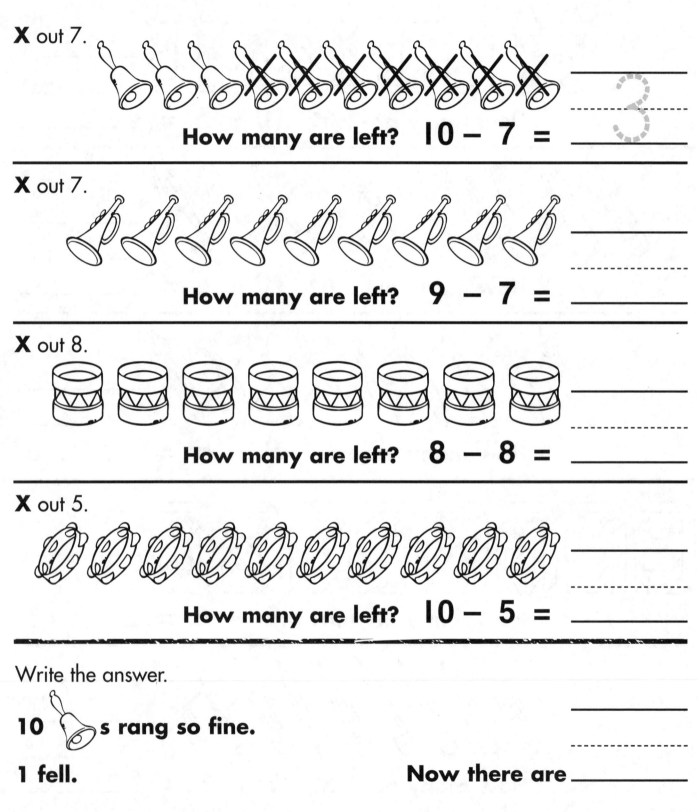

How many are left?   10 − 7 = _____ 3

X out 7.

How many are left?   9 − 7 = _____

X out 8.

How many are left?   8 − 8 = _____

X out 5.

How many are left?   10 − 5 = _____

Write the answer.

10 🔔 s rang so fine. _____

1 fell.   **Now there are** _____

Fresh Fruit

Cross out and subtract.

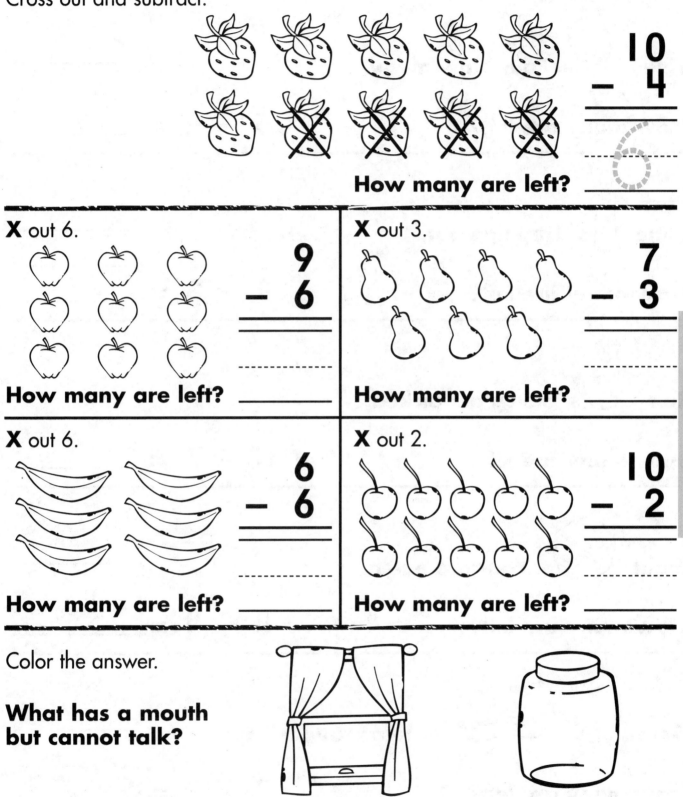

$$\begin{array}{r} 10 \\ -\ 4 \\ \hline \end{array}$$

How many are left? _6_

X out 6.

$$\begin{array}{r} 9 \\ -\ 6 \\ \hline \end{array}$$

How many are left? _____

X out 3.

$$\begin{array}{r} 7 \\ -\ 3 \\ \hline \end{array}$$

How many are left? _____

X out 6.

$$\begin{array}{r} 6 \\ -\ 6 \\ \hline \end{array}$$

How many are left? _____

X out 2.

$$\begin{array}{r} 10 \\ -\ 2 \\ \hline \end{array}$$

How many are left? _____

Color the answer.

What has a mouth but cannot talk?

Subtraction Stories

Write the answer.

Five ⬭s. Four blow away.

How many are left?   5 – 4 = _____

Nine 🕯s. Three go out.

How many are left?   9 – 3 = _____

Ten 🌼s. Seven get picked.

How many are left?   10 – 7 = _____

Eight 🍪s. Four are eaten.

How many are left?   8 – 4 = _____

Seven 🐛s. Two crawl away.

How many are left?   7 – 2 = _____

Solving subtraction story problems

Check It!

Subtract. Then add to check.

5 − 3 = __2__  ✓ 2 + 3 = __5__

9 − 5  = _____ ✓ 4 + 5 = _____

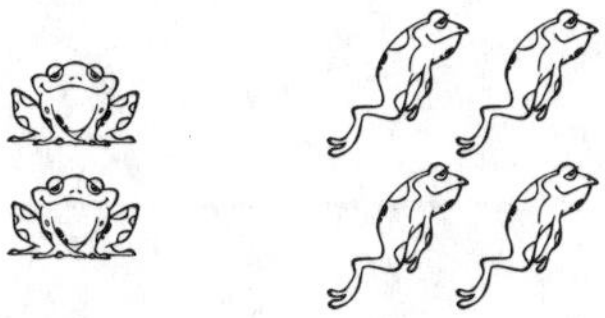

6 − 4 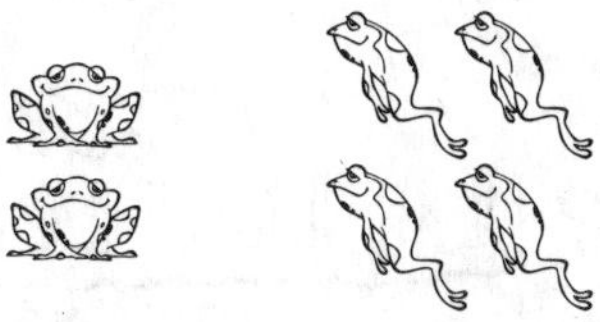 = _____ ✓ 2 + 4 = _____

10 − 3  = _____ ✓ 7 + 3 = _____

9 − 6  = _____ ✓ 3 + 6 = _____

Party Time

Write how many are left.

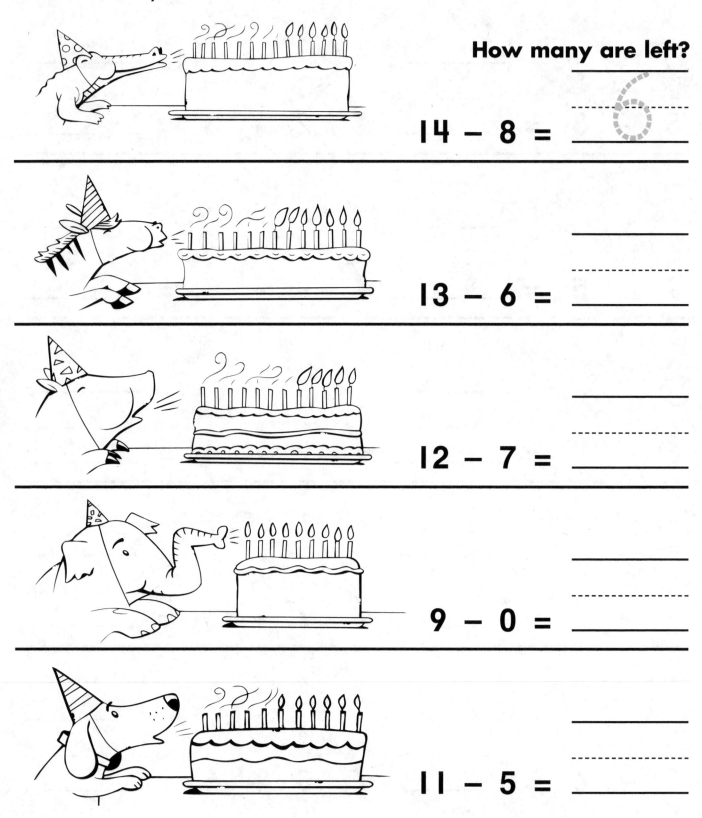

How many are left?

14 − 8 = _____

13 − 6 = _____

12 − 7 = _____

9 − 0 = _____

11 − 5 = _____

Subtracting numbers 0-9 from numbers through 14

Home Sweet Home

Cross out and subtract. Write how many are left.

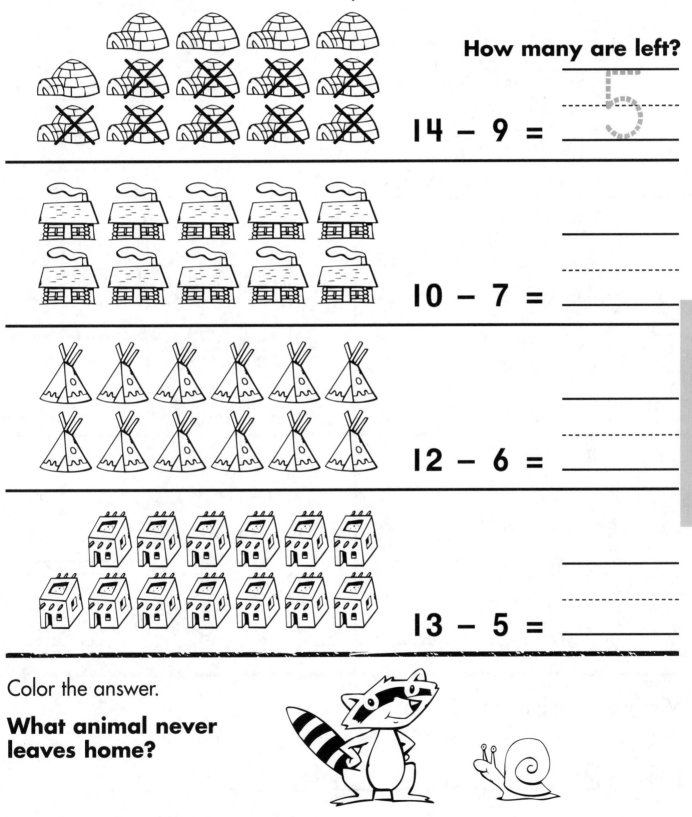

How many are left?

$14 - 9 =$ _____ 5

$10 - 7 =$ _____

$12 - 6 =$ _____

$13 - 5 =$ _____

Color the answer.

What animal never leaves home?

Down We Go

Cross out and subtract. Write how many are left.

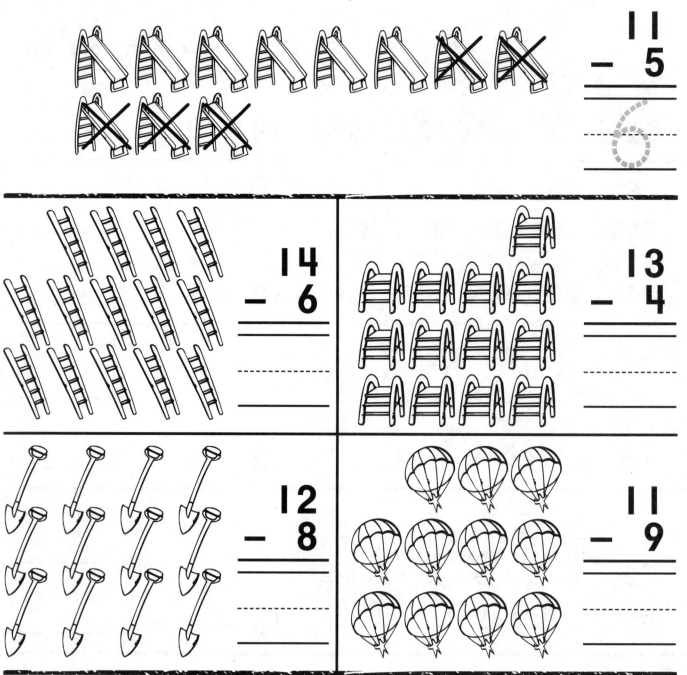

$$\begin{array}{r} 11 \\ -\ 5 \\ \hline \end{array}$$

6

$$\begin{array}{r} 14 \\ -\ 6 \\ \hline \end{array}$$

$$\begin{array}{r} 13 \\ -\ 4 \\ \hline \end{array}$$

$$\begin{array}{r} 12 \\ -\ 8 \\ \hline \end{array}$$

$$\begin{array}{r} 11 \\ -\ 9 \\ \hline \end{array}$$

Write the missing numbers.

14, 12, _____, 8, _____, 4, 2

Subtracting numbers 0-9 from numbers through 14 in vertical form

Have a Nice Trip

Cross out and subtract. Write how many are left.

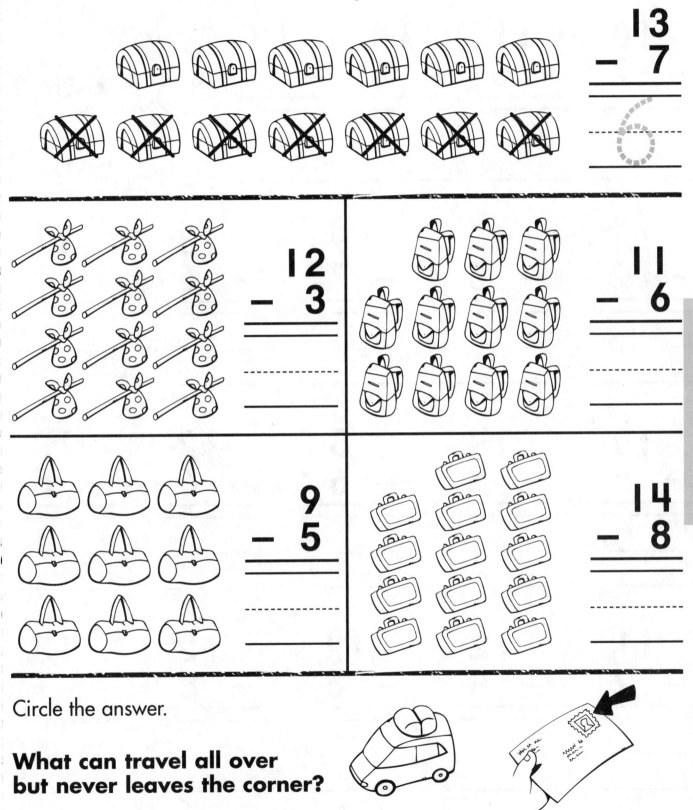

$$\begin{array}{r} 13 \\ -\ 7 \\ \hline 6 \end{array}$$

$$\begin{array}{r} 12 \\ -\ 3 \\ \hline \end{array}$$

$$\begin{array}{r} 11 \\ -\ 6 \\ \hline \end{array}$$

$$\begin{array}{r} 9 \\ -\ 5 \\ \hline \end{array}$$

$$\begin{array}{r} 14 \\ -\ 8 \\ \hline \end{array}$$

Circle the answer.

What can travel all over but never leaves the corner?

Review

Subtract.

10 − 7	11 − 6	14 − 5	13 − 3

12 − 9	10 − 5	9 − 7	13 − 6	11 − 7

10 − 6	14 − 8	8 − 6	12 − 6	13 − 5

11 − 2	12 − 4	14 − 6	12 − 8	13 − 7

Reviewing subtraction facts through 14

I Need Some More

Subtract.
Write how many more are
needed to make 10.

needed

needed

$$\begin{array}{r} 10 \\ -\ 5 \\ \hline \end{array}$$

$$\begin{array}{r} 10 \\ -\ 7 \\ \hline \end{array}$$

$$\begin{array}{r} 10 \\ -\ 6 \\ \hline \end{array}$$

Color the correct answer box.

has 8 🌿 s.

He wants 10 🌿 s.

How many more 🌿 s does 🎅 need?

$$\boxed{2} \quad \boxed{3}$$

Nuts and Bolts

Subtract. Write how many are left.

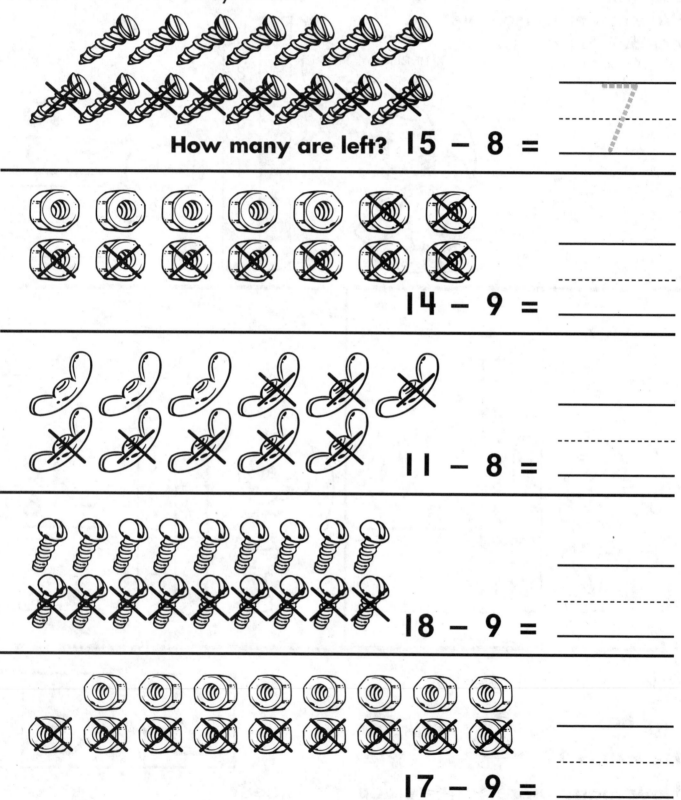

How many are left? $15 - 8 =$ 7

$14 - 9 =$ _____

$11 - 8 =$ _____

$18 - 9 =$ _____

$17 - 9 =$ _____

Subtracting numbers 0-9 from numbers through 18

Too Many Tools

Cross out and subtract. Write how many are left.

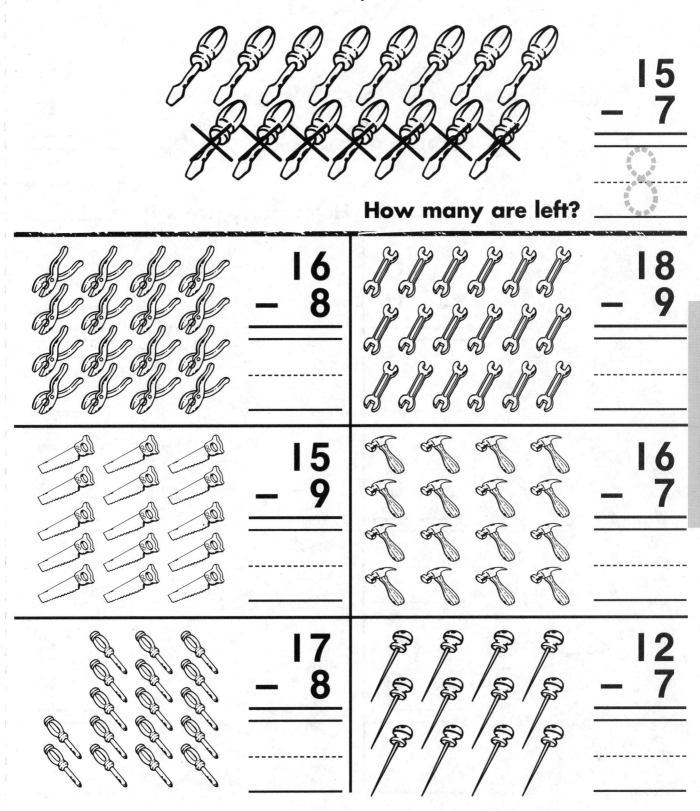

$$\begin{array}{r} 15 \\ -7 \\ \hline \end{array}$$

How many are left? _____

$$\begin{array}{r} 16 \\ -8 \\ \hline \end{array}$$

$$\begin{array}{r} 18 \\ -9 \\ \hline \end{array}$$

$$\begin{array}{r} 15 \\ -9 \\ \hline \end{array}$$

$$\begin{array}{r} 16 \\ -7 \\ \hline \end{array}$$

$$\begin{array}{r} 17 \\ -8 \\ \hline \end{array}$$

$$\begin{array}{r} 12 \\ -7 \\ \hline \end{array}$$

Subtraction

Zoom Along

Cross out and subtract. Write how many are left.

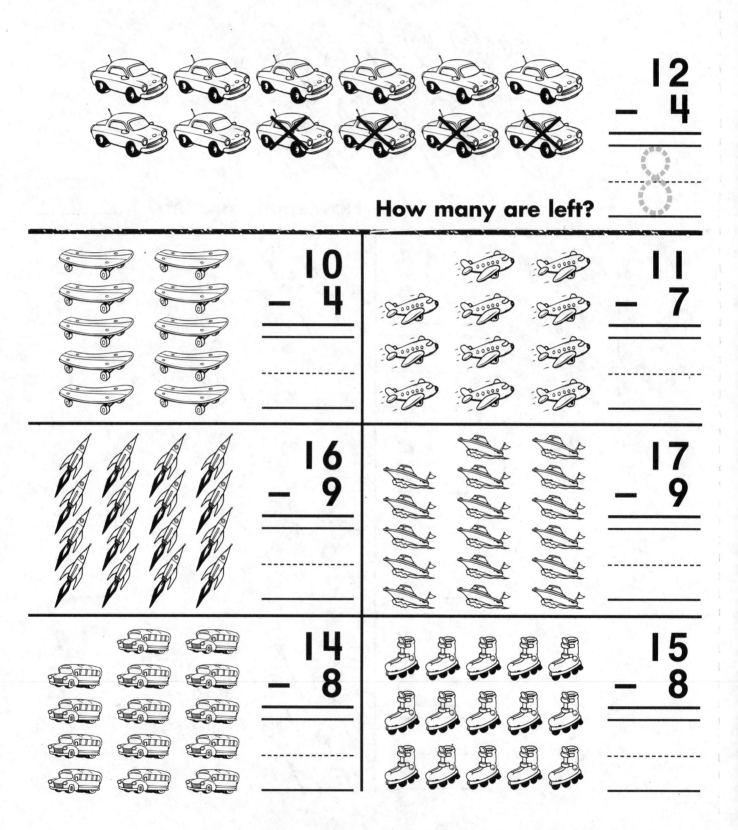

$$\begin{array}{r} 12 \\ -\ 4 \\ \hline 8 \end{array}$$

How many are left? _____

$$\begin{array}{r} 10 \\ -\ 4 \\ \hline \end{array}$$

$$\begin{array}{r} 11 \\ -\ 7 \\ \hline \end{array}$$

$$\begin{array}{r} 16 \\ -\ 9 \\ \hline \end{array}$$

$$\begin{array}{r} 17 \\ -\ 9 \\ \hline \end{array}$$

$$\begin{array}{r} 14 \\ -\ 8 \\ \hline \end{array}$$

$$\begin{array}{r} 15 \\ -\ 8 \\ \hline \end{array}$$

Subtracting numbers 0-9 from numbers through 18 in vertical form

Review

Subtract.

10 − 7	12 − 6	18 − 9	16 − 7	12 − 8
3				
15 − 7	13 − 9	17 − 8	11 − 8	14 − 6
13 − 5	11 − 6	15 − 8	16 − 9	
13 − 7	15 − 9	17 − 9	16 − 8	12 − 7

Tens Take Away

Cross out groups of ten.
First subtract the ones column.
Then subtract the tens column.

tens	ones
9	0
− 3	0
6	0

How many are left?

tens	ones
8	0
− 4	0

tens	ones
7	0
− 5	0

First subtract the ones.
Then subtract the tens.

$$
\begin{array}{r} 80 \\ -30 \\ \hline \end{array}
\qquad
\begin{array}{r} 60 \\ -20 \\ \hline \end{array}
\qquad
\begin{array}{r} 50 \\ -40 \\ \hline \end{array}
$$

$$
\begin{array}{r} 40 \\ -10 \\ \hline \end{array}
\qquad
\begin{array}{r} 60 \\ -30 \\ \hline \end{array}
\qquad
\begin{array}{r} 90 \\ -80 \\ \hline \end{array}
\qquad
\begin{array}{r} 30 \\ -20 \\ \hline \end{array}
\qquad
\begin{array}{r} 50 \\ -20 \\ \hline \end{array}
$$

Subtracting multiples of 10

You Can Do It!

First subtract the ones. Then subtract the tens.

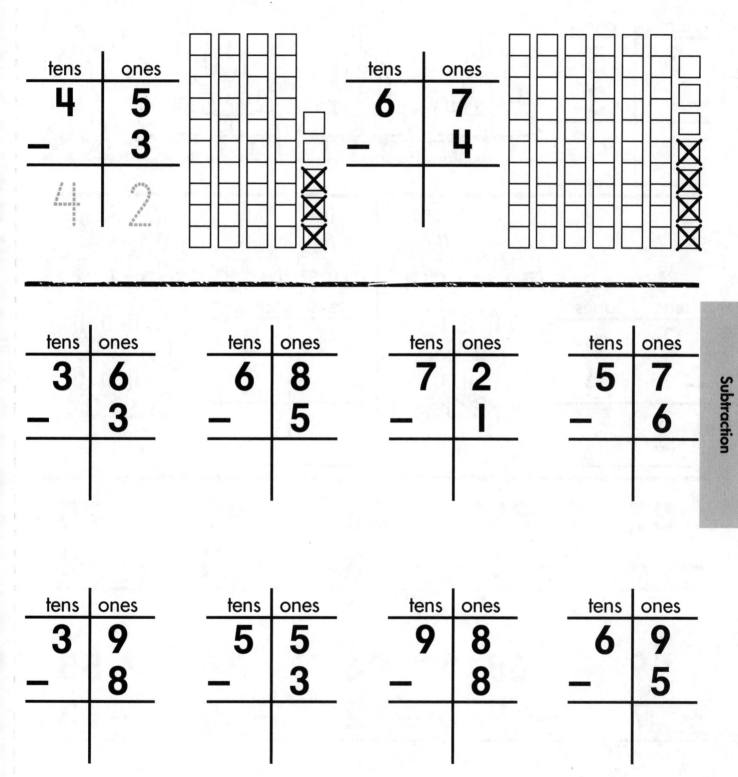

	tens	ones
	4	5
−		3
	4	2

	tens	ones
	6	7
−		4

	tens	ones
	3	6
−		3

	tens	ones
	6	8
−		5

	tens	ones
	7	2
−		1

	tens	ones
	5	7
−		6

	tens	ones
	3	9
−		8

	tens	ones
	5	5
−		3

	tens	ones
	9	8
−		8

	tens	ones
	6	9
−		5

Brush Off

Subtract the ones. Write how many are left.

tens	ones
3	5
−	3
3	2

tens	ones
2	6
−	4

tens	ones
4	8
−	2

$$87 - 6$$ $$54 - 1$$ $$63 - 3$$ $$99 - 4$$ $$75 - 2$$

$$49 - 7$$ $$68 - 4$$ $$96 - 2$$ $$36 - 5$$ $$55 - 3$$

Subtracting 1-digit numbers from 2-digit numbers without regrouping

Practice Makes Purr-fect

Color the spaces to match the answers in the code.

8 = yellow	20 = red
12 = orange	30 = green

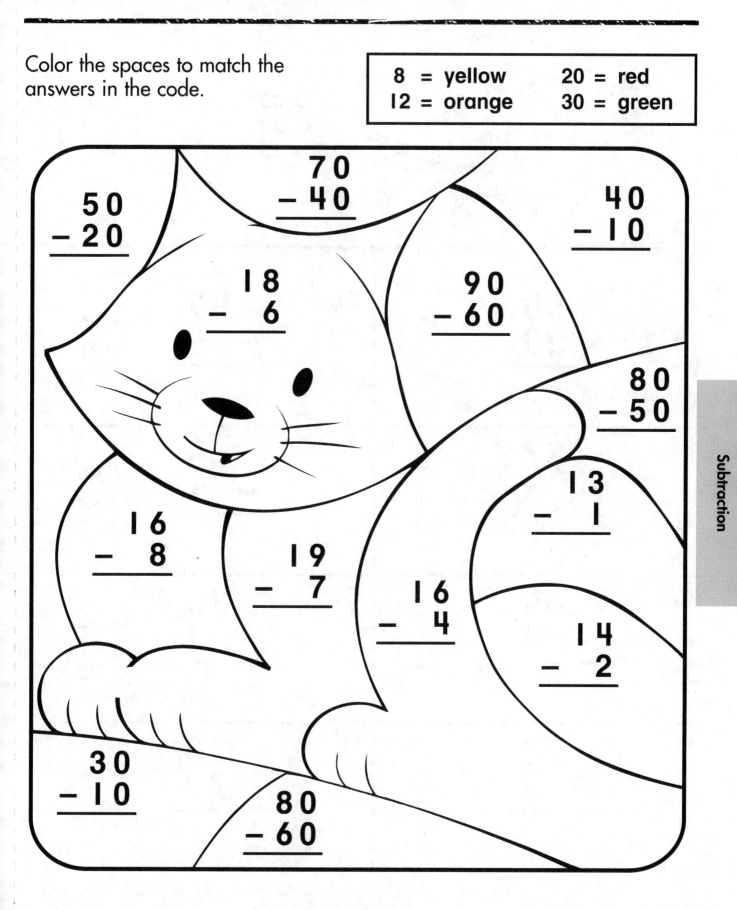

Practice Test

$$\begin{array}{r} 40 \\ -20 \\ \hline 20 \end{array}$$

○ 30
● 20
○ 10

A.
$$\begin{array}{r} 60 \\ -20 \\ \hline \end{array}$$
○ 60
○ 50
○ 40

E.
$$\begin{array}{r} 89 \\ -9 \\ \hline \end{array}$$
○ 90
○ 81
○ 80

B.
$$\begin{array}{r} 37 \\ -5 \\ \hline \end{array}$$
○ 32
○ 31
○ 30

F.
$$\begin{array}{r} 64 \\ -1 \\ \hline \end{array}$$
○ 68
○ 65
○ 63

C.
$$\begin{array}{r} 54 \\ -3 \\ \hline \end{array}$$
○ 52
○ 51
○ 50

G.
$$\begin{array}{r} 38 \\ -7 \\ \hline \end{array}$$
○ 32
○ 31
○ 30

D.
$$\begin{array}{r} 78 \\ -3 \\ \hline \end{array}$$
○ 76
○ 75
○ 74

H.
$$\begin{array}{r} 90 \\ -70 \\ \hline \end{array}$$
○ 30
○ 20
○ 10

Testing subtraction skills

Detect the Difference

Subtract, then circle the number that matches your answer.

$$\begin{array}{r} 57 \\ -\ 2 \\ \hline \end{array}$$

59 (55)

$$\begin{array}{r} 40 \\ -10 \\ \hline \end{array}$$

20 30

$$\begin{array}{r} 91 \\ -\ 0 \\ \hline \end{array}$$

91 90

$$\begin{array}{r} 68 \\ -\ 6 \\ \hline \end{array}$$

64 62

$$\begin{array}{r} 70 \\ -20 \\ \hline \end{array}$$

50 90

$$\begin{array}{r} 10 \\ -10 \\ \hline \end{array}$$

10 0

$$\begin{array}{r} 84 \\ -\ 3 \\ \hline \end{array}$$

82 81

$$\begin{array}{r} 99 \\ -\ 3 \\ \hline \end{array}$$

96 95

$$\begin{array}{r} 78 \\ -\ 5 \\ \hline \end{array}$$

74 73

$$\begin{array}{r} 60 \\ -10 \\ \hline \end{array}$$

50 70

$$\begin{array}{r} 58 \\ -\ 2 \\ \hline \end{array}$$

54 56

$$\begin{array}{r} 90 \\ -60 \\ \hline \end{array}$$

20 30

Winning Scores

Circle the greater score. Subtract to find out by how many points the home team won.

HOME	(8)
VISITOR	4
	4

HOME	23
VISITOR	0

HOME	18
VISITOR	9

HOME	15
VISITOR	5

HOME	17
VISITOR	8

HOME	75
VISITOR	5

HOME	36
VISITOR	2

HOME	27
VISITOR	3

HOME	14
VISITOR	7

Subtraction review

Answer Key

As the child completes the pages in this section, review his or her answers. When you take the time to correct the work and explain mistakes, you're showing your child that you feel learning is important.

page 67

Hats Off

Subtract.

How many are left? $5 - 3 = 2$

How many are left? $5 - 4 = 1$

How many are left? $3 - 1 = 2$

How many are left? $4 - 3 = 1$

Color the answer.
What has a head and a foot, but no body?

Subtracting numbers 0-5 from numbers to 5   67

page 68

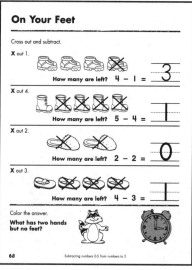

On Your Feet

Cross out and subtract.

X out 1.
How many are left? $4 - 1 = 3$

X out 4.
How many are left? $5 - 4 = 1$

X out 2.
How many are left? $2 - 2 = 0$

X out 3.
How many are left? $4 - 3 = 1$

Color the answer.
What has two hands but no feet?

68   Subtracting numbers 0-5 from numbers to 5

page 69

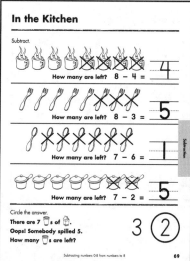

In the Kitchen

Subtract.

How many are left? $8 - 4 = 4$

How many are left? $8 - 3 = 5$

How many are left? $7 - 6 = 1$

How many are left? $7 - 2 = 5$

Circle the answer.
There are 7 cups of.
Oops! Somebody spilled 5.
How many cups are left?

3 (2)

Subtracting numbers 0-8 from numbers to 8   69

page 70

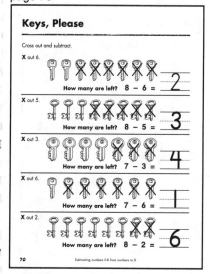

Keys, Please

Cross out and subtract.

X out 6.
How many are left? $8 - 6 = 2$

X out 5.
How many are left? $8 - 5 = 3$

X out 3.
How many are left? $7 - 3 = 4$

X out 6.
How many are left? $7 - 6 = 1$

X out 2.
How many are left? $8 - 2 = 6$

70   Subtracting numbers 0-8 from numbers to 8

page 71

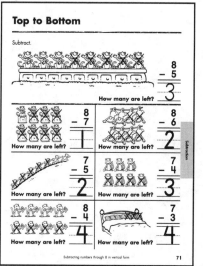

Top to Bottom

Subtract.

$8 - 5 = 3$
How many are left?

$8 - 7 = 1$
How many are left?

$8 - 6 = 2$
How many are left?

$7 - 5 = 2$
How many are left?

$7 - 4 = 3$
How many are left?

$8 - 4 = 4$
How many are left?

$7 - 3 = 4$
How many are left?

Subtracting numbers through 8 in vertical form   71

page 72

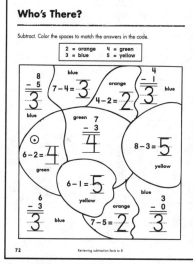

Who's There?

Subtract. Color the spaces to match the answers in the code.

2 = orange   4 = green
3 = blue   5 = yellow

$8 - 5 = 3$ blue
$7 - 4 = 3$
blue

$4 - 1 = 3$ blue
orange

$4 - 2 = 2$

green
$7 - 3 = 4$

$6 - 2 = 4$ green

$8 - 3 = 5$ yellow

$6 - 1 = 5$ yellow

$6 - 3 = 3$ blue
$7 - 5 = 2$ orange

$3 - 0 = 3$ blue

72   Reviewing subtraction facts to 8

page 73

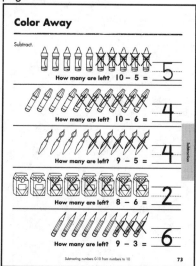

Color Away

Subtract.

How many are left? $10 - 5 = 5$

How many are left? $10 - 6 = 4$

How many are left? $9 - 5 = 4$

How many are left? $8 - 6 = 2$

How many are left? $9 - 3 = 6$

Subtracting numbers 0-10 from numbers to 10   73

page 74

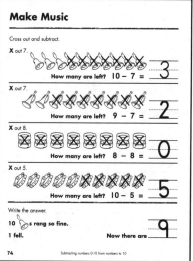

Make Music

Cross out and subtract.

X out 7.
How many are left? $10 - 7 = 3$

X out 7.
How many are left? $9 - 7 = 2$

X out 8.
How many are left? $8 - 8 = 0$

X out 5.
How many are left? $10 - 5 = 5$

Write the answer.
10 bells rang so fine.
1 fell.   Now there are 9

74   Subtracting numbers 0-10 from numbers to 10

page 75

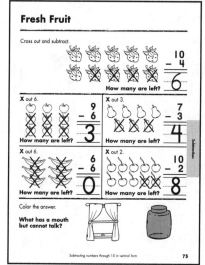

Fresh Fruit

Cross out and subtract.

$10 - 4 = 6$
How many are left?

X out 6.
$9 - 6 = 3$
How many are left?

X out 3.
$7 - 3 = 4$
How many are left?

X out 6.
$6 - 6 = 0$
How many are left?

X out 2.
$10 - 2 = 8$
How many are left?

Color the answer.
What has a mouth but cannot talk?

Subtracting numbers through 10 in vertical form   75

Subtraction Stories

Write the answer.

Five s. Four blow away.
How many are left? $5 - 4 = $ **1**

Nine s. Three go out.
How many are left? $9 - 3 = $ **6**

Ten s. Seven get picked.
How many are left? $10 - 7 = $ **3**

Eight s. Four are eaten.
How many are left? $8 - 4 = $ **4**

Seven s. Two crawl away.
How many are left? $7 - 2 = $ **5**

76   Solving subtraction story problems

Check It!

Subtract. Then add to check.

$5 - 3 = $ **2** ✓ $2 + 3 = $ **5**

$9 - 5 = $ **4** ✓ $4 + 5 = $ **9**

$6 - 4 = $ **2** ✓ $2 + 4 = $ **6**

$10 - 3 = $ **7** ✓ $7 + 3 = $ **10**

$9 - 6 = $ **3** ✓ $3 + 6 = $ **9**

Using addition facts to check subtraction   77

Party Time

Write how many are left.

How many are left? $14 - 8 = $ **6**

$13 - 6 = $ **7**

$12 - 7 = $ **5**

$9 - 0 = $ **9**

$11 - 5 = $ **6**

78   Subtracting numbers 0-9 from numbers through 14

Home Sweet Home

Cross out and subtract. Write how many are left.

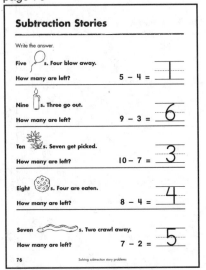

How many are left?
$14 - 9 = $ **5**

$10 - 7 = $ **3**

$12 - 6 = $ **6**

$13 - 5 = $ **8**

Color the answer.
What animal never leaves home?

Subtracting numbers 0-9 from numbers through 14   79

Down We Go

Cross out and subtract. Write how many are left.

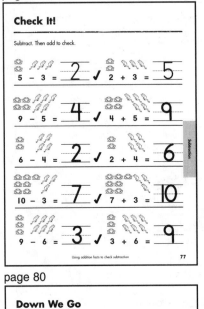

$\begin{array}{r} 11 \\ - 5 \\ \hline 6 \end{array}$

$\begin{array}{r} 14 \\ - 6 \\ \hline 8 \end{array}$
$\begin{array}{r} 13 \\ - 4 \\ \hline 9 \end{array}$

$\begin{array}{r} 12 \\ - 8 \\ \hline 4 \end{array}$
$\begin{array}{r} 11 \\ - 9 \\ \hline 2 \end{array}$

Write the missing numbers.

14, 12, **10**, 8, **6**, 4, 2

80   Subtracting numbers 0-9 from numbers through 14 in vertical form

Have a Nice Trip

Cross out and subtract. Write how many are left.

$\begin{array}{r} 13 \\ - 7 \\ \hline 6 \end{array}$

$\begin{array}{r} 12 \\ - 3 \\ \hline 9 \end{array}$
$\begin{array}{r} 11 \\ - 5 \\ \hline 6 \end{array}$

$\begin{array}{r} 9 \\ - 5 \\ \hline 4 \end{array}$
$\begin{array}{r} 14 \\ - 8 \\ \hline 6 \end{array}$

Circle the answer.
What can travel all over but never leaves the corner?

Subtracting numbers 0-9 from numbers through 14 in vertical form   81

Review

Subtract.

$\begin{array}{r} 10 \\ - 7 \\ \hline 3 \end{array}$
$\begin{array}{r} 11 \\ - 6 \\ \hline 5 \end{array}$
$\begin{array}{r} 14 \\ - 5 \\ \hline 9 \end{array}$
$\begin{array}{r} 13 \\ - 3 \\ \hline 10 \end{array}$

$\begin{array}{r} 12 \\ - 9 \\ \hline 3 \end{array}$
$\begin{array}{r} 10 \\ - 5 \\ \hline 5 \end{array}$
$\begin{array}{r} 9 \\ - 7 \\ \hline 2 \end{array}$
$\begin{array}{r} 13 \\ - 6 \\ \hline 7 \end{array}$
$\begin{array}{r} 11 \\ - 7 \\ \hline 4 \end{array}$

$\begin{array}{r} 10 \\ - 6 \\ \hline 4 \end{array}$
$\begin{array}{r} 14 \\ - 8 \\ \hline 6 \end{array}$
$\begin{array}{r} 8 \\ - 6 \\ \hline 2 \end{array}$
$\begin{array}{r} 12 \\ - 6 \\ \hline 6 \end{array}$
$\begin{array}{r} 13 \\ - 5 \\ \hline 8 \end{array}$

$\begin{array}{r} 11 \\ - 2 \\ \hline 9 \end{array}$
$\begin{array}{r} 12 \\ - 4 \\ \hline 8 \end{array}$
$\begin{array}{r} 14 \\ - 6 \\ \hline 8 \end{array}$
$\begin{array}{r} 12 \\ - 8 \\ \hline 4 \end{array}$
$\begin{array}{r} 13 \\ - 7 \\ \hline 6 \end{array}$

82   Reviewing subtraction facts through 14

I Need Some More

Subtract.
Write how many more are
needed to make 10.

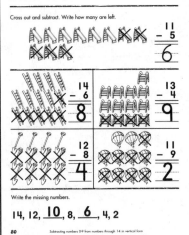

$\begin{array}{r} 10 \\ - 5 \\ \hline 5 \end{array}$

$\begin{array}{r} 10 \\ - 7 \\ \hline 3 \end{array}$
$\begin{array}{r} 10 \\ - 6 \\ \hline 4 \end{array}$

Color the correct answer box.
has 8 s.
He wants 10 s.
How many more s does need?   **2** 3

Using subtraction to find out how many more are needed   83

Nuts and Bolts

Subtract. Write how many are left.

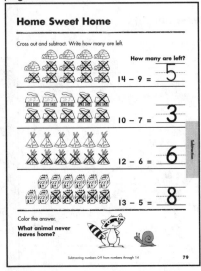

How many are left? $15 - 8 = $ **7**

$14 - 9 = $ **5**

$11 - 8 = $ **3**

$18 - 9 = $ **9**

$17 - 9 = $ **8**

84   Subtracting numbers 0-9 from numbers through 18

page 85

Too Many Tools

Cross out and subtract. Write how many are left.

$$\begin{array}{r} 15 \\ -\ 7 \\ \hline 8 \end{array}$$

How many are left?

$$\begin{array}{r} 16 \\ -\ 8 \\ \hline 8 \end{array} \qquad \begin{array}{r} 18 \\ -\ 9 \\ \hline 9 \end{array}$$

$$\begin{array}{r} 15 \\ -\ 6 \\ \hline 9 \end{array} \qquad \begin{array}{r} 16 \\ -\ 7 \\ \hline 9 \end{array}$$

$$\begin{array}{r} 17 \\ -\ 8 \\ \hline 9 \end{array} \qquad \begin{array}{r} 12 \\ -\ 7 \\ \hline 5 \end{array}$$

Subtracting numbers 0-9 from numbers through 18 in vertical form 85

page 86

Zoom Along

Cross out and subtract. Write how many are left.

$$\begin{array}{r} 12 \\ -\ 4 \\ \hline 8 \end{array}$$

How many are left?

$$\begin{array}{r} 10 \\ -\ 4 \\ \hline 6 \end{array} \qquad \begin{array}{r} 11 \\ -\ 7 \\ \hline 4 \end{array}$$

$$\begin{array}{r} 16 \\ -\ 9 \\ \hline 7 \end{array} \qquad \begin{array}{r} 17 \\ -\ 9 \\ \hline 8 \end{array}$$

$$\begin{array}{r} 14 \\ -\ 7 \\ \hline 7 \end{array} \qquad \begin{array}{r} 15 \\ -\ 8 \\ \hline 7 \end{array}$$

86   Subtracting numbers 0-9 from numbers through 18 in vertical form

page 87

Review

Subtract.

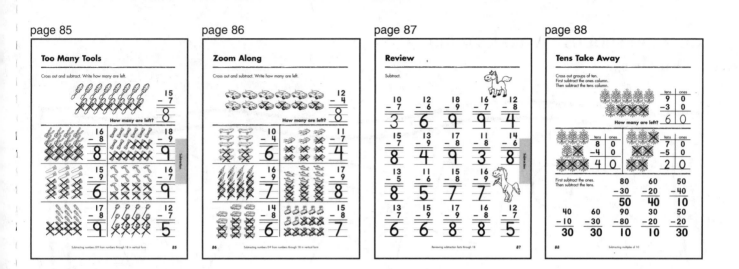

$\begin{array}{r}10\\-7\\\hline3\end{array}$	$\begin{array}{r}12\\-6\\\hline6\end{array}$	$\begin{array}{r}18\\-9\\\hline9\end{array}$	$\begin{array}{r}16\\-7\\\hline9\end{array}$	$\begin{array}{r}12\\-8\\\hline4\end{array}$
$\begin{array}{r}15\\-7\\\hline8\end{array}$	$\begin{array}{r}13\\-9\\\hline4\end{array}$	$\begin{array}{r}17\\-8\\\hline9\end{array}$	$\begin{array}{r}11\\-8\\\hline3\end{array}$	$\begin{array}{r}14\\-6\\\hline8\end{array}$
$\begin{array}{r}13\\-5\\\hline8\end{array}$	$\begin{array}{r}11\\-6\\\hline5\end{array}$	$\begin{array}{r}15\\-8\\\hline7\end{array}$	$\begin{array}{r}16\\-9\\\hline7\end{array}$	
$\begin{array}{r}13\\-7\\\hline6\end{array}$	$\begin{array}{r}15\\-9\\\hline6\end{array}$	$\begin{array}{r}17\\-9\\\hline8\end{array}$	$\begin{array}{r}16\\-8\\\hline8\end{array}$	$\begin{array}{r}12\\-7\\\hline5\end{array}$

Reviewing subtraction facts through 18   87

page 88

Tens Take Away

Cross out groups of ten.
First subtract the ones column.
Then subtract the tens column.

	tens	ones
	9	0
–	3	0
	6	0

How many are left? 60

	tens	ones
	8	0
–	4	0
	4	0

	tens	ones
	7	0
–	5	0
	2	0

First subtract the ones.
Then subtract the tens.

$$\begin{array}{r}80\\-30\\\hline50\end{array} \quad \begin{array}{r}60\\-20\\\hline40\end{array} \quad \begin{array}{r}50\\-40\\\hline10\end{array}$$

$$\begin{array}{r}40\\-10\\\hline30\end{array} \quad \begin{array}{r}60\\-30\\\hline30\end{array} \quad \begin{array}{r}90\\-80\\\hline10\end{array} \quad \begin{array}{r}30\\-20\\\hline10\end{array} \quad \begin{array}{r}50\\-20\\\hline30\end{array}$$

88   Subtracting multiples of 10

page 89

You Can Do It!

First subtract the ones. Then subtract the tens.

tens	ones		tens	ones
4	5		6	7
	3			4
4	2		6	3

tens	ones		tens	ones		tens	ones		tens	ones
3	6		6	8		7	2		5	7
	3			5			1			6
3	3		6	3		7	1		5	1

tens	ones		tens	ones		tens	ones		tens	ones
3	9		5	5		9	8		6	9
	8			3			8			5
3	1		5	2		9	0		6	4

Subtracting 1-digit numbers from 2-digit numbers without regrouping   89

page 90

Brush Off

Subtract the ones. Write how many are left.

tens	ones
3	5
	3
3	2

tens	ones		tens	ones
2	6		4	8
	4			2
2	2		4	6

$$\begin{array}{r}87\\-6\\\hline81\end{array} \quad \begin{array}{r}54\\-1\\\hline53\end{array} \quad \begin{array}{r}63\\-3\\\hline60\end{array} \quad \begin{array}{r}99\\-4\\\hline95\end{array} \quad \begin{array}{r}75\\-2\\\hline73\end{array}$$

$$\begin{array}{r}49\\-7\\\hline42\end{array} \quad \begin{array}{r}68\\-4\\\hline64\end{array} \quad \begin{array}{r}96\\-2\\\hline94\end{array} \quad \begin{array}{r}36\\-5\\\hline31\end{array} \quad \begin{array}{r}55\\-3\\\hline52\end{array}$$

90   Subtracting 1-digit numbers from 2-digit numbers without regrouping

page 91

Practice Makes Purr-fect

Color the spaces to match the answers in the code.

8 = yellow	20 = red
12 = orange	30 = green

green $\begin{array}{r}50\\-20\end{array}$ $\begin{array}{r}70\\-40\end{array}$ green $\begin{array}{r}40\\-10\end{array}$

orange $\begin{array}{r}18\\-6\end{array}$ $\begin{array}{r}90\\-60\end{array}$ green

$\begin{array}{r}80\\-50\end{array}$ green

$\begin{array}{r}16\\-8\end{array}$ $\begin{array}{r}19\\-7\end{array}$ $\begin{array}{r}13\\-1\end{array}$ orange

yellow $\begin{array}{r}16\\-4\end{array}$ orange

$\begin{array}{r}14\\-2\end{array}$

orange   orange

$\begin{array}{r}30\\-10\end{array}$ red $\begin{array}{r}80\\-60\end{array}$ red

Reviewing subtraction   91

page 92

Practice Test

$$\begin{array}{r}40\\-20\\\hline20\end{array}$$

- ○ 30
- ● 20
- ○ 10

A.	$\begin{array}{r}60\\-20\\\hline40\end{array}$	○ 60 ○ 30 ● 40	E.	$\begin{array}{r}89\\-9\\\hline80\end{array}$ ○ 90 ○ 81 ● 80
B.	$\begin{array}{r}37\\-5\\\hline32\end{array}$	● 32 ○ 31 ○ 30	F.	$\begin{array}{r}64\\-1\\\hline63\end{array}$ ○ 68 ○ 65 ● 63
C.	$\begin{array}{r}54\\-3\\\hline51\end{array}$	○ 52 ● 51 ○ 50	G.	$\begin{array}{r}38\\-7\\\hline31\end{array}$ ○ 32 ● 31 ○ 30
D.	$\begin{array}{r}78\\-3\\\hline75\end{array}$	○ 76 ● 75 ○ 74	H.	$\begin{array}{r}90\\-70\\\hline20\end{array}$ ○ 30 ● 20 ○ 10

92   Testing subtraction skills

page 93

Detect the Difference

Subtract, then circle the number that matches your answer.

$$\begin{array}{r}57\\-2\\\hline\end{array}$$ 59 (55) $$\begin{array}{r}40\\-10\\\hline\end{array}$$ 20 (30)

$$\begin{array}{r}91\\-0\\\hline\end{array}$$ (91) 90 $$\begin{array}{r}68\\-6\\\hline\end{array}$$ 64 (62)

$$\begin{array}{r}70\\-20\\\hline\end{array}$$ (50) 90 $$\begin{array}{r}10\\-10\\\hline\end{array}$$ 10 (0) $$\begin{array}{r}84\\-3\\\hline\end{array}$$ 82 (81) $$\begin{array}{r}99\\-3\\\hline\end{array}$$ (96) 95

$$\begin{array}{r}78\\-5\\\hline\end{array}$$ 74 (73) $$\begin{array}{r}60\\-10\\\hline\end{array}$$ (50) 70 $$\begin{array}{r}58\\-2\\\hline\end{array}$$ 54 (56) $$\begin{array}{r}90\\-60\\\hline\end{array}$$ 20 (30)

Subtracting 1-digit numbers from 2-digit numbers without regrouping   93

page 94

Winning Scores

Circle the greater score. Subtract to find out by how many points the home team won.

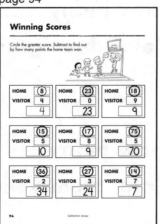

HOME (8)	HOME (23)	HOME (18)
VISITOR 4	VISITOR 0	VISITOR 9
4	23	9

HOME (15)	HOME (17)	HOME (75)
VISITOR 5	VISITOR 8	VISITOR 5
10	9	70

HOME (36)	HOME (27)	HOME (14)
VISITOR 2	VISITOR 3	VISITOR 7
34	24	7

94   Subtraction review

Subtraction

Count and Color

Count the shapes. Write how many.

How many ☐**s?** _____
Color them red. _____

How many △**s?** _____
Color them green. _____

How many ○**s?** _____
Color them blue. _____

How many ▭**s?** _____
Color them yellow. _____

Identifying and counting shapes

Graph It!

Color the graph to show how many of each shape is on page 98.

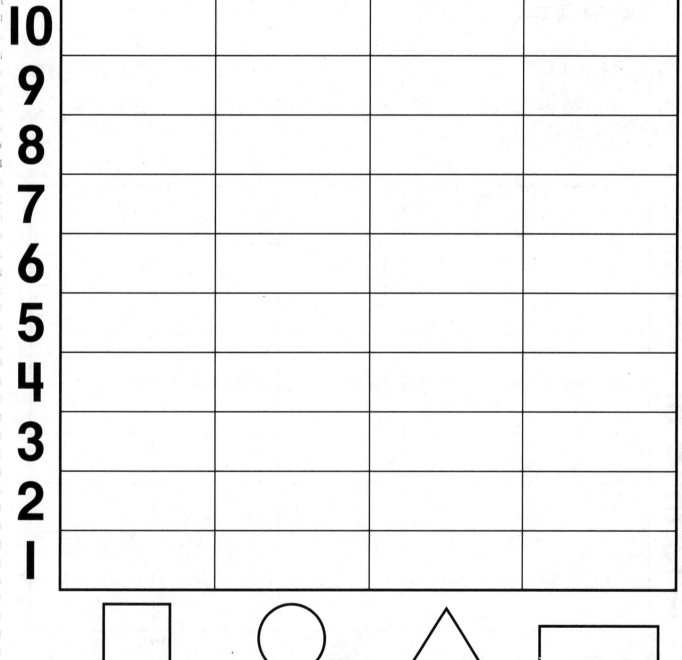

10
9
8
7
6
5
4
3
2
1

Garden Graph

Count how many the rabbit picked.
Color the graph to show the number of each.

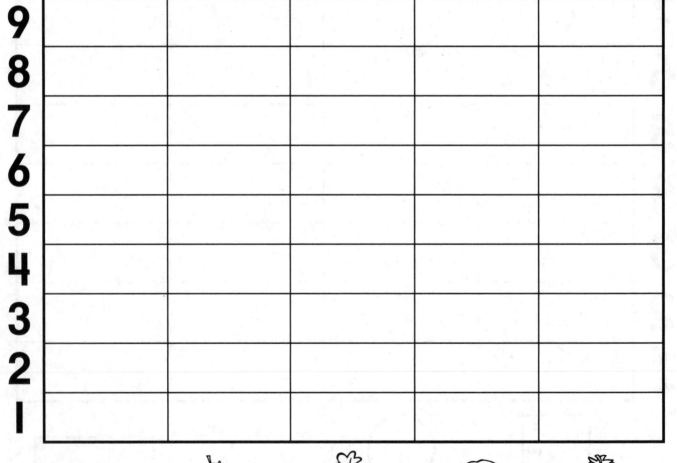

Completing a graph

What's Next?

Draw the shape that comes next.
Color each pattern using the code.

◯ = blue   △ = red

▢ = green   ▭ = yellow

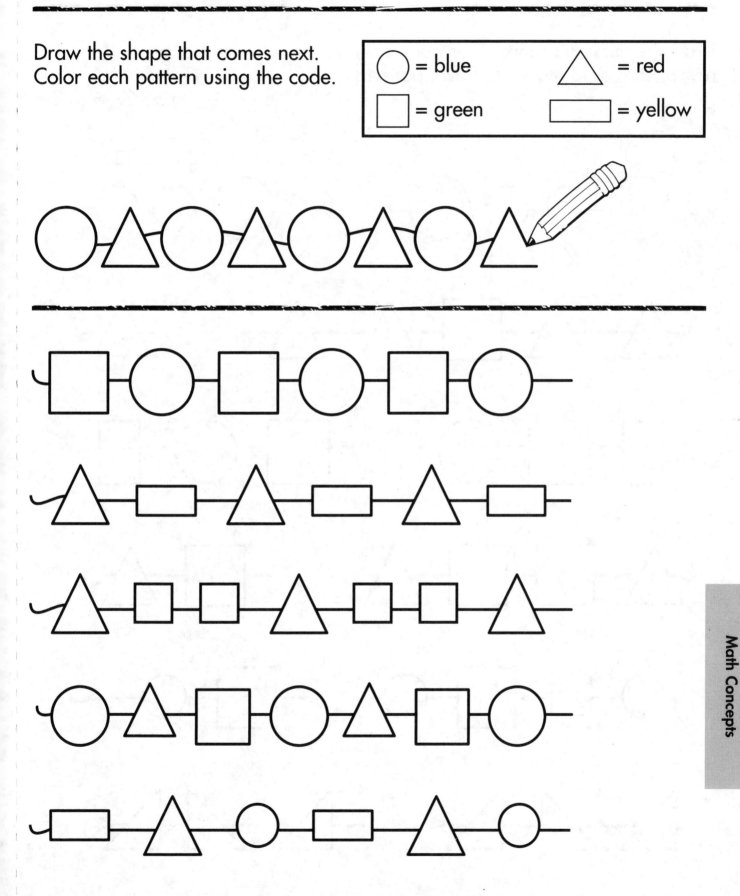

What's Missing?

Draw the missing shapes. Then color each row of shapes to make your own patterns.

Recognizing and completing shape patterns

Shape Puzzlers

Look closely. How many triangles do you see? Write the number.

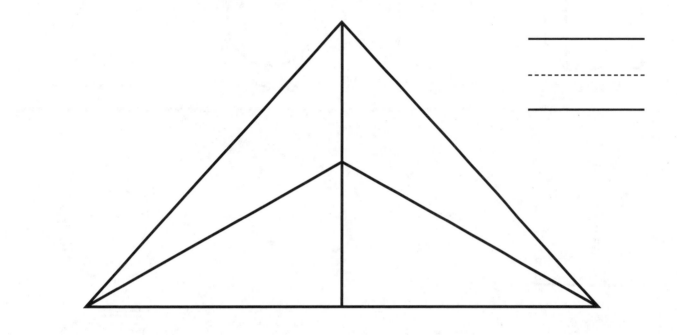

Look closely. How many rectangles do you see? Write the number.

Shape Search

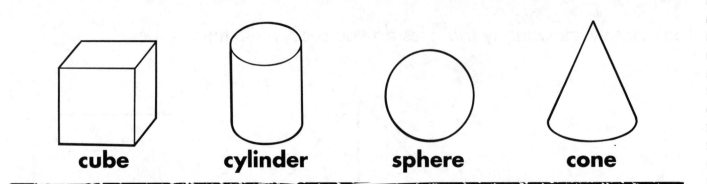

cube   cylinder   sphere   cone

Match.

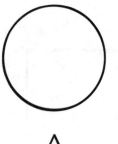

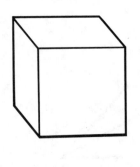

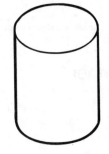

     Matching three-dimensional shapes

Shaping Up

Color the circle.

Color the rectangle.

Continue the pattern.

Color the sphere.

Color the cylinder.

Color the cube.

Color the cone.

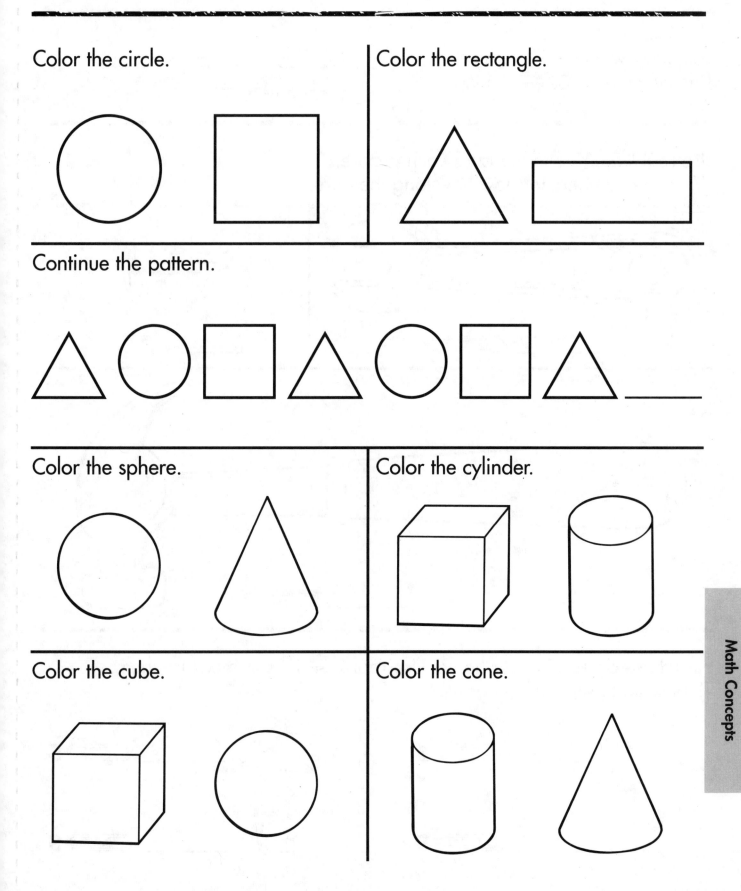

How Long?

You can use 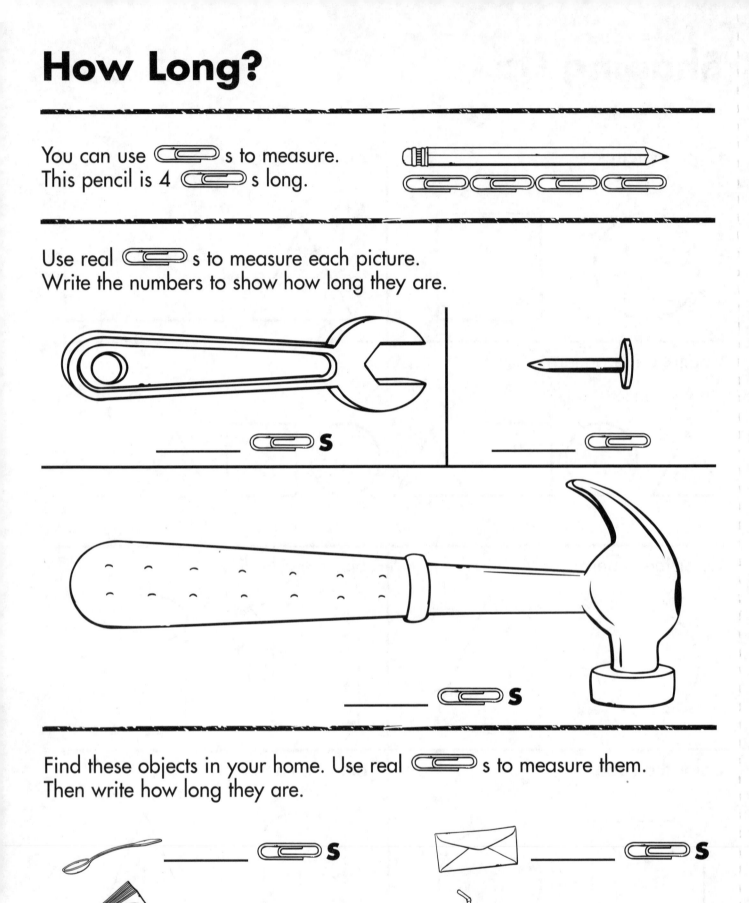s to measure.
This pencil is 4 s long.

Use real s to measure each picture.
Write the numbers to show how long they are.

_____ s

_____ s

_____ s

Find these objects in your home. Use real s to measure them.
Then write how long they are.

_____ s

_____ s

_____ s

_____ s

Measuring length with nonstandard units

Inching Along

5 inches

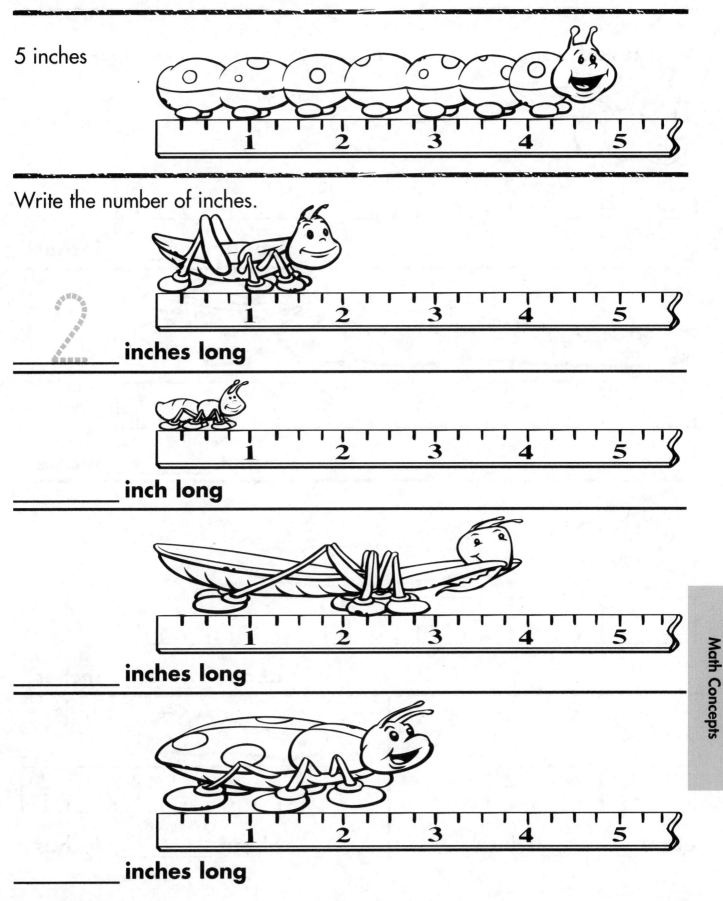

Write the number of inches.

_____ inches long

_____ inch long

_____ inches long

_____ inches long

Math Concepts

Inch by Inch

Measure each worm to the nearest inch. Write about how many inches.

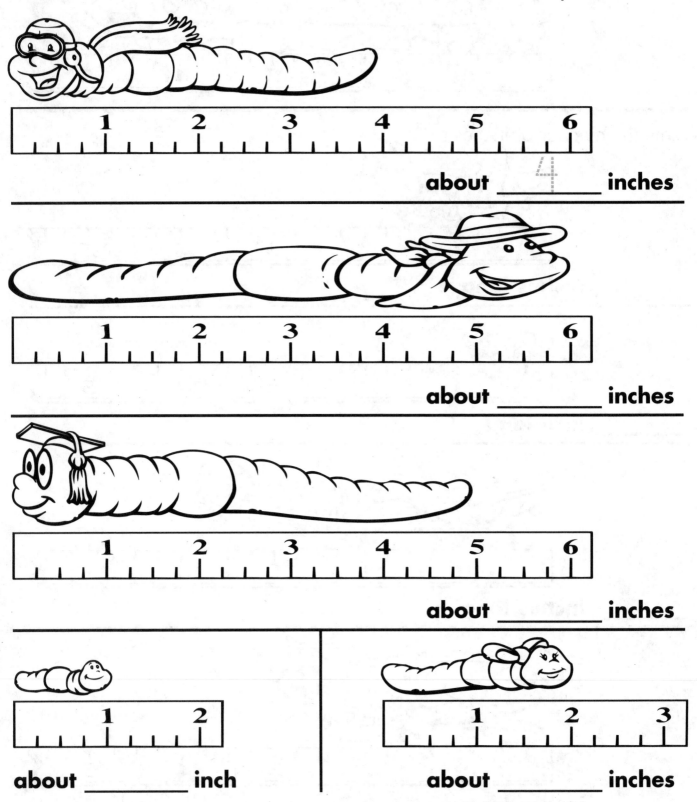

about ___4___ inches

about _____ inches

about _____ inches

about _____ inch

about _____ inches

Pretty Ribbons

Measure each ribbon to the nearest inch. Write the number.
Color the **longest** ribbon red. Color the **shortest** ribbon blue.

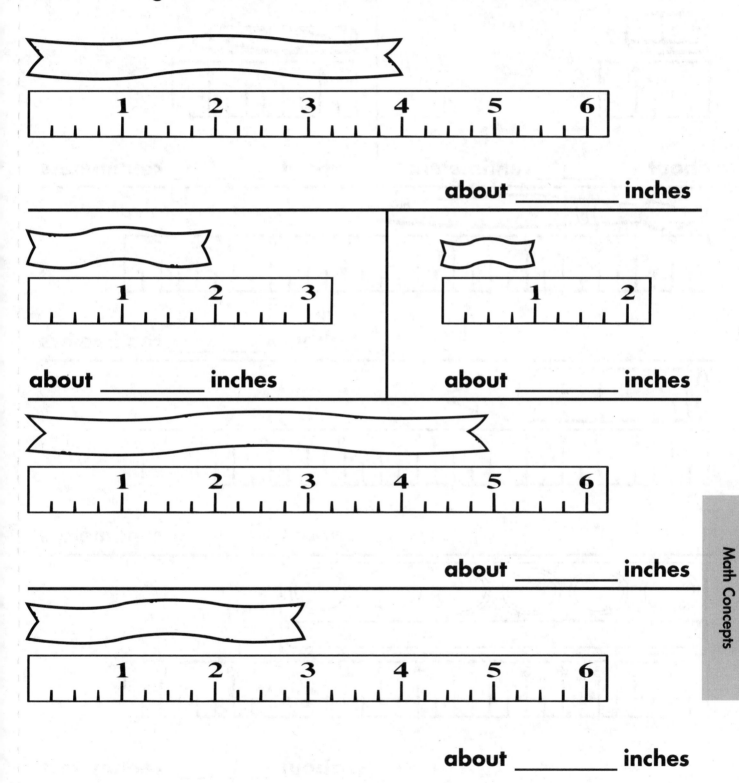

about _____ inches

about _____ inches

about _____ inches

about _____ inches

about _____ inches

Math Concepts

Art Fun

Measure each object to the nearest centimeter. Write about how many centimeters.

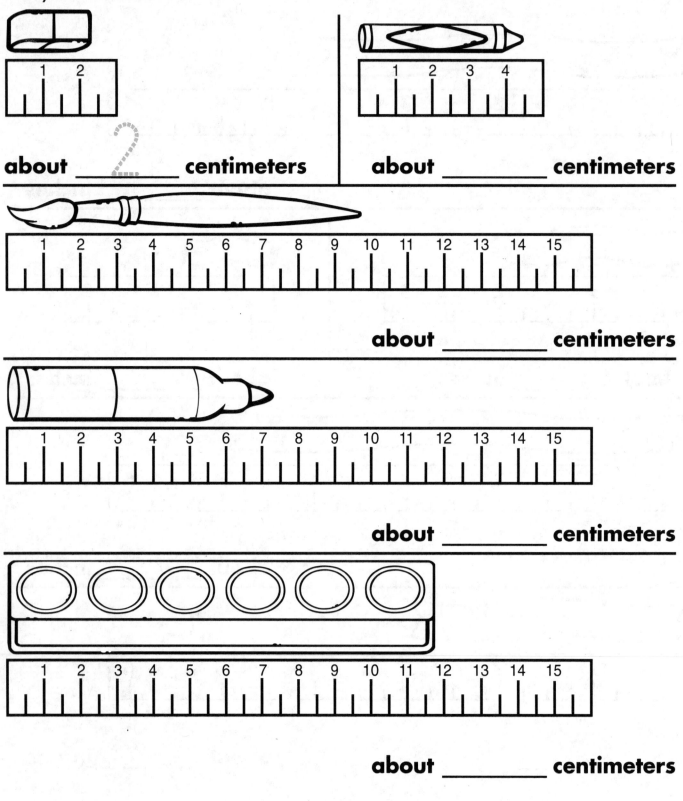

about _____2_____ centimeters

about _____ centimeters

about _____ centimeters

about _____ centimeters

about _____ centimeters

Measuring length in centimeters

Find Sam's Sneaker

Measure each sneaker.
Sam's sneaker is
9 centimeters long.
Find and color it.

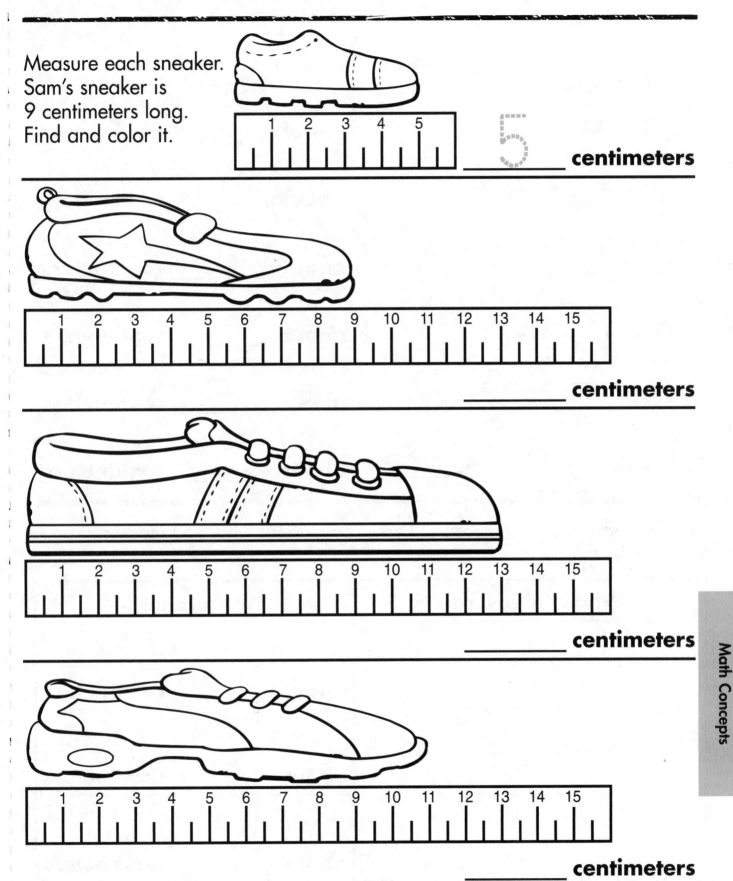

1 2 3 4 5

_____ centimeters

1 2 3 4 5 6 7 8 9 10 11 12 13 14 15

_____ centimeters

1 2 3 4 5 6 7 8 9 10 11 12 13 14 15

_____ centimeters

1 2 3 4 5 6 7 8 9 10 11 12 13 14 15

_____ centimeters

Measuring length in centimeters

Measure at Home

Use a centimeter ruler to measure these things around your home. Write the lengths.

about _____ centimeters

about _____ centimeters

about _____ centimeters

about _____ centimeters

about _____ centimeters

about _____ centimeters

Look for more things to measure. Draw a picture of what you measured and write the length.

What I Measured	Measurement
	about _____ centimeters
	about _____ centimeters
	about _____ centimeters

Measuring length in centimeters

How Much Does It Hold?

less than 1 liter   **1 liter**   **more than 1 liter**

Color all the things that hold **more than 1 liter** red.
Color all the things that hold **less than 1 liter** yellow.

Math Concepts

Cups, Pints, and Quarts

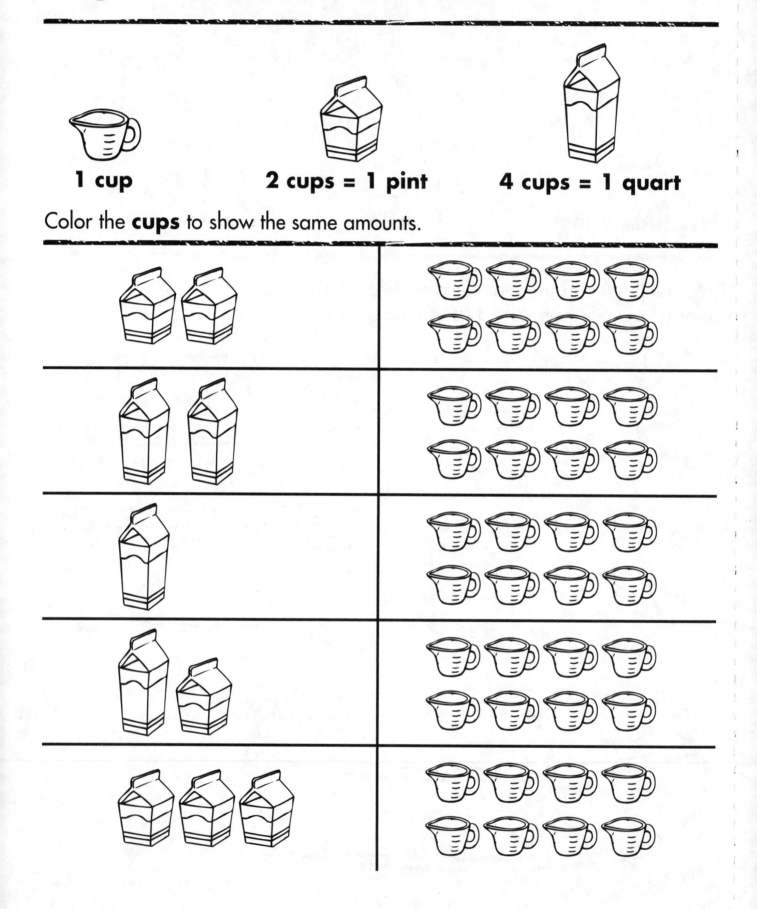

1 cup　　　　**2 cups = 1 pint**　　　　**4 cups = 1 quart**

Color the **cups** to show the same amounts.

Comparing the capacity of cups, pints, and quarts

Weighing Pounds

This spaghetti weighs 1 **pound**.
Another way to write **pound** is **lb**.

Color the things that weigh **more than** 1 lb. red.

Color the things that weigh **less than** 1 lb. blue.

Math Concepts

Kilograms

**less than
1 kilogram**

**about 1
kilogram**

**more than
1 kilogram**

Another way to write **kilogram** is **kg**.

Color the things that are **less than** [1 kg.] green.

Color the things that are **more than** [1 kg] orange.

Comparing weights to 1 kilogram

Review I

Circle the correct answer.

A [ruler marked 1 2 3] can measure _____.   inches   pounds

2 [measuring cup]s equal _____.   [one milk carton]   [two milk cartons]

This [ruler marked 1 2 3] can measure _____.   kilograms   centimeters

A [tiger] weighs _____.   more than [1 lb. weight]   less than [1 lb. weight]

A [milk carton] equals _____.   [three measuring cups]   [two milk cartons]

A [feather] is _____.   less than [1 kg. weight]   more than [1 kg. weight]

Review II

Write the length.

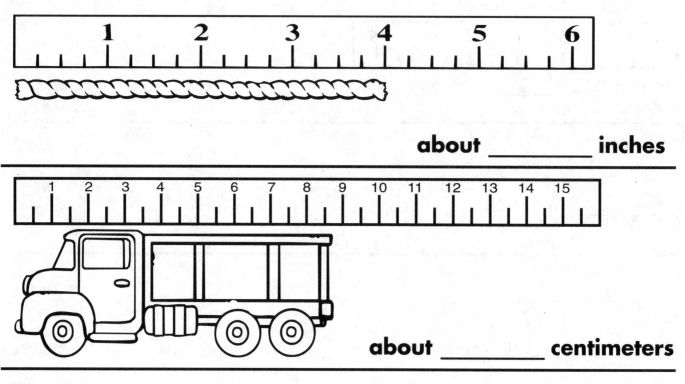

about _____ inches

about _____ centimeters

Color the cups to show the same amount.

Circle the answer that tells about each object's weight.

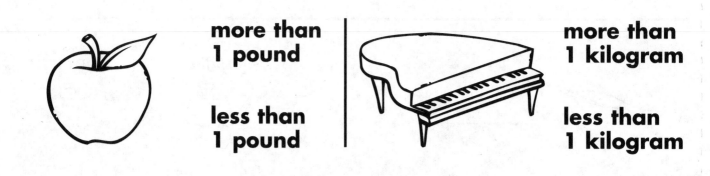

more than
1 pound

less than
1 pound

more than
1 kilogram

less than
1 kilogram

Reviewing length, capacity, and weight

Equal Parts

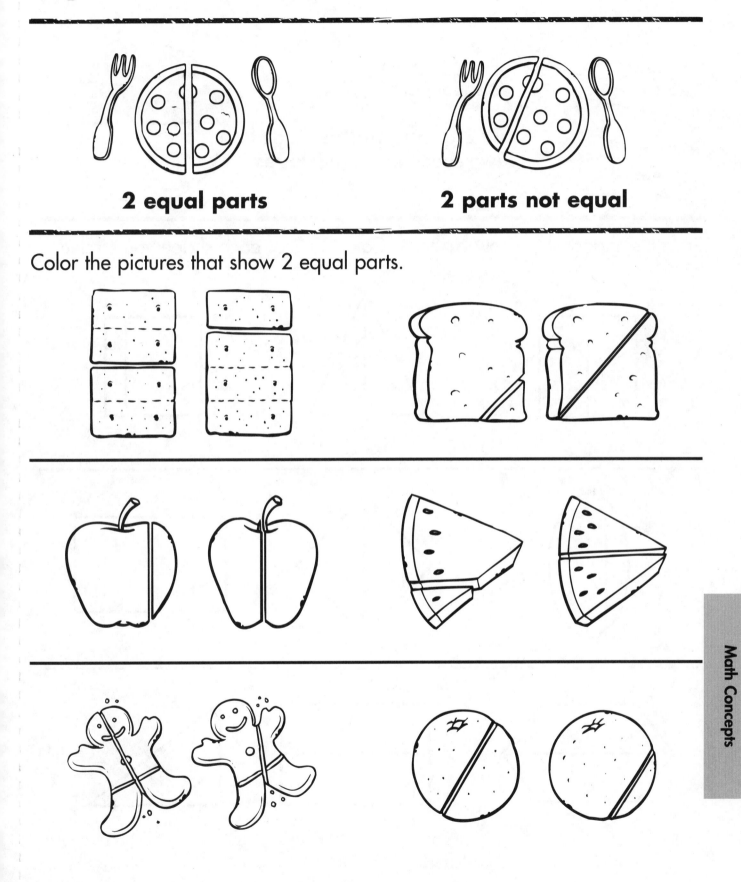

2 equal parts

2 parts not equal

Color the pictures that show 2 equal parts.

What is a Half?

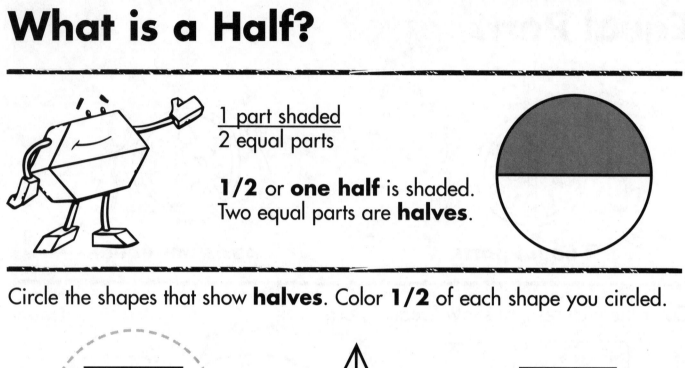

1 part shaded
2 equal parts

1/2 or **one half** is shaded.
Two equal parts are **halves**.

Circle the shapes that show **halves**. Color **1/2** of each shape you circled.

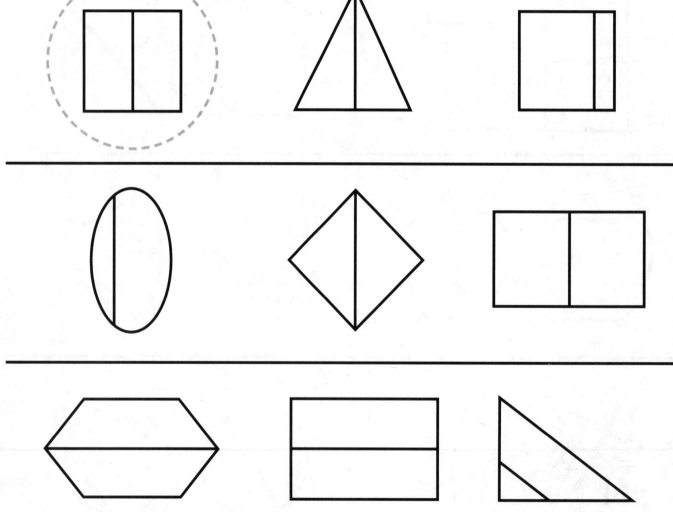

Recognizing halves as two equal parts

What is a Fourth?

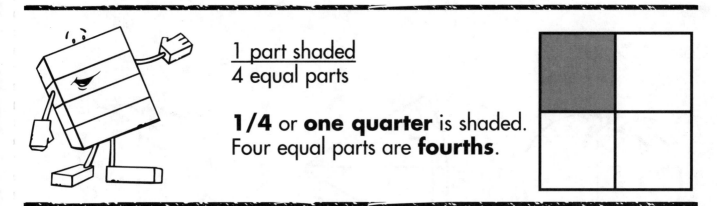

1 part shaded
4 equal parts

1/4 or **one quarter** is shaded.
Four equal parts are **fourths**.

Circle the shapes that show **fourths**. Color **1/4** of each shape you circled.

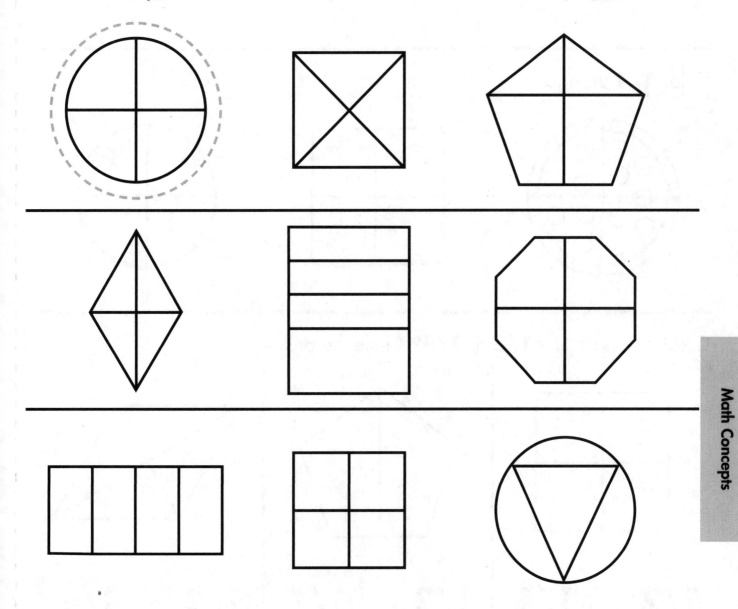

Math Concepts

Halves and Fourths

Color **1/2** red.

 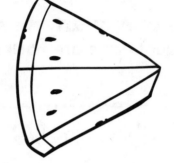 

Color **1/4** orange.

Color one part. Is it **1/2** or **1/4**? Circle the answer.

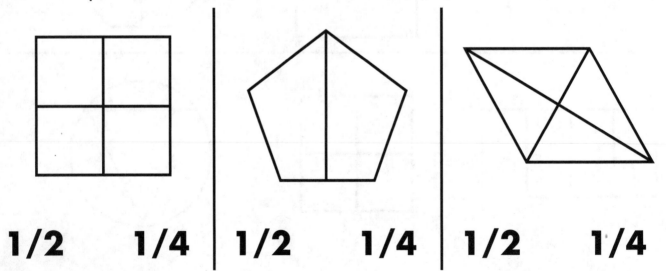

1/2   **1/4** | **1/2**   **1/4** | **1/2**   **1/4**

Recognizing halves and fourths

Answer Key

As the child completes the pages in this section, review his or her answers. When you take the time to correct the work and explain mistakes, you're showing your child that you feel learning is important.

page 98

Count and Color

Count the shapes. Write how many.

How many ☐s? **9** Color them red.

How many △s? **7** Color them green.

How many ○s? **6** Color them blue.

How many ▭s? **4** Color them yellow.

98   Identifying and counting shapes

page 99

Graph It!

Color the graph to show how many of each shape is on page 98.

Completing a graph   99

page 100

Garden Graph

Count how many the rabbit picked. Color the graph to show the number of each.

100   Completing a graph

page 101

What's Next?

Draw the shape that comes next. Color each pattern using the code.

○ = blue △ = red
☐ = green ▭ = yellow

Recognizing and completing shape patterns   101

page 102

What's Missing?

Draw the missing shapes. Then color each row of shapes to make your own patterns.

102   Recognizing and completing shape patterns

page 103

Shape Puzzlers

Look closely. How many triangles do you see? Write the number.

7

Look closely. How many rectangles do you see? Write the number.

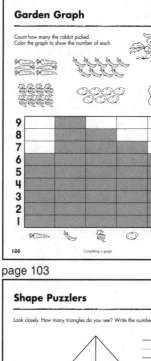

How many can you find?

Using visual discrimination to identify triangles and rectangles   103

page 104

Shape Search

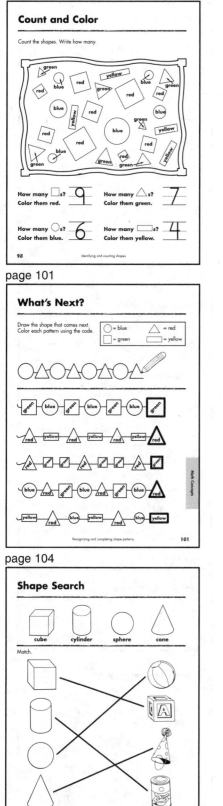

cube   cylinder   sphere   cone

Match.

104   Matching three-dimensional shapes

page 105

Shaping Up

Color the circle.

Color the rectangle.

Continue the pattern.

Color the sphere.

Color the cylinder.

Color the cube.

Color the cone.

Reviewing shape and pattern skills   105

page 106

How Long?

You can use ⬭s to measure. This pencil is 4 ⬭s long.

Use real ⬭s to measure each picture. Write the numbers to show how long they are.

3 ⬭s

☐ ⬭s

5 ⬭s

Find these objects in your home. Use real ⬭s to measure them. Then write how long they are.

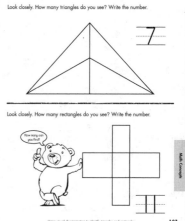

☐s   ☐s

Answers may vary.

☐s   ☐s

106   Measuring length with nonstandard units

Inching Along

5 inches

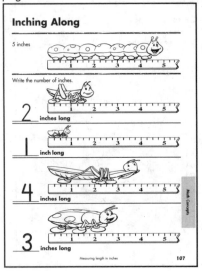

Write the number of inches.

2 inches long

1 inch long

4 inches long

3 inches long

Measuring length in inches   107

Inch by Inch

Measure each worm to the nearest inch. Write about how many inches.

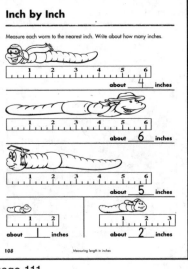

about 4 inches

about 6 inches

about 5 inches

about 1 inches   about 2 inches

108   Measuring length in inches

Pretty Ribbons

Measure each ribbon to the nearest inch. Write the number.
Color the **longest** ribbon red. Color the **shortest** ribbon blue.

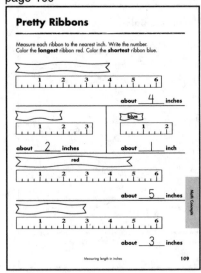

about 4 inches

blue

about 2 inches   about 1 inch

red

about 5 inches

about 3 inches

Measuring length in inches   109

Art Fun

Measure each object to the nearest centimeter. Write about how many centimeters.

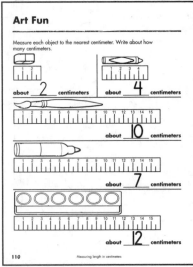

about 2 centimeters   about 4 centimeters

about 10 centimeters

about 7 centimeters

about 12 centimeters

110   Measuring length in centimeters

Find Sam's Sneaker

Measure each sneaker.
Sam's sneaker is
9 centimeters long.
Find and color it.

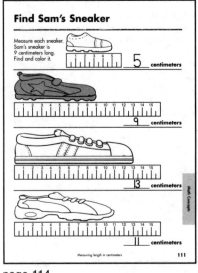

5 centimeters

9 centimeters

13 centimeters

11 centimeters

Measuring length in centimeters   111

Measure at Home

Use a centimeter ruler to measure these things around your home. Write the lengths.

about _____ centimeters

about _____ centimeters

Answers may vary.   about _____ centimeters

about _____ centimeters

about _____ centimeters

about _____ centimeters

Look for more things to measure. Draw a picture of what you measured and write the length.

What I Measured	Measurement
Answers may vary.	about _____ centimeters
	about _____ centimeters
	about _____ centimeters

112   Measuring length in centimeters

How Much Does It Hold?

less than 1 liter   1 liter   more than 1 liter

Color all the things that hold **more than 1 liter** red.
Color all the things that hold **less than 1 liter** yellow.

yellow   yellow

yellow   red

yellow   red   red

red

113   Comparing the capacity of containers with 1 liter

Cups, Pints, and Quarts

1 cup   2 cups = 1 pint   4 cups = 1 quart

Color the **cups** to show the same amounts.

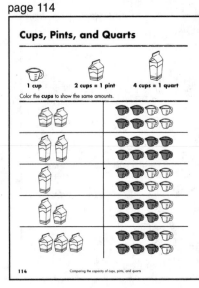

114   Comparing the capacity of cups, pints, and quarts

Weighing Pounds

This spaghetti weighs 1 **pound**.
Another way to write **pound** is lb.

Color the things that weigh **more than** 1 lb red.

Color the things that weigh **less than** 1 lb blue.

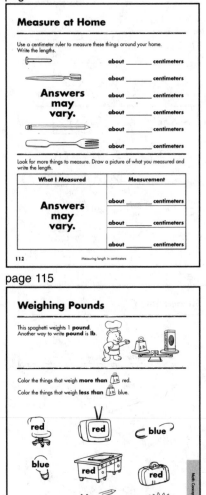

red   red   blue

blue   red   red

blue

blue   blue

115   Comparing weights to 1 pound

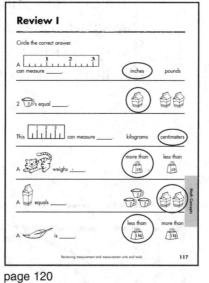

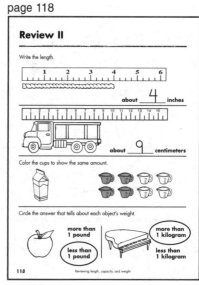

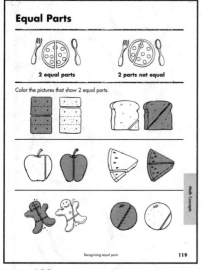

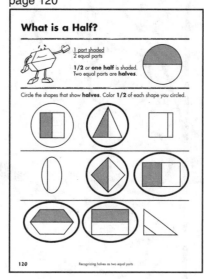

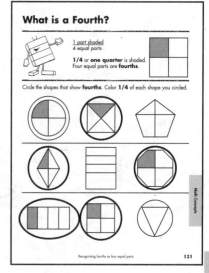

Halves and Fourths

Color 1/2 red.

Color 1/4 orange.

Color one part. Is it 1/2 or 1/4? Circle the answer.

1/2   (1/4)   (1/2)   1/4   1/2   (1/4)

122   Recognizing halves and fourths

Math Concepts

It's Time

The numbers show the time.
The short hand shows the **hour**.
The long hand shows the **minutes**.
The time is 4 o'clock.

Write the clock numbers.
Color the clock.

Write the numbers.

The hour hand is on _____.

The minute hand is on _____.

It is _____ o'clock.

Recognizing numerals on a clock and clock parts

What Time Is It?

The **minute hand** is on 12.
The **hour hand** is on 3.
It is 3 o'clock.

Color the hour hand red. Circle the correct time.

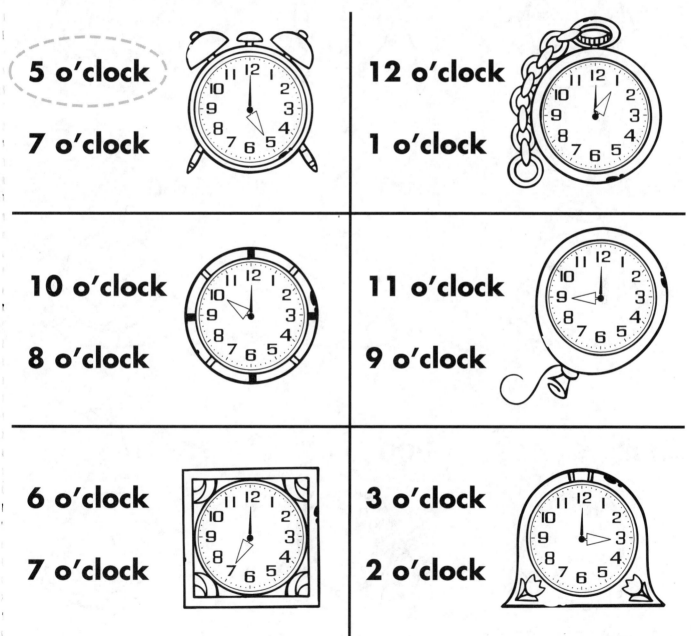

5 o'clock

7 o'clock

12 o'clock

1 o'clock

10 o'clock

8 o'clock

11 o'clock

9 o'clock

6 o'clock

7 o'clock

3 o'clock

2 o'clock

Party Time

Draw the hour hand on each clock to show the time. Color the party hats.

7:00

2:00

5:00

11:00

8:00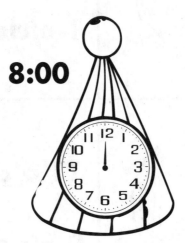

1:00

4:00

9:00

10:00

Showing time to the hour on an analog clock

Digital Time

A **digital clock** tells time with just numbers.
First it tells the hour. Then it tells the minutes.

hour → 7:00

minutes

Write the time on the digital clocks.

So Many Clocks

4 o'clock   **4:00**

Draw lines to match the clocks that show the same time.

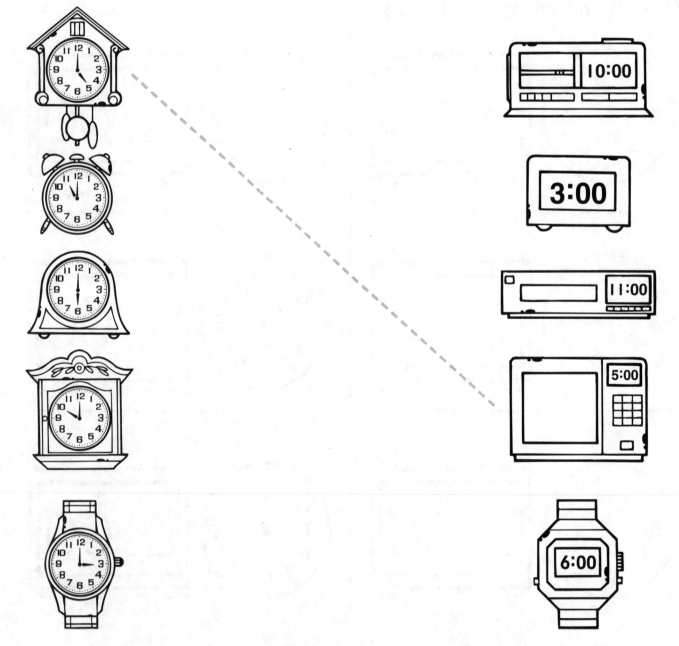

Now and Later

Now it is **2 o'clock**.

One hour **later** it will be **3 o'clock**.

Draw clock hands to show the time one hour **later**. Write the time.

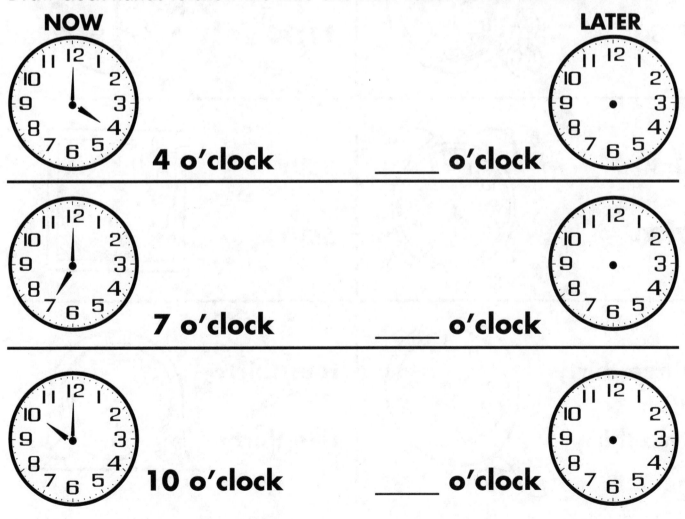

NOW

LATER

4 o'clock

_____ o'clock

7 o'clock

_____ o'clock

10 o'clock

_____ o'clock

Showing the time one hour later

131

Time to the Half Hour

The minute hand is on the 6.
The hour hand is **between** the 8 and 9.
The time is **8:30** or **eight-thirty**.

Circle the correct time.

9:30

8:30

1:30

11:30

8:30

7:30

5:30

6:30

three-thirty

two-thirty

four-thirty

five-thirty

Snack Time

The minute hand is on the 6.
The hour hand is **between** 3 and 4.
The time is **3:30** or **three-thirty**.

Draw the hour hand to show the time. Remember, the hour hand will be **between** two numbers on the clock.

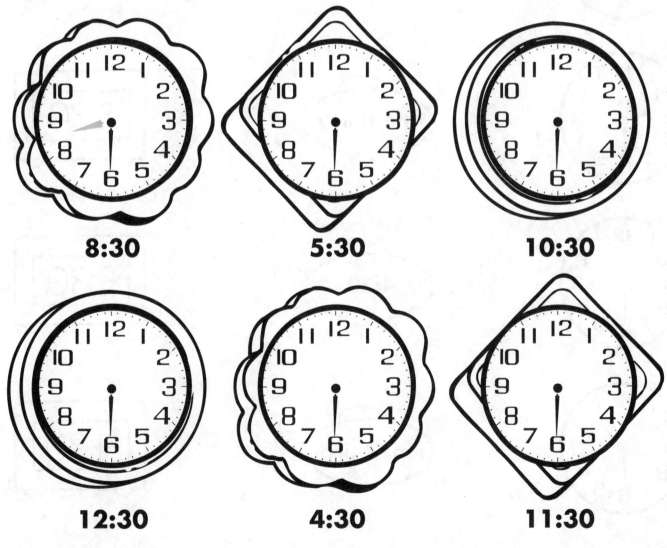

8:30   **5:30**   **10:30**

12:30   **4:30**   **11:30**

Showing time to the half hour   **133**

Fishing for Time

Draw a line from each clock to the time it shows. Then color the clocks and fish using the code.

one-thirty = red   8:30 = green

4:30 = yellow   nine-thirty = blue

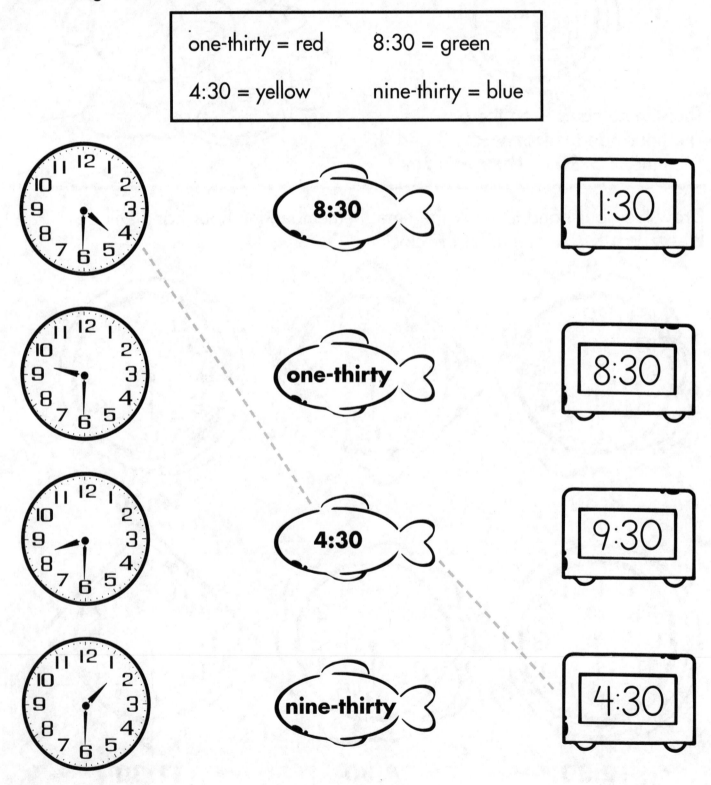

Matching analog and digital clocks to time to the half hour

Time to Clown Around

Write the time.

1:30

_____ _____ _____

_____ _____ _____

_____ _____ _____

Racing Time

Write the time.

7:00

_____　　_____　　_____

_____　　_____　　_____

_____　　_____　　_____

　　　　Reading and writing time to the hour and half hour

Penny Pockets

A **penny** is worth **one cent**.
Another way to write **one cent** is **1¢**.

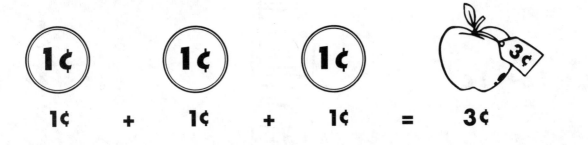

1¢   +   1¢   +   1¢   =   3¢

Color each penny brown. Write how many. Color the pocket in each row that has more pennies.

_____ pennies   _____ pennies

_____ pennies   _____ pennies

Identifying the value of a penny (one cent piece)

Penny Jars

Draw lines to match the pennies with the amounts.

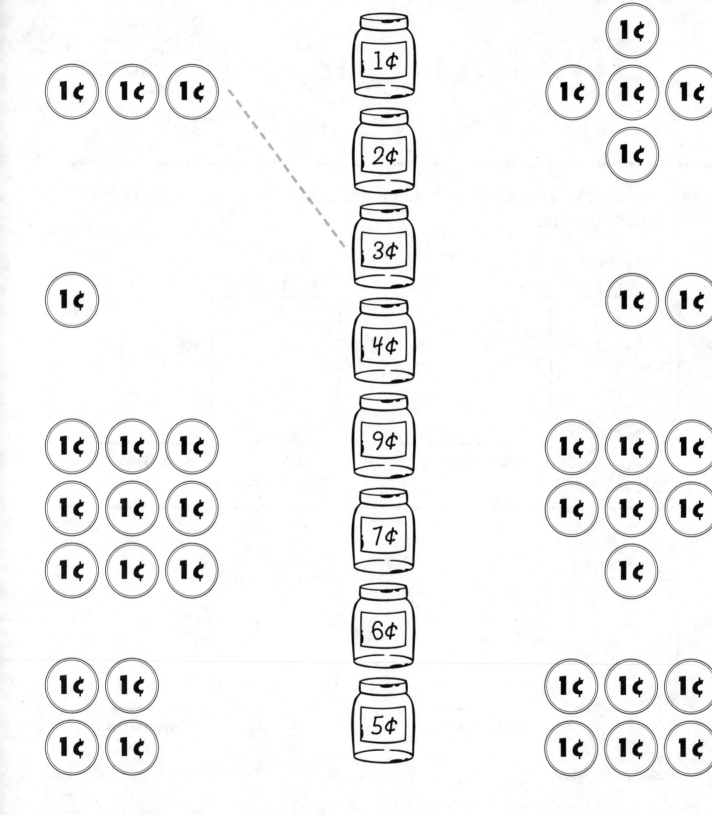

Matching groups of pennies to amounts

Be a Nickel Detective

A **nickel** is worth **five cents** or **5¢**.

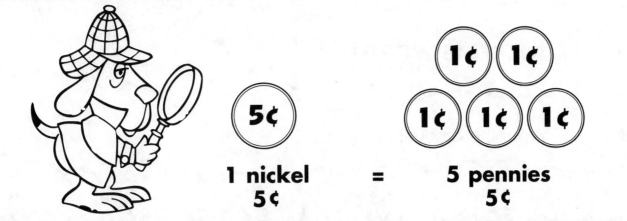

1 nickel
5¢

=

5 pennies
5¢

Color each nickel yellow. Color each penny brown.
Circle the group with the most nickels.

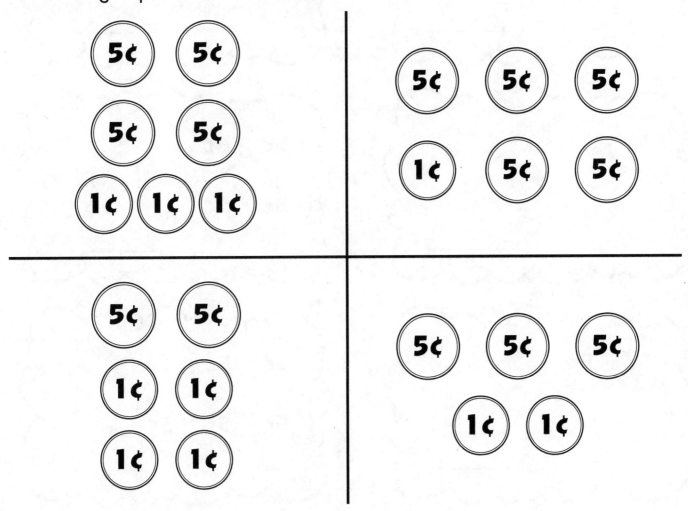

Identifying the value of a nickel (five cent piece)

Counting Nickels

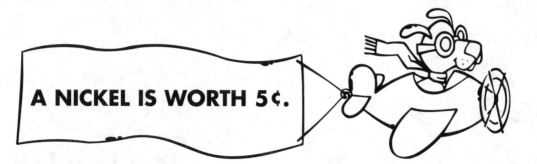

A NICKEL IS WORTH 5¢.

Count by 5's. Write the amount.

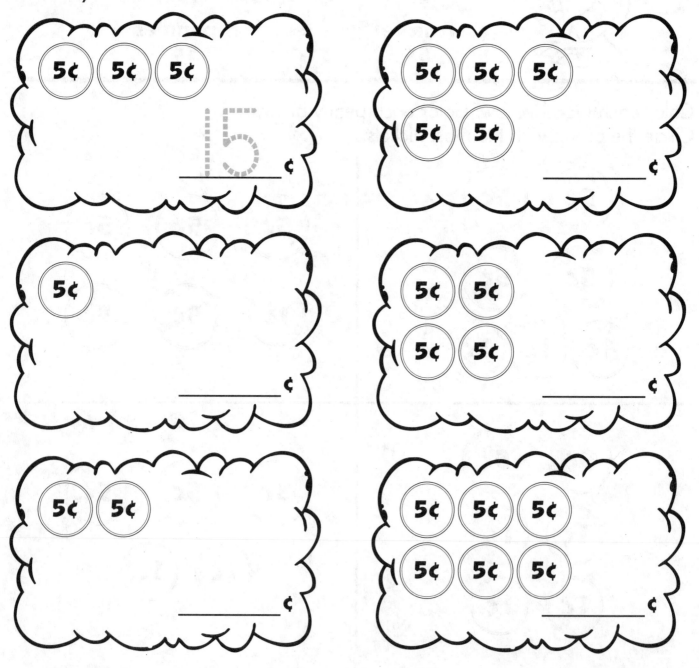

5¢ 5¢ 5¢

_____¢

5¢ 5¢ 5¢
5¢ 5¢

_____¢

5¢

_____¢

5¢ 5¢
5¢ 5¢

_____¢

5¢ 5¢

_____¢

5¢ 5¢ 5¢
5¢ 5¢ 5¢

_____¢

Counting nickels

Coin Count

Count the money in each bank and write the amount. Color the bank with the **most** money pink. Color the one with the **least** money blue.

A Dime a Glass

A **dime** is worth **ten cents** or **10¢**.

1 dime   =   10 pennies
10¢   10¢

Count the money. Write the amount.

1¢ 1¢ 1¢ 1¢ 1¢ 1¢ 1¢ 1¢ 1¢ 1¢ _____ ¢

10¢ _____ ¢

10¢ 10¢ 1¢ _____ ¢

10¢ 1¢ 1¢ 1¢ _____ ¢

10¢ 1¢ 1¢ 1¢ 1¢ 1¢ _____ ¢

142

Counting Dimes

Count by 10's. Write the amount.

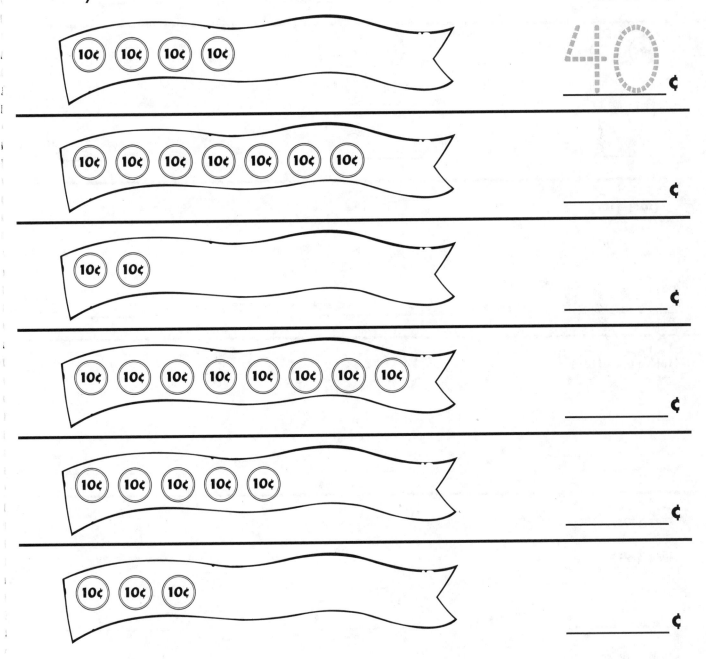

40 ¢

_____ ¢

_____ ¢

_____ ¢

_____ ¢

_____ ¢

Adding Money

Count the money in each group. Add to find the total for the row.

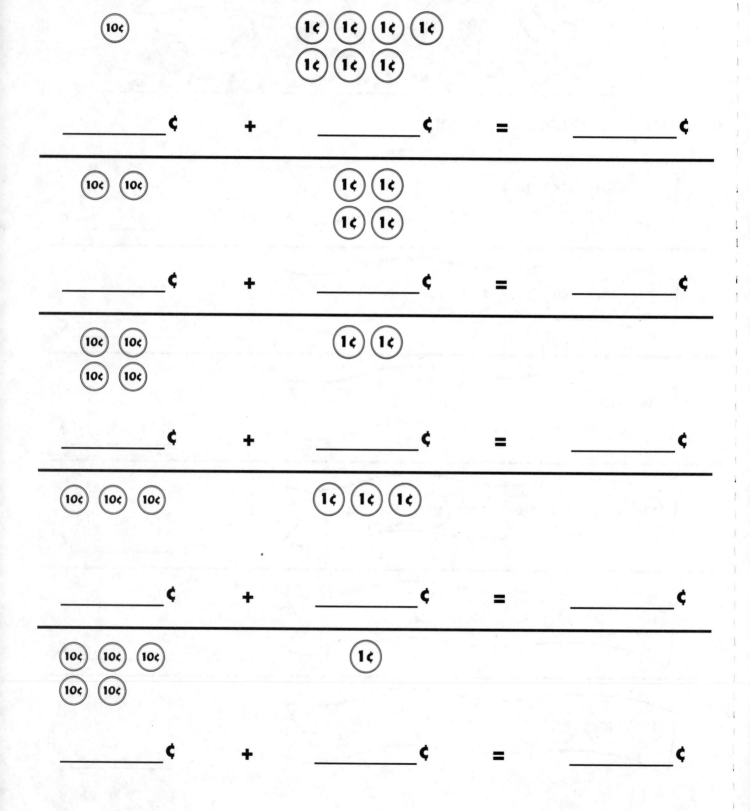

_____¢ + _____¢ = _____¢

_____¢ + _____¢ = _____¢

_____¢ + _____¢ = _____¢

_____¢ + _____¢ = _____¢

_____¢ + _____¢ = _____¢

Counting dimes and pennies

Quarters Anyone?

A **quarter** is worth **twenty-five cents** or **25¢**.

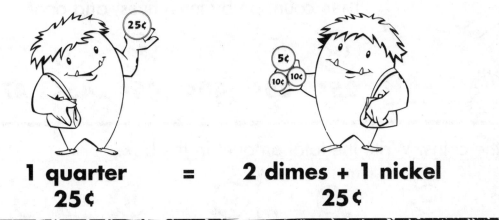

1 quarter	=	2 dimes + 1 nickel
25¢		25¢

Count the money in each purse. Color the purse red if you can trade its coins for a quarter or quarters.

Identifying the value of a quarter (twenty-five cent piece)

Coin Collections

Start with the coin that is worth the most.
Then count on by tens, fives, and ones.

25¢	10¢	5¢	5¢	1¢	1¢
25¢	35¢	40¢	45¢	46¢	47¢

47¢

Count the coins. Write the total amount in the box.

25¢	10¢	10¢	5¢	1¢	1¢
25¢	35¢	45¢	50¢	_____¢	_____¢

25¢	10¢	10¢	10¢	10¢	10¢
_____¢	_____¢	_____¢	_____¢	_____¢	_____¢

25¢	10¢	10¢	5¢	5¢	1¢
_____¢	_____¢	_____¢	_____¢	_____¢	_____¢

25¢	10¢	5¢	1¢	1¢	1¢
_____¢	_____¢	_____¢	_____¢	_____¢	_____¢

25¢	10¢	5¢	5¢	5¢	5¢
_____¢	_____¢	_____¢	_____¢	_____¢	_____¢

Counting quarters, dimes, nickels, and pennies to find money values

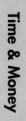

Drawing Coins

Draw coins to show the amount. You may draw any coins you wish.

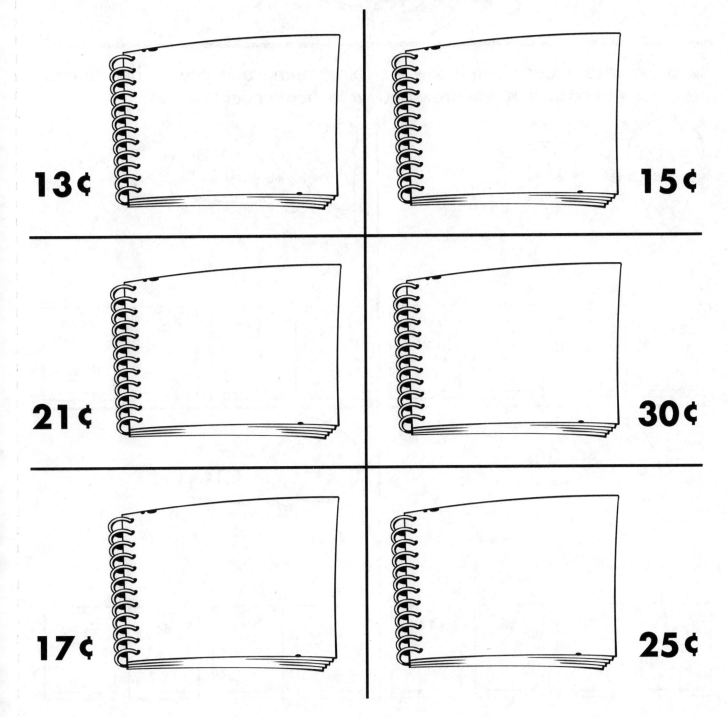

13¢

15¢

21¢

30¢

17¢

25¢

Snack Bar

I can use 1 quarter and 1 dime.

35¢

Read the price of each item. Draw the coins you need to buy it. Then count how many of each coin you drew and write the number.

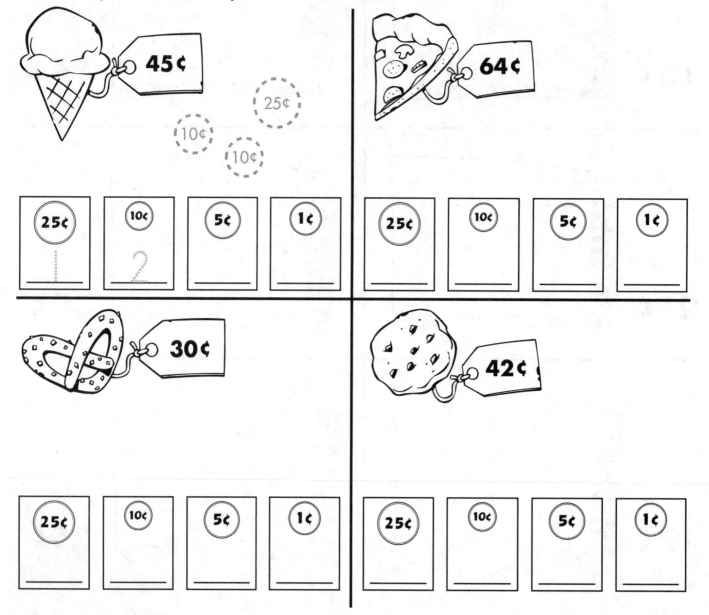

Solving problems using money

Review

Count the money. Write the amount.

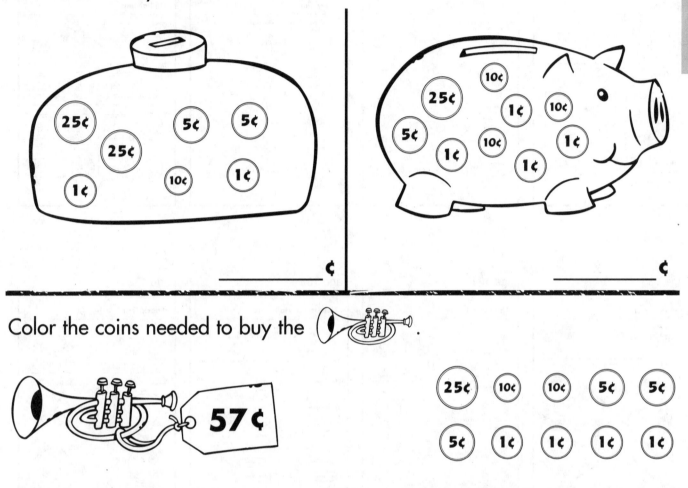

_____ ¢   _____ ¢

Color the coins needed to buy the .

57¢

25¢	10¢	10¢	5¢	5¢
5¢	1¢	1¢	1¢	1¢

Read each problem and circle the answer.

Bob has 1 dime,
2 nickels, and 5 pennies.

Can he trade for a quarter?

Kara has 1 quarter,
and 2 dimes. Lynn has
3 dimes, 2 nickels, and
2 pennies.

Who has more money?

yes   **no**   **Kara**   **Lynn**

Reviewing quarters, dimes, nickels, and pennies and their values   **149**

Answer Key

As the child completes the pages in this section, review his or her answers. When you take the time to correct the work and explain mistakes, you're showing your child that you feel learning is important.

page 126

It's Time

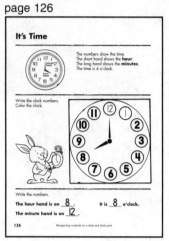

page 127

What Time Is It?

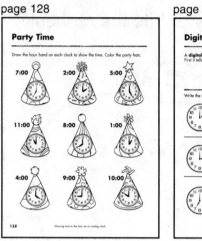

page 128

Party Time

Draw the hour hand on each clock to show the time. Color the party hats.

page 129

Digital Time

page 130

So Many Clocks

page 131

Now and Later

page 132

Time to the Half Hour

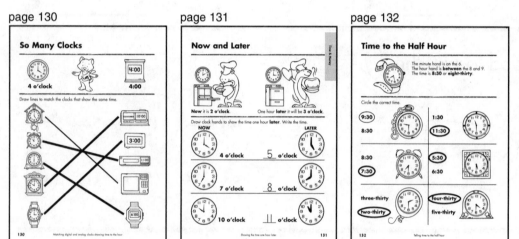

page 133

Snack Time

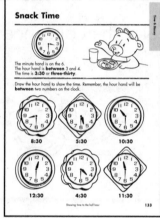

page 134

Fishing for Time

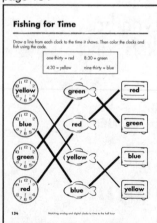

page 135

Time to Clown Around

page 136

Racing Time

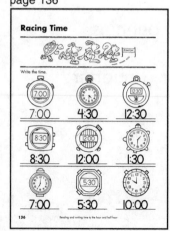

page 137

Penny Pockets

page 138

Penny Jars

Draw lines to match the pennies with the amounts.

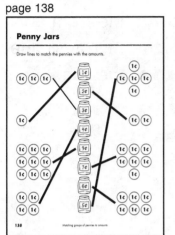

138   Matching groups of pennies to amounts

page 139

Be a Nickel Detective

A **nickel** is worth **five cents** or 5¢.

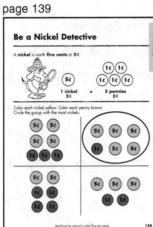

1 nickel = 5 pennies
5¢   5¢

Color each nickel yellow. Color each penny brown.
Circle the group with the most nickels.

Identifying the value of a nickel (five cent piece)   139

page 140

Counting Nickels

A NICKEL IS WORTH 5¢.

Count by 5's. Write the amount.

15   25
5   20
10   30

140   Counting nickels

page 141

Coin Count

Count the money in each bank and write the amount. Color the bank with the **most** money pink. Color the one with the **least** money blue.

blue   7 ¢   9 ¢

15 ¢   pink   17 ¢

15 ¢   8 ¢

Counting nickels and pennies   141

page 142

A Dime a Glass

A **dime** is worth **ten cents** or 10¢.

1 dime = 10 pennies
10¢   10¢

Count the money. Write the amount.

10 ¢
10 ¢
21 ¢
13 ¢
15 ¢

142   Identifying the value of a dime (ten cent piece)

page 143

Counting Dimes

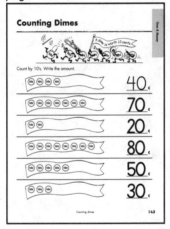

A dime is worth 10 cents

Count by 10's. Write the amount.

40 ¢
70 ¢
20 ¢
80 ¢
50 ¢
30 ¢

Counting dimes   143

page 144

Adding Money

Count the money in each group. Add to find the total for the row.

10 ¢ + 7 ¢ = 17 ¢
20 ¢ + 4 ¢ = 24 ¢
40 ¢ + 2 ¢ = 42 ¢
30 ¢ + 3 ¢ = 33 ¢
50 ¢ + 1 ¢ = 51 ¢

144   Counting dimes and pennies

page 145

Quarters Anyone?

A **quarter** is worth **twenty-five cents** or 25¢.

1 quarter = 2 dimes + 1 nickel
25¢   25¢

Count the money in each purse. Color the purse red if you can trade its coins for a quarter or quarters.

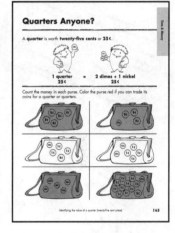

Identifying the value of a quarter (twenty-five cent piece)   145

page 146

Coin Collections

Start with the coin that is worth the most. Then count on by tens, fives, and ones.
25¢ 35¢ 40¢ 45¢ 46¢ 47¢   47

Count the coins. Write the total amount in the box.

25¢ 35¢ 45¢ 50¢ 51¢ 52¢   52
25¢ 35¢ 45¢ 55¢ 65¢ 75¢   75
25¢ 35¢ 45¢ 50¢ 55¢ 56¢   56
25¢ 35¢ 40¢ 41¢ 42¢ 43¢   43
25¢ 35¢ 40¢ 45¢ 50¢ 55¢   55

146   Counting quarters, dimes, nickels, and pennies to find money values

page 147

Drawing Coins

1¢   5¢   10¢   25¢

Draw coins to show the amount. You may draw any coins you wish.

Answers may vary.   Answers may vary.
13¢   15¢

Answers may vary.   Answers may vary.
21¢   30¢

Answers may vary.   Answers may vary.
17¢   25¢

Drawing coins to show amounts   147

page 148

Snack Bar

I can see 1 quarter and 1 dime.
35¢

Read the price of each item. Draw the coins you need to buy it. Then count how many of each coin you drew and write the number.

45¢
Answers may vary.   64¢
2
2   1   4
30¢
42¢
1   1   1   1   2

148   Solving problems using money

page 149

Review

Count the money. Write the amount.

72 ¢   64 ¢

Color the coins needed to buy the
57¢

Read each problem and circle the answer.

Bob has 1 dime, 2 nickels, and 5 pennies.
Can he trade for a quarter?
yes   no

Kara has 1 quarter, and 2 dimes. Lynn has 3 dimes, 2 nickels, and 2 pennies.
Who has more money?
Kara   Lynn

Reviewing quarters, dimes, nickels, and pennies and their values   149

Lamb in the Sun

Say the name of each picture. Color the lamb and sun. Draw a line from each picture that has the same beginning sound as **lamb** to the lamb. Draw a line from each picture that has the same beginning sound as **sun** to the sun.

Ss

 **Ll**

Recognizing the initial consonant sounds of **Ll** and **Ss**

Monkeys and Tigers

Say the name of each picture. Color the monkeys and tigers. Draw a line from each picture that has the same beginning sound as **monkey** to the monkeys. Draw a line from each picture that has the same beginning sound as **tiger** to the tigers.

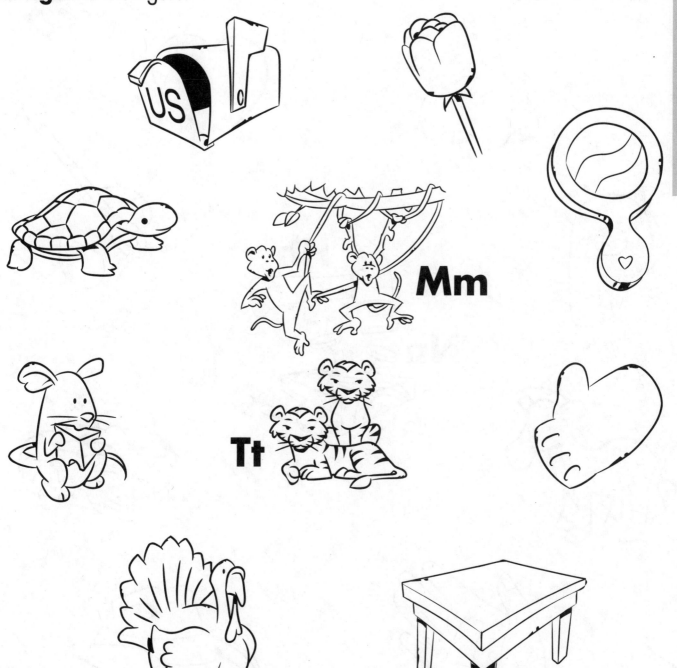

Recognizing the initial consonant sounds of **Mm** and **Tt**

Hammer and Nails

Say the name of each picture. Color the hammer and nails. Draw a line from each picture that has the same beginning sound as **hammer** to the hammer. Draw a line from each picture that has the same beginning sound as **nail** to the nails.

Recognizing the initial consonant sounds of **Hh** and **Nn**

Dog Sees a Windmill

Say the name of each picture. Color the dog and windmill. Draw a line from each picture that has the same beginning sound as **dog** to the dog. Draw a line from each picture that has the same beginning sound as **windmill** to the windmill.

Recognizing the initial consonant sounds of **Dd** and **Ww**

Two Sounds of Gg

Hard Sound

When **g** comes before **a**, **o**, or **u**, it has a hard sound like in **gum**.

g<u>oo</u>se **g<u>a</u>ve** **g<u>u</u>m**

Soft Sound

When **g** comes before **e**, **i**, or **y**, it often has a soft sound like **j**.

g<u>e</u>neral **g<u>y</u>psy**
g<u>i</u>ngerbread

The letter **g** does not always have the soft sound before **e** or **i**. Sometimes it has the hard sound, like in **girl**, **get**, and **give**.

Say each word. Circle the **g** and the letter that comes after it. Color the picture if the word has the soft sound of **g**.

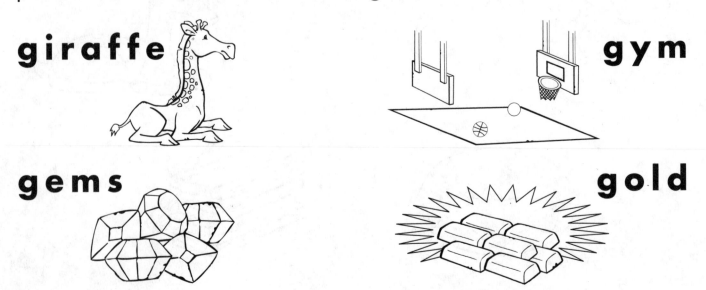

giraffe

gym

gems

gold

Recognizing the hard and soft consonant sounds of **Gg**

A Rose for Bear

Say the name of each picture. Color the rose and bear. Draw a line from each picture that has the same beginning sound as **rose** to the rose. Draw a line from each picture that has the same beginning sound as **bear** to the bear.

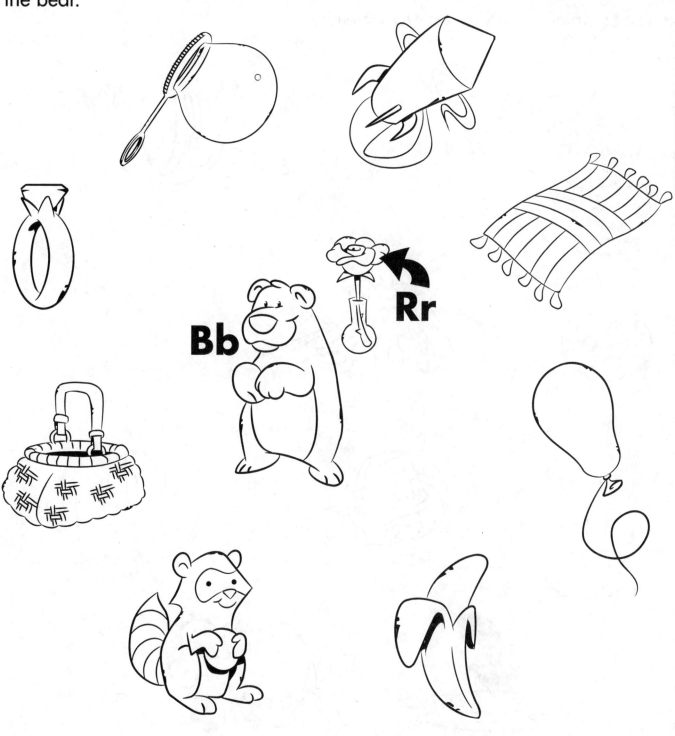

Rr

Bb

Violin and Yo-Yo

Say the name of each picture. Color the **violin** purple and the **yo-yo** yellow. Color the rest of the pictures using the code.

Same beginning sound as **violin** = purple
Same beginning sound as **yo-yo** = yellow

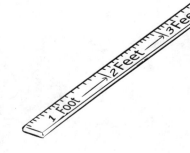

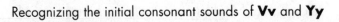

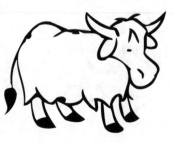

Recognizing the initial consonant sounds of **Vv** and **Yy**

Pandas Around a Fire

Say the name of each picture. Color the **pandas** pink and the **fire** red.
Color the rest of the pictures using the code.

Same beginning sound as **panda** = pink
Same beginning sound as **fire** = red

Two Sounds of Cc

Hard Sound

When **c** comes before **a**, **o**, or **u**, it has a hard sound like **k**.

<u>c</u>at   <u>c</u>ub   <u>c</u>ot

Soft Sound

When **c** comes before **e**, **i**, or **y**, it has a soft sound like **s**.

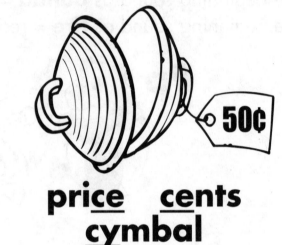

50¢

pri<u>c</u>e   <u>c</u>ents
<u>c</u>ymbal

Say each word. Circle the word if it has the hard **c** sound. Draw a box around the word if it has the soft **c** sound.

celery   **car**   **cup**

cone   **mice**   **cube**

fence   **comb**   **lace**

Kettle Juggler

Say the name of each picture. Color the kettles and juggler. Draw a line from each picture that has the same beginning sound as **kettle** to the kettles. Draw a line from each picture that has the same beginning sound as **juggler** to the juggler.

Kk

Jj

Queen and Zebra

Say the name of each picture. Color the queen and zebra. Draw a line from each picture that has the same beginning sound as **queen** to the queen. Draw a line from each picture that has the same beginning sound as **zebra** to the zebra.

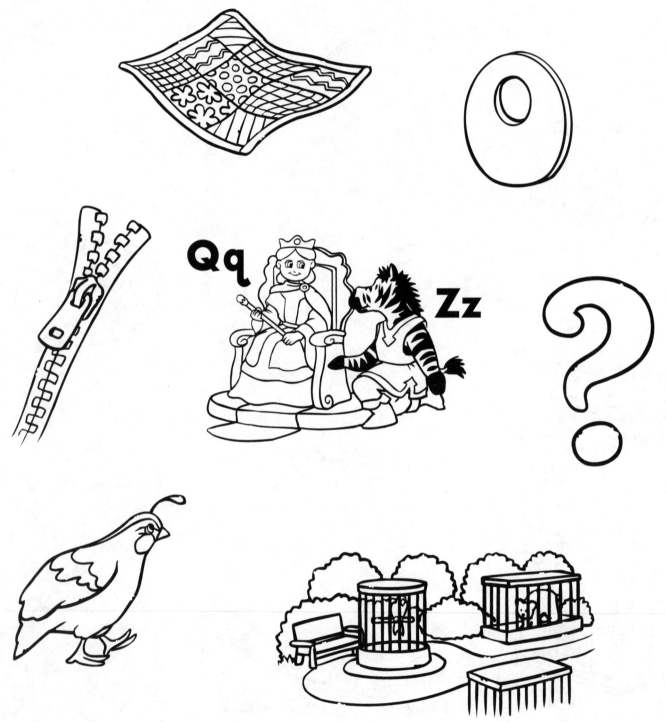

Recognizing the initial consonant sounds of **Qq** and **Zz**

Two Sounds of Xx

Say the name of each picture. Listen for the sound at the end of each word.

six

fox

The letter **x** makes another sound sometimes. When it is at the beginning of a word, **x** often makes the same sound as **z**.

xylophone

Say the name of each picture. Draw a line to the word that names it, then color the picture.

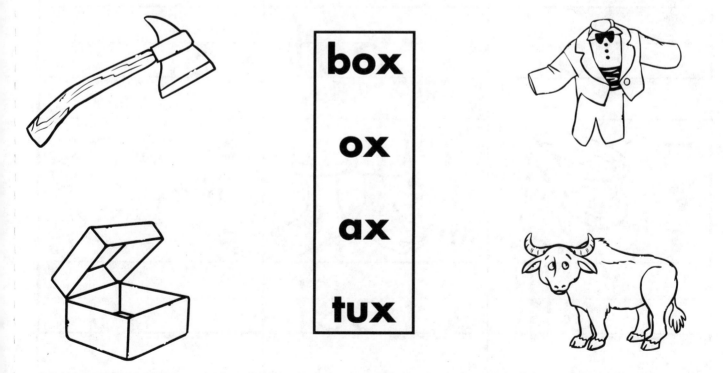

box

ox

ax

tux

What's Missing?

Circle the missing letter in each word, then write it to finish the word. Color the pictures.

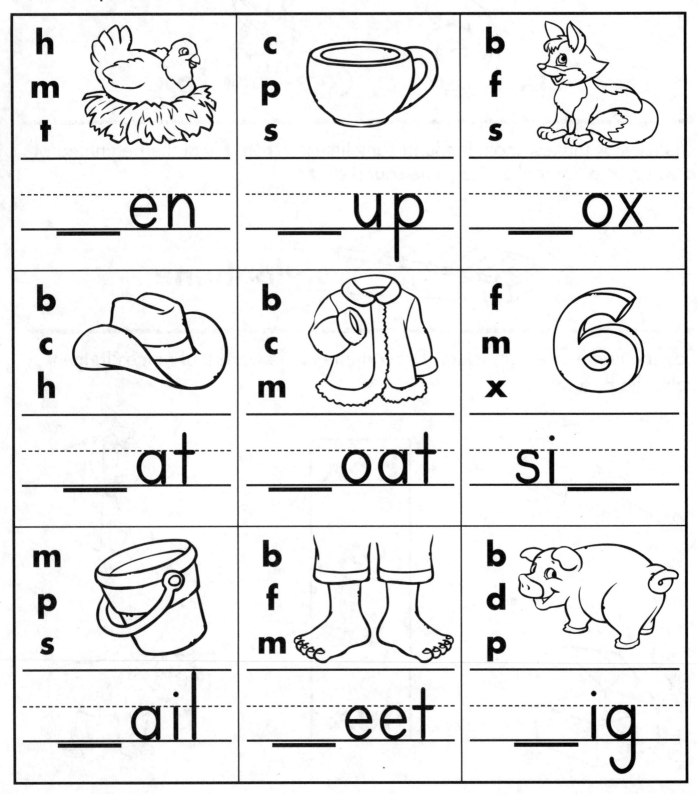

h **m** **t**	**c** **p** **s**	**b** **f** **s**
____ en	____ up	____ ox
b **c** **h**	**b** **c** **m**	**f** **m** **x**
____ at	____ oat	si ____
m **p** **s**	**b** **f** **m**	**b** **d** **p**
____ ail	____ eet	____ ig

Reviewing consonant sounds

Hearing Endings

Say the name of each picture, then fill in the circle next to the word that names it. Color the pictures.

○ **map**   ○ **man**   ○ **bun**   ○ **bud**   ○ **fan**   ○ **fat**

○ **bell**   ○ **bet**   ○ **ham**   ○ **hat**   ○ **miss**   ○ **mitt**

○ **win**   ○ **wig**   ○ **cub**   ○ **cup**   ○ **cot**   ○ **cob**

○ **hen**   ○ **hem**   ○ **bob**   ○ **box**   ○ **wet**   ○ **web**

Recognizing the sounds of consonants in final position

Consonant Blends with l

Some **consonants** can be put together to make a **blend**.

The **blend bl** has the sound you hear in the word **blue**.
The **blend pl** has the sound you hear in the word **planes**.
The **blend fl** has the sound you hear in the word **fly**.

Color the planes blue. Then read the sentence.

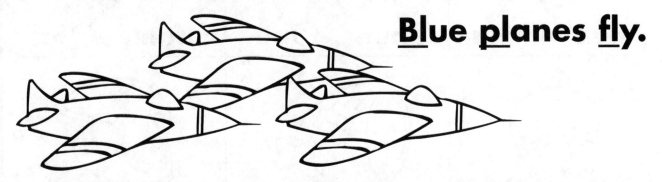

Blue planes fly.

Circle the **blends** at the beginning of each word.

clock

slide

glove

black

Write another word that has a consonant blend with the letter **l**.

_____

_____

_____

Recognizing and writing two-letter initial consonant blends with **l**

Consonant Blends with r

The **blend *dr*** has the sound you hear in the word **<u>dr</u>ew**.

The **blend *gr*** has the sound you hear in the word **<u>gr</u>een**.

The **blend *tr*** has the sound you hear in the word **<u>tr</u>ee**.

Color the tree green. Then read the sentence.

He **<u>dr</u>ew** a **<u>gr</u>een** **<u>tr</u>ee**.

Use the words in the box to write the name of each picture. Notice the **blend** at the beginning of each word.

bricks	dragon	crown	grass

Write another word that has a consonant blend with the letter **r**.

Recognizing and writing two-letter initial consonant blends with **r**

Consonant Blends with s

The **blend sp** has the sound you hear in the word **spider**.
The **blend st** has the sound you hear in the word **story**.
The **blend sc** has the sound you hear in the word **scary**.

Read the sentence.

This **spider story** is **scary**!

Use the words in the box to write the name of each picture. Notice the **blend** at the beginning of each word.

smile	snail	skate	sweater

Write another word that has a consonant blend with the letter **s**.

Blend or Brend?

Circle each word that begins with the wrong **blend**. Rewrite it using the correct **blend**.

praying catch

_____
- - - - - - - - - - - - - - - - -
_____

glowing tall

- - - - - - - - - - - - - - - - -
_____

go in the snore

- - - - - - - - - - - - - - - - -
_____

letter flom a friend

_____
- - - - - - - - - - - - - - - - -
_____

pet stider

- - - - - - - - - - - - - - - - -
_____

Blend at the End

A word may begin or end with a **blend**.

s<u>k</u>ate   **ma<u>sk</u>**

Circle the two-consonant **blend** at the end of each word.

ant	must	felt
band	**lamp**	**ink**
ask	**lift**	**last**

Write four of the ending **blends** you circled.

_____   _____   _____   _____

_____   _____   _____   _____

Use the words above to write the name of each picture.

_____   _____

S and Two Partners

Some **blends** join **s** with *two* other consonants.

He has **<u>str</u>ing**, a **<u>spr</u>ing**, and a **<u>scr</u>ew**.

Use the words in the box to write the name of each picture. Notice the three-consonant **blend** at the beginning of each word.

spray scrub strong straw

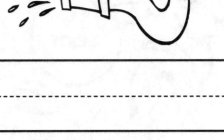

_____

- - - - - - - - - - - - - - - - -

_____

_____

- - - - - - - - - - - - - - - - -

_____

Recognizing and writing three-consonant blends with **s**

Where's the Blend?

Look at the words on the apples. If you see a **blend** at the beginning of the word, color the apple red. If you see a **blend** at the end of the word, color the apple yellow. Then color the rest of the picture.

Reviewing consonant blends: initial and in final position

Apple Has Short a

<u>a</u>pple　　**b<u>a</u>t**

Say the name of each picture. If you hear the short **a** sound, write **a** to finish the word.

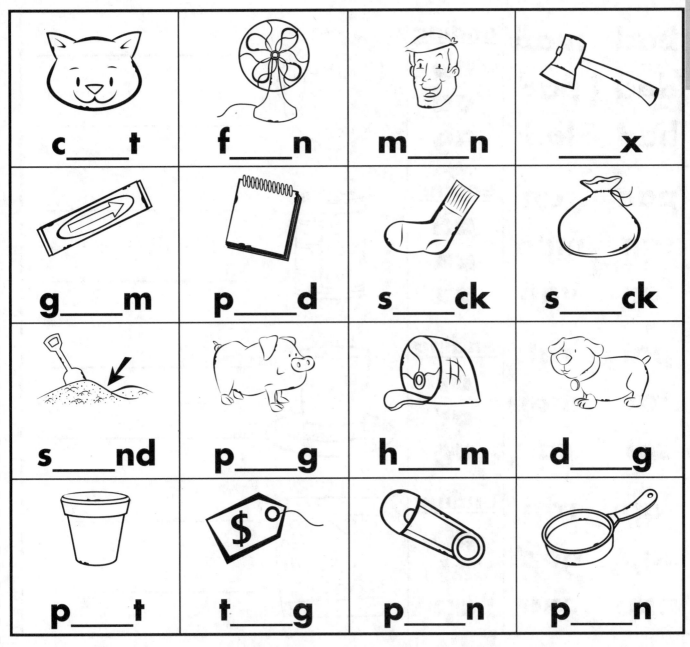

c___t	f___n	m___n	___x
g___m	p___d	s___ck	s___ck
s___nd	p___g	h___m	d___g
p___t	t___g	p___n	p___n

Meet Some Short a Families

tag   **bag**

Read the rhyming words in the first box in each row and circle the ending they share. Use the picture clue to write one more rhyming word.

		ending		
bad	mad	**ab** **ad** **ag**		_____
dad	pad			
had	lad			
pan	ran	**ad** **an** **ax**		_____
tan	man			
fan	van			
pat	rat	**at** **ar** **ag**		_____
fat	mat			
sat	cat			
lap	rap	**ab** **at** **ap**		_____
tap	gap			
nap	cap			

       Recognizing word families with short **a**

Egg Has Short e

__e__gg   b__e__ll

Say the name of each picture. If you hear the short **e** sound, write **e** to finish the word.

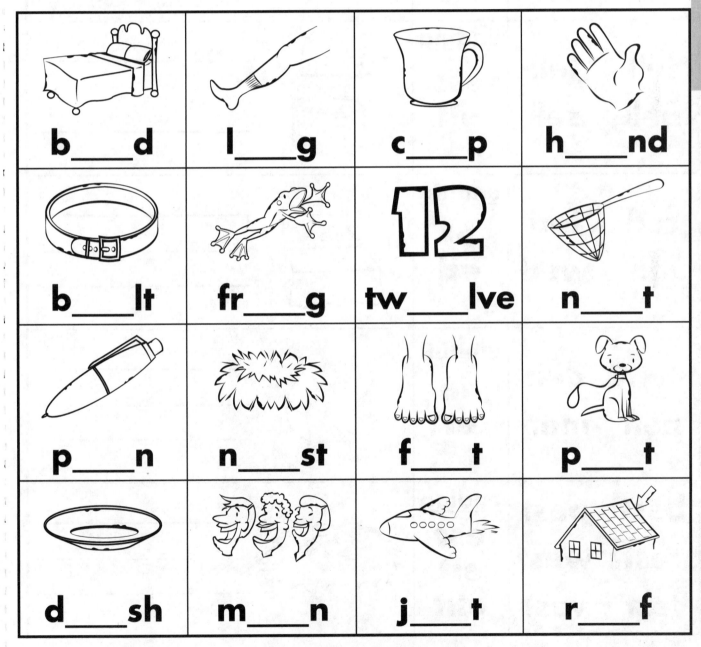

b____d	l__g	c__p	h__nd
b__lt	fr__g	tw____lve	n__t
p____n	n__st	f____t	p____t
d__sh	m__n	j__t	r__f

Recognizing the sound of short **e**; completing words with short **e**

Meet Some Short e Families

Read the rhyming words in the first box in each row and circle the ending they share. Use the picture clue to write one more rhyming word.

bet pet met wet set let	ending el et ed		_____ ------------------------ _____
fell tell bell sell	ending ess ell		_____ ------------------------ _____
red fed led wed	ending et ed		_____ ------------------------ _____
ten den pen men	ending en et		_____ ------------------------ _____
best pest rest west test vest	ending est elt ent		_____ ------------------------ _____

Recognizing word families with short e

Hill Has Short i

h**i**ll   d**i**g

Say the name of each picture. If you hear the short **i** sound, write **i** to finish the word.

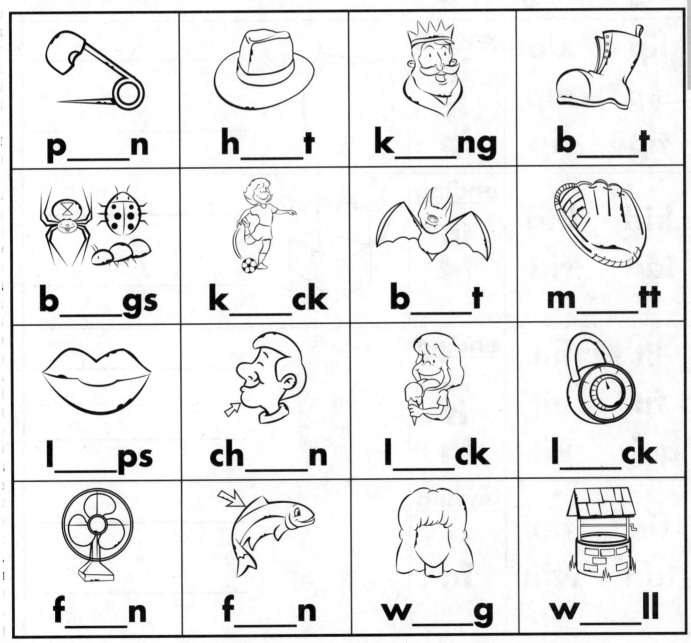

p___n	h___t	k___ng	b___t
b___gs	k___ck	b___t	m___tt
l___ps	ch___n	l___ck	l___ck
f___n	f___n	w___g	w___ll

Meet Some Short i Families

Read the rhyming words in the first box in each row and circle the ending they share. Use the picture clue to write one more rhyming word.

big dig fig jig rig wig	ending **it** **in** **ig**	_____ - - - - - - - - - _____
lip zip sip dip tip rip	ending **in** **ir** **ip**	_____ - - - - - - - - - _____
hid bid kid rid	ending **ip** **id**	_____ - - - - - - - - - _____
lit hit fit bit quit kit	ending **is** **it** **ig**	_____ - - - - - - - - - _____
fin tin kin win	ending **it** **in**	_____ - - - - - - - - - _____

Ox Has Short o

<u>o</u>x

s<u>o</u>ck

Say the name of each picture. If you hear the short **o** sound, write **o** to finish the word.

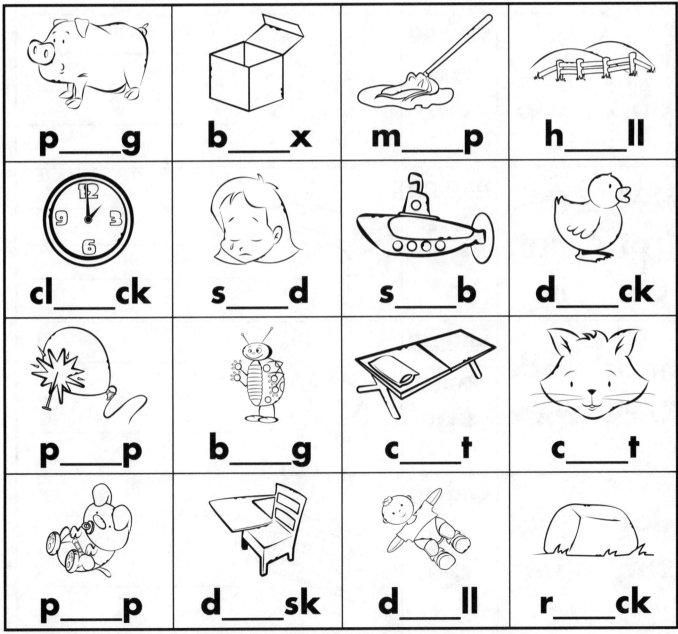

p___g	b___x	m___p	h___ll
cl___ck	s___d	s___b	d___ck
p___p	b___g	c___t	c___t
p___p	d___sk	d___ll	r___ck

Recognizing the sound of short **o**; completing words with short **o**

Meet Some Short o Families

Read the rhyming words in the first box in each row and circle the ending they share. Use the picture clue to write one more rhyming word.

		ending		
bob mob		ob		_____
job rob		op		_____
hop mop		od		_____
pop sop		op		_____
lot got		on		_____
rot not		og		_____
pot hot		ot		_____
dock sock		ock		_____
flock rock		ogs		_____
dog jog		og		_____
fog hog		op		_____

Recognizing word families with short o

Up Has Short u

u̱p   b<u>u</u>g

Say the name of each picture. If you hear the short **u** sound, write **u** to finish the word.

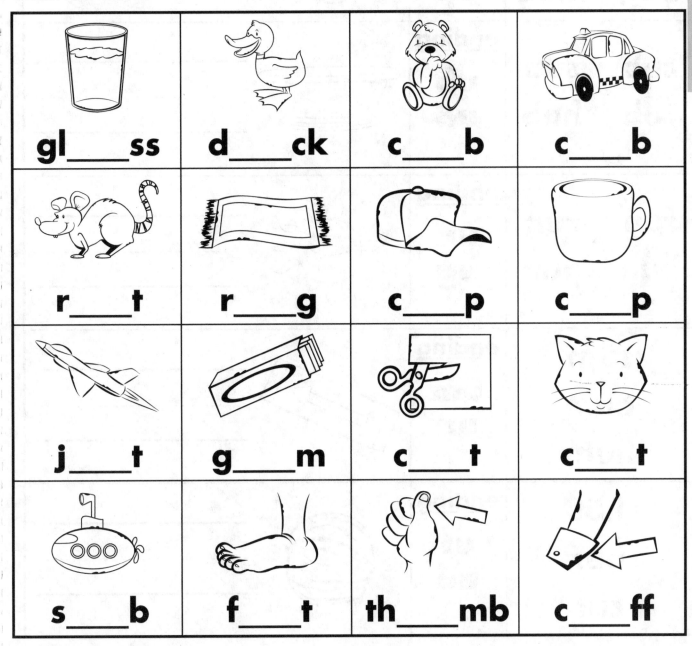

gl___ss	d___ck	c___b	c___b
r___t	r___g	c___p	c___p
j___t	g___m	c___t	c___t
s___b	f___t	th___mb	c___ff

Recognizing the sound of short **u**; completing words with short **u**

181

Meet Some Short u Families

Read the rhyming words in the first box in each row and circle the ending they share. Use the picture clue to write one more rhyming word.

		ending		
rug	tug	ub		
hug	dug	**ug**		
bug	mug	up		
cub	sub	ending		
rub	hub	**ub** ud		
fun	run	ending		
bun	pun	**un** ug		
sum		ending		
bum		**um** un		
hum				
hut		ending		
but		**ut** ud		
cut				

Short Vowel Art

Read the word in each space and listen for the vowel sound. Then color the spaces using the code to show the vowels being used in the words.

short **a** = orange	short **i** = red	short **u** = green
short **e** = blue	short **o** = purple	☆ = yellow

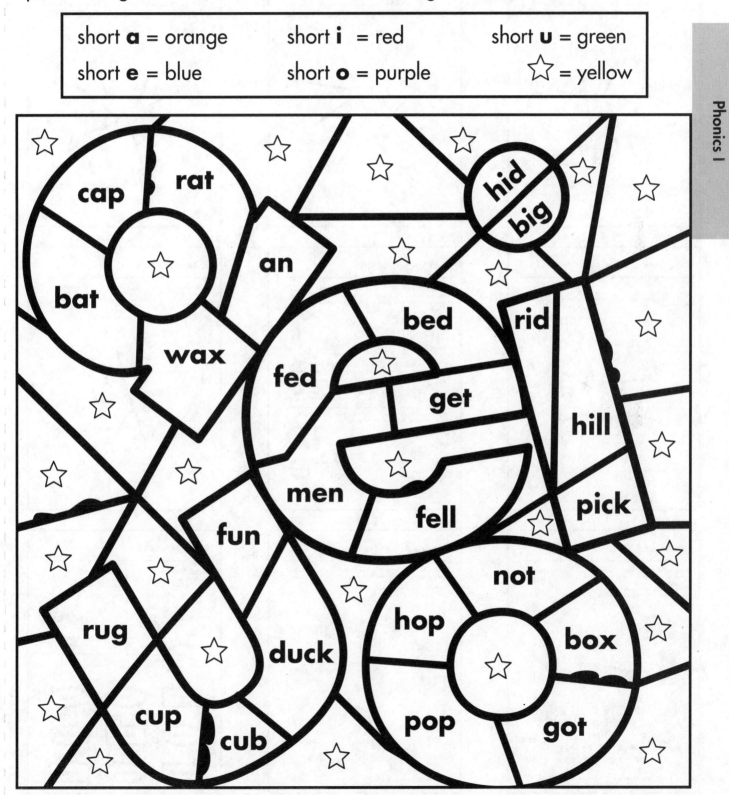

Reviewing the short sounds of the vowels **a**, **e**, **i**, **o**, and **u**

Answer Key

As the child completes the pages in this section, review his or her answers. When you take the time to correct the work and explain mistakes, you're showing your child that you feel learning is important.

page 152

Lamb in the Sun

Say the name of each picture. Color the lamb and sun. Draw a line from each picture that has the same beginning sound as **lamb** to the lamb. Draw a line from each picture that has the same beginning sound as **sun** to the sun.

152 — Recognizing the initial consonant sounds of Ll and Ss

page 153

Monkeys and Tigers

Say the name of each picture. Color the monkeys and tigers. Draw a line from each picture that has the same beginning sound as **monkey** to the monkeys. Draw a line from each picture that has the same beginning sound as **tiger** to the tigers.

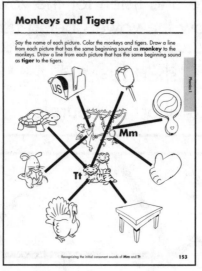

Recognizing the initial consonant sounds of Mm and Tt — 153

page 154

Hammer and Nails

Say the name of each picture. Color the hammer and nails. Draw a line from each picture that has the same beginning sound as **hammer** to the hammer. Draw a line from each picture that has the same beginning sound as **nail** to the nails.

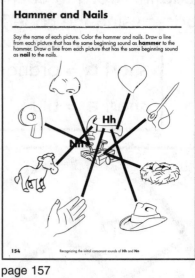

154 — Recognizing the initial consonant sounds of Hh and Nn

page 155

Dog Sees a Windmill

Say the name of each picture. Color the dog and windmill. Draw a line from each picture that has the same beginning sound as **dog** to the dog. Draw a line from each picture that has the same beginning sound as **windmill** to the windmill.

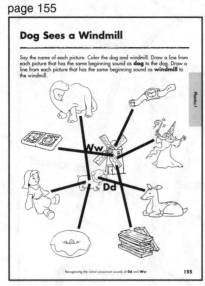

Recognizing the initial consonant sounds of Dd and Ww — 155

page 156

Two Sounds of Gg

Hard Sound
When **g** comes before **a**, **o**, or **u**, it has a hard sound like **gum**.

goose   gave   gum

Soft Sound
When **g** comes before **e**, **i**, or **y**, it often has a soft sound like **J**.

general   gypsy   gingerbread

The letter **g** does not always have the soft sound before **e** or **i**. Sometimes it has the hard sound, like in **girl**, **get**, and **give**.

Say each word. Circle the **g** and the letter that comes after it. Color the picture if the word has the soft sound of **g**.

gi affe   gy m

ge ms   go d

156 — Recognizing the hard and soft consonant sounds of Gg

page 157

A Rose for Bear

Say the name of each picture. Color the rose and bear. Draw a line from each picture that has the same beginning sound as **rose** to the rose. Draw a line from each picture that has the same beginning sound as **bear** to the bear.

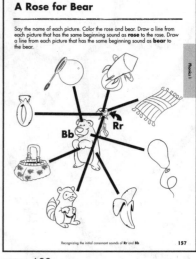

Recognizing the initial consonant sounds of Rr and Bb — 157

page 158

Violin and Yo-Yo

Say the name of each picture. Color the **violin** purple and the **yo-yo** yellow. Color the rest of the pictures using the code.

Same beginning sound as **violin** = purple
Same beginning sound as **yo-yo** = yellow

yellow   Yy

Vv
purple

purple   purple

yellow

yellow

purple

purple

yellow   yellow

158 — Recognizing the initial consonant sounds of Vv and Yy

page 159

Pandas Around a Fire

Say the name of each picture. Color the **pandas** pink and the **fire** red. Color the rest of the pictures using the code.

Same beginning sound as **panda** = pink
Same beginning sound as **fire** = red

Pp

Ff

red   red

pink

red   pink   pink

red   pink

Recognizing the initial consonant sounds of Pp and Ff — 159

page 160

Two Sounds of Cc

Hard Sound
When **c** comes before **a**, **o**, or **u**, it has a hard sound like **k**.

cat   cub   cot

Soft Sound
When **c** comes before **e**, **i**, or **y**, it has a soft sound like **s**.

price   cents   cymbal
50¢

Say each word. Circle the word if it has the hard **c** sound. Draw a box around the word if it has the soft **c** sound.

celery   car   cup

cone   mice   cube

fence   comb   lace

160 — Recognizing the hard and soft consonant sounds of Cc

184   Answers

page 161

Kettle Juggler

Say the name of each picture. Color the kettles and juggler. Draw a line from each picture that has the same beginning sound as **kettle** to the kettles. Draw a line from each picture that has the same beginning sound as **juggler** to the juggler.

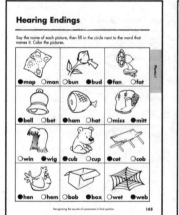

Recognizing the initial consonant sounds of **Kk** and **Jj**   161

page 162

Queen and Zebra

Say the name of each picture. Color the queen and zebra. Draw a line from each picture that has the same beginning sound as **queen** to the queen. Draw a line from each picture that has the same beginning sound as **zebra** to the zebra.

162   Recognizing the initial consonant sounds of **Qq** and **Zz**

page 163

Two Sounds of Xx

Say the name of each picture. Listen for the sound at the end of each word.

six   fox

The letter **x** makes another sound sometimes. When it is at the beginning of a word, **x** often makes the same sound as **z**.

xylophone

Say the name of each picture. Draw a line to the word that names it, then color the picture.

box
ox
ax
tux

Recognizing the two consonant sounds of **Xx**   163

page 164

What's Missing?

Circle the missing letter in each word, then write it to finish the word. Color the pictures.

h e n   c u p   f o x
h a t   c o a t   s i x
p a i l   f e e t   p i g

164   Reviewing consonant sounds

Phonics I

page 165

Hearing Endings

Say the name of each picture, then fill in the circle next to the word that names it. Color the pictures.

● map ○ man   ○ bun ● bud   ● fan ○ fat
● bell ○ bet   ● ham ○ hat   ○ miss ● mitt
○ win ● wig   ○ cub ○ cup   ● cot ○ cob
● hen ○ hem   ○ bob ● box   ○ wet ● web

Recognizing the sounds of consonants in final position   165

page 166

Consonant Blends with l

Some **consonants** can be put together to make a **blend**.
The **blend bl** has the sound you hear in the word **blue**.
The **blend pl** has the sound you hear in the word **planes**.
The **blend fl** has the sound you hear in the word **fly**.

Color the planes blue. Then read the sentence.

Blue planes fly.

Circle the **blends** at the beginning of each word.

cl ock   sli de
gl ove   bl ack

Write another word that has a consonant blend with the letter **l**.

Answers may vary.

166   Recognizing and writing two-letter initial consonant blends with l

page 167

Consonant Blends with r

The **blend dr** has the sound you hear in the word **drew**.
The **blend gr** has the sound you hear in the word **green**.
The **blend tr** has the sound you hear in the word **tree**.
Color the tree green. Then read the sentence.

He **drew** a **green tree**.

Use the words in the box to write the name of each picture. Notice the **blend** at the beginning of each word.

| bricks | dragon | crown | grass |

crown   grass
bricks   dragon

Write another word that has a consonant blend with the letter **r**.

Answers may vary.

Recognizing and writing two-letter initial consonant blends with r   167

page 168

Consonant Blends with s

The **blend sp** has the sound you hear in the word **spider**.
The **blend st** has the sound you hear in the word **story**.
The **blend sc** has the sound you hear in the word **scary**.
Read the sentence.

This **spider story** is **scary**!

Use the words in the box to write the name of each picture. Notice the **blend** at the beginning of each word.

| snail | snail | skate | sweater |

snail   sweater
smile   skate

Write another word that has a consonant blend with the letter **s**.

Answers may vary.

168   Recognizing and writing two-letter initial consonant blends with s

page 169

Blend or Brend?

Circle each word that begins with the wrong **blend**. Rewrite it using the correct **blend**.

praying atch   playing
glowing all   growing
go in the snore   store
letter flom friend   from
pet stider   spider

Reviewing initial consonant blends   169

page 170

Blend at the End

A word may begin or end with a **blend**.

skate   mask

Circle the two-consonant **blend** at the end of each word.

ant   must   felt
band   lamp   ink
ask   lft   last

Write four of the ending **blends** you circled.

Answers may vary.

Use the words above to write the name of each picture.

lamp   ant

170   Recognizing two-consonant blends in final position

page 171

S and Two Partners

Some **blends** join **s** with two other consonants.

He has **string**, a **spring**, and a **screw**.

Use the words in the box to write the name of each picture. Notice the three-consonant **blend** at the beginning of each word.

| spray | scrub | strong | straw |

straw   spray
scrub   strong

Recognizing and writing three-consonant blends with s   171

page 172

Where's the Blend?

Look at the words on the apples. If you see a **blend** at the beginning of the word, color the apple red. If you see a **blend** at the end of the word, color the apple yellow. Then color the rest of the picture.

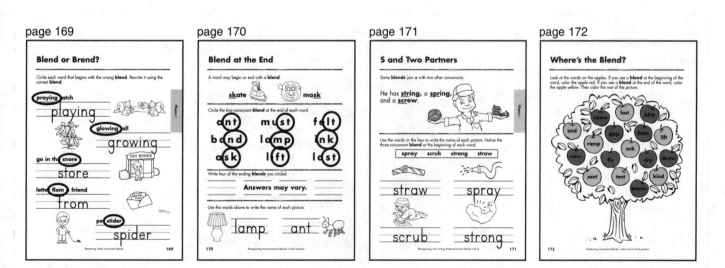

172   Reviewing consonant blends: initial and in final position

Answers

185

page 173

Apple Has Short a

page 174

Meet Some Short a Families

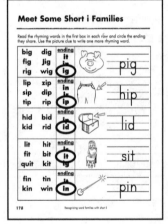

page 175

Egg Has Short e

page 176

Meet Some Short e Families

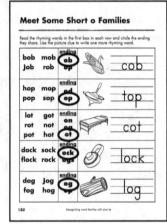

page 177

Hill Has Short i

page 178

Meet Some Short i Families

page 179

Ox Has Short o

page 180

Meet Some Short o Families

page 181

Up Has Short u

page 182

Meet Some Short u Families

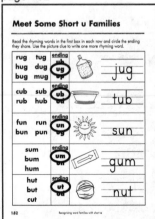

page 183

Short Vowel Art

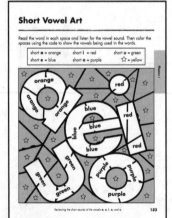

186

Answers

Silent e and Long Vowels

When a vowel is followed by a single consonant and the letter **e**, it usually takes its long sound. The **e** at the end of the word makes no sound—it's a **silent e**.

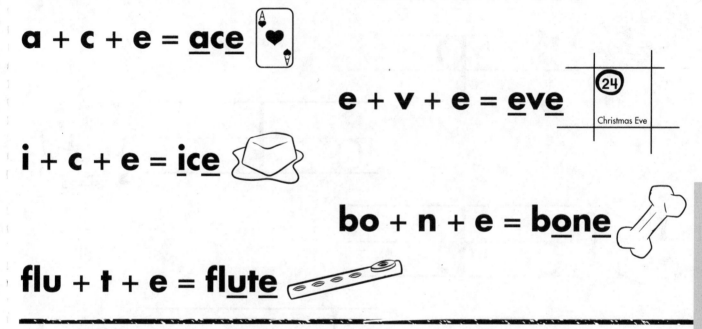

a + c + e = <u>ace</u>

e + v + e = <u>eve</u>

24
Christmas Eve

i + c + e = <u>ice</u>

bo + n + e = b<u>one</u>

flu + t + e = fl<u>ute</u>

Sound out each word. Draw a circle around the **long vowel** and a square around the **silent e**.

line   make   here

nose   cube

Read the word below. Rewrite it, adding a **silent e** at the end. What new word did you make?

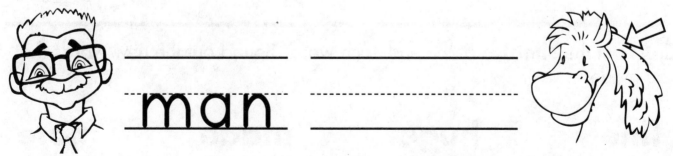

man _____

Phonics II

Silent e Word Play

Say the name of each picture. Fill in the missing vowel and the **silent e** to complete the word.

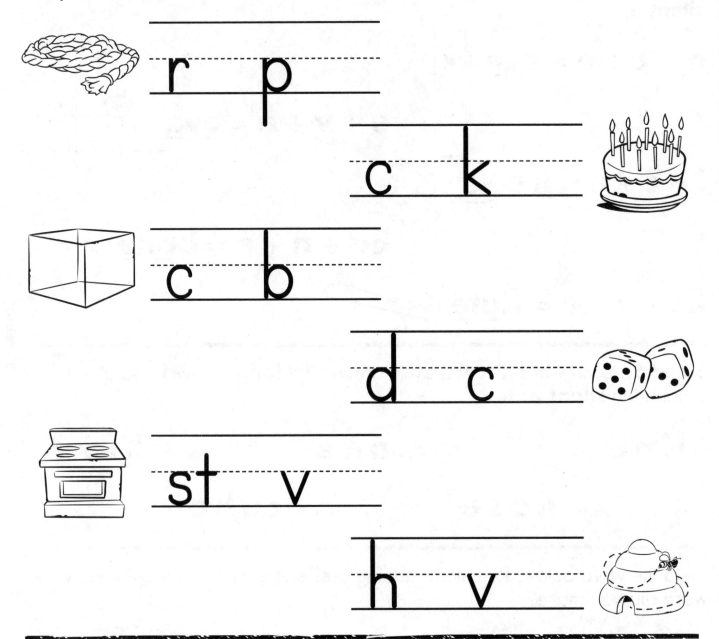

r ___ p

c ___ k

c ___ b

d ___ c

st ___ v

h ___ v

Cross out the **silent e** at the end each word. Sound out the new words that you made.

fine   **huge**   **made**   **note**

Recognizing the effect of **silent e** on vowel sounds

Hearing the Long a Sound

The words **lake** and **train** have the long **a** sound.

lake  **train**

Say the names of the two pictures in each box. Color the one with the long **a** sound.

Identifying the long **a** sound

189

Strain Your Brain!

Usually, **ai** has the long **a** sound.

n<u>ai</u>l

 **br<u>ai</u>d**

Write words from the box to complete each sentence. Circle **ai** in each word you write.

| hail | rain | mail | pail | paint | laid |

_____

The _____ is full of

_____ .

Will the (cloud) bring _____

or _____ ?

I _____ the

_____ on the table.

Recognizing and writing words with long **a** spelled **ai**

Another Way to Make Long a

Usually, **ay** has the long **a** sound.

h<u>ay</u>

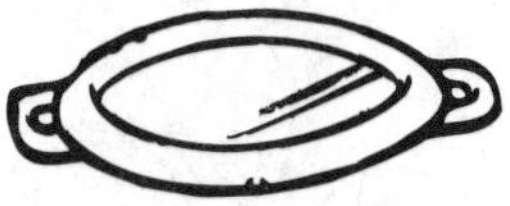

tr<u>ay</u>

Write words from the box to complete each sentence. Circle **ay** in each word you write.

clay	pay	day	play	gray	stay

Every _____ I

_____ with friends.

I _____ inside when

the clouds are _____ .

Did you _____

for the _____ ?

Hearing the Long e Sound

The words **weed** and **meat** have the long **e** sound.

weed   **meat**

Say the names of the two pictures in each box. Color the one with the long **e** sound.

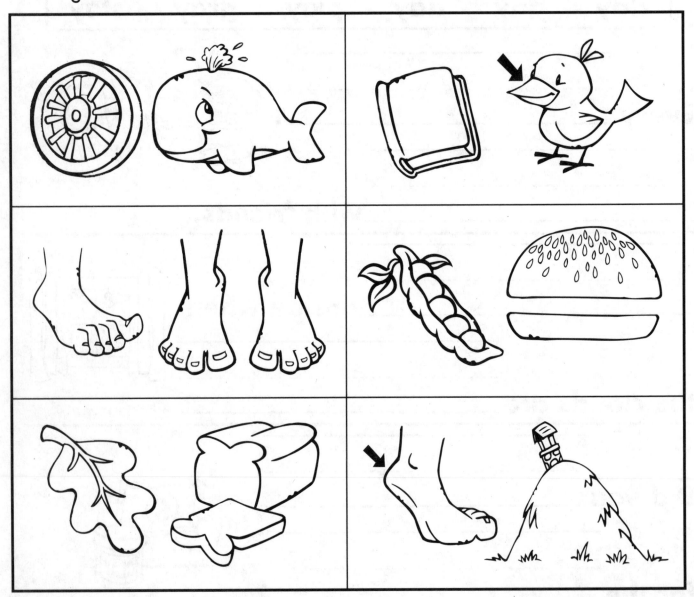

Identifying the long **e** sound

Neat!

Usually, **ea** has the long **e** sound.

leaf

seal

Write words from the box to complete each sentence. Circle **ea** in each word you write.

| meal | eat | tea | team | leap | cream |

_____

We will_____ our

_____ now.

_____

Everyone on the_____

can_____ high.

_____

I put_____

in my_____.

We Keep Up with e

When the only vowel in a word is one **e** at the end, that **e** usually has a long sound.

b<u>e</u>   **h<u>e</u>**   **sh<u>e</u>**   **m<u>e</u>**   **w<u>e</u>**

Usually, **ee** has the long **e** sound.

kn<u>ee</u>   **m<u>ee</u>t**

Circle the word that completes each sentence.

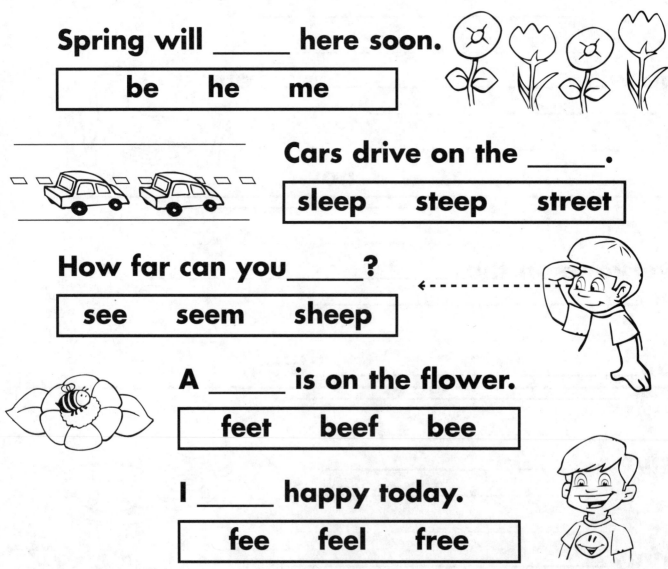

Spring will _____ here soon.

| be | he | me |

Cars drive on the _____.

| sleep | steep | street |

How far can you _____?

| see | seem | sheep |

A _____ is on the flower.

| feet | beef | bee |

I _____ happy today.

| fee | feel | free |

Hearing the Long i Sound

The words **kite** and **light** have the long **i** sound.

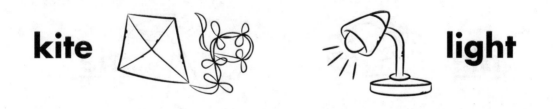

kite   **light**

Say the names of the two pictures in each box. Color the one with the long **i** sound.

Identifying the long **i** sound

Like, Lie, Light—All Long i

Usually, **ie** has the long **i** sound.

p<u>ie</u>  t<u>ie</u>

Usually, **igh** has the long **i** sound.

n<u>igh</u>t  r<u>igh</u>t

Cross out the word in each box that does not have the long **i** sound.

tie fight ~~fit~~	die did light
lie might fin	night pie pin
tight tin nice	bright tint sigh

Recognizing words with long **i** spelled **ie** and **igh**

Hearing the Long o Sound

The words **nose** and **coat** have the long **o** sound.

nose   **coat**

Say the names of the two pictures in each box. Color the one with the long **o** sound.

Phonics II

Partners with o

Usually, **oe** at the end of a word has the long **o** sound.

d<u>oe</u>

h<u>oe</u>

Usually, **oa** has the long **o** sound.

c<u>oa</u>st

fl<u>oa</u>t

Match each word with its picture.

toe

boat

coal

toast

soap

coat

Recognizing words with long **o** spelled **oe** and **oa**

Which Long o Word Fits?

When **o** is at the end of a word, it often takes its long sound.

"H<u>o</u>, h<u>o</u>, h<u>o</u>!"

In many words, **ow** has the long **o** sound.

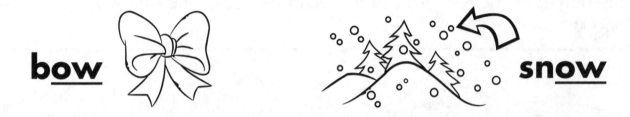

b<u>ow</u>   sn<u>ow</u>

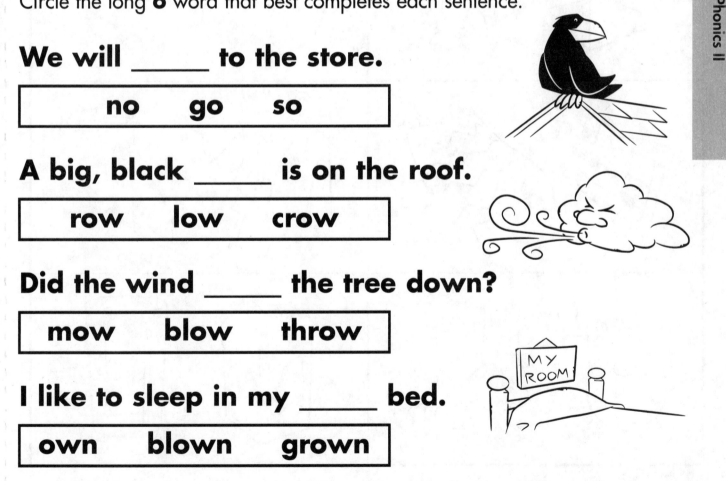

Circle the long **o** word that best completes each sentence.

We will _____ to the store.

no	go	so

A big, black _____ is on the roof.

row	low	crow

Did the wind _____ the tree down?

mow	blow	throw

I like to sleep in my _____ bed.

own	blown	grown

Hearing the Long u Sound

The words **mule** and **fruit** have the long **u** sound.

mule   fruit

Say the names of the two pictures in each box. Color the one with the long **u** sound.

Partners with u

Usually, **ue** has the long **u** sound.

gl<u>ue</u>

 **T<u>ue</u>sday**

In some words, **ui** has the long **u** sound.

fr<u>ui</u>t

 **j<u>ui</u>ce**

Match each word with its picture.

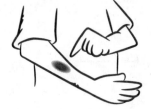

fruit

clue

glue

bruise

cruise

suit

Recognizing words with long **u** spelled **ue** and **ui**

Y as a Vowel

The letter **y** can be used as a vowel as well as a consonant.
Sometimes it has the long **i** sound, as in **fly**.

Sometimes it has the
long **e** sound, as in **happy**.

Say each word aloud. If it has the long **i** sound, write **i** on the line. If it has the long **e** sound, write **e**. Then color the pictures.

cry____

fry____

silly____

family____

city____

hydrant____

Recognizing the two vowel sounds of **y**: long **i** and long **e**

Are You Ready for ar?

Usually, **ar** has the vowel sound you hear in **ba̲r̲n**.

ba̲r̲n

Circle the correct name for each picture.

| aim   arm | pack   park | star   stay |
| make   mark | cat   cart | party   pantry |

Write **ar** to complete each word below. Then read the words aloud.

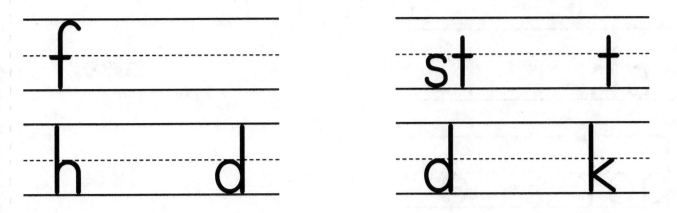

Don't Forget or!

Usually, **or** has the vowel sound you hear in **f<u>or</u>k**.

fork

Circle the correct name for each picture.

cook cork	bone born	stork stock
hose horse	stare store	corn cone

Write **or** to complete each word on the left. Then draw lines to match each **or** word with its opposite.

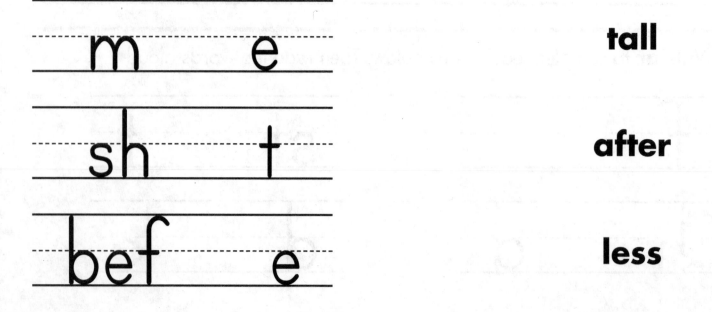

m____e   **tall**

sh____t   **after**

bef____e   **less**

Recognizing the sounds of **r**-controlled vowels

The Early Bird Gets the Worm

The vowel sound is the same in each of the words below.

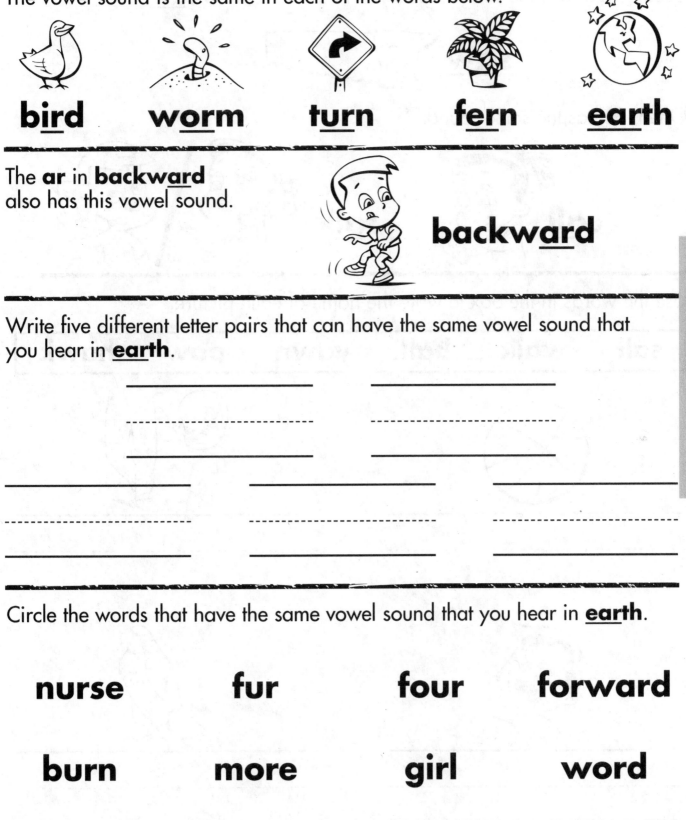

b<u>ir</u>d **w<u>or</u>m** **t<u>ur</u>n** **f<u>er</u>n** **<u>ear</u>th**

The **ar** in **backw<u>ar</u>d** also has this vowel sound.

backw<u>ar</u>d

Write five different letter pairs that can have the same vowel sound that you hear in **earth**.

_____   _____

_____   _____

_____   _____

_____   _____

_____

Circle the words that have the same vowel sound that you hear in **earth**.

nurse   **fur**   **four**   **forward**

burn   **more**   **girl**   **word**

Different Letters, Same Sound

Usually, **aw** has the vowel sound you hear in the word **saw**.

s<u>aw</u>

Often, **al** has the same sound.

c<u>al</u>l   **t<u>al</u>k**

Use the words in the box to write the name of each picture.

| salt | walk | ball | yawn | paw | hawk |

Recognizing the vowel sounds of **a**/consonant combinations

A Moose on the Moon

In some words, **oo** has the vowel sound you hear in **m<u>oo</u>n**.

m<u>oo</u>n

f<u>oo</u>d

m<u>oo</u>se

Match each word with its picture.

boot

goose

noon

roof

tools

tooth

balloon

igloo

Let's Buy Some New Glue

Often, **ew** and **ue** have the same vowel sound as the **oo** in m**oo**n.

New Glue on *Sale!*

n**ew**　　　gl**ue**

Choose a word that best completes each sentence and write it on the line.

When will the tulips _____ **?**

| blew | bloom | blue |

Ron _____ **a picture.**

| drew | droop | due |

Mom put meat in the _____ **.**

| clue | gloom | stew |

Anna _____ **the ball.**

| true | threw | troop |

Completing short sentences; recognizing the long double **o** sound of **ew** and **ue**

Looking at oo

In some words, **oo** has the vowel sound you hear in the word **look**.

Match each word with its picture.

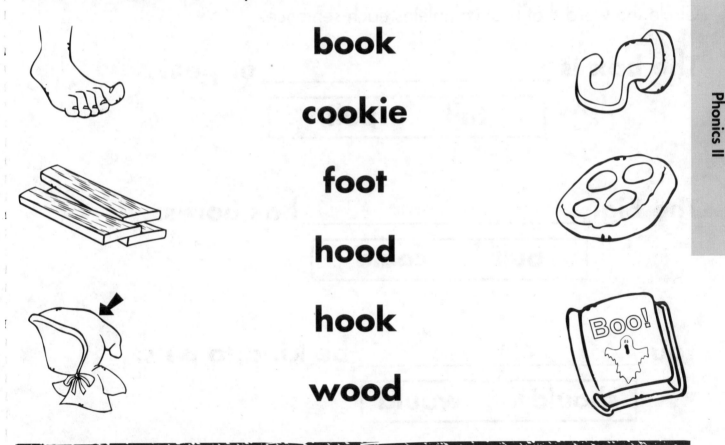

book

cookie

foot

hood

hook

wood

Underline each word with the same vowel sound as **foot**.

stood   **took**   **tooth**   **good**   **boot**   **look**

Some Special Words

The words in the box below all have the same vowel sound as **look**.

could	**would**	**bull**
put	**should**	**full**

The **l** in the words **could**, **would**, and **should** is silent—it has no sound.

Circle the word that best completes each sentence.

The box is _____ of pens.

full	**pull**

The big _____ has horns.

bull	**could**

You _____ be kind to pets.

should	**would**

I _____ my bike away.

pull	**put**

Completing short sentences; recognizing the short double **o** sound of **ou** and **u**

Surprise Spellings

In some words, **ie** has the long **e** sound.

chief **field** **believe** **piece**

In a few words, **eigh** has the long **a** sound.

neighbor **eight** **sleigh** **weigh**

Circle the word that best completes each sentence.

I live next door to my ___. | **neighbor** **chief**

Look how much I ___! | **eight** **weigh**

Flowers grow in that ___. | **field** **piece**

Recognizing irregular spellings of the **a** and **e** long vowel sounds

The Joyful Noise of oi and oy!

Both **oi** and **oy** have the same vowel sound.

b<u>oy</u>   **b<u>oi</u>l**

Underline **oi** or **oy** in each word.

oil	choice	noise	point
join	annoy	toy	joy

Rewrite the **oi** and **oy** words in each sentence on the lines below.

The boy will boil a hot dog.

_____   _____

An oyster is not noisy.

_____   _____

Point to the cowboy.

_____   _____

And Now About ow and ou

Both **ow** and **ou** can have the same vowel sound.

br<u>ow</u>n 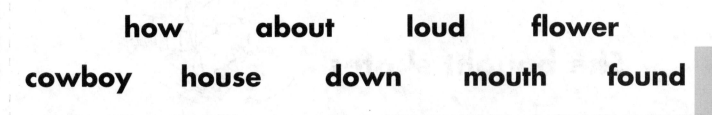 r<u>ou</u>nd

Underline **ow** or **ou** in each word.

how   about   loud   flower

cowboy   house   down   mouth   found

Rewrite the **ow** and **ou** words in each sentence on the lines below.

The clown likes to laugh and shout.

_____   _____

The cowboy sniffs the flower.

_____   _____

Now we will sit on the ground.

_____   _____

Ought We to Trust ou?

There are different sounds for **ou**. Say each word below and listen for the **ou** sound.

c**ou**ld	c**ou**ch	c**ou**gh

When **ou** is followed by **ght**, the **gh** is silent and only the **t** is heard.

She b**ou**ght skates

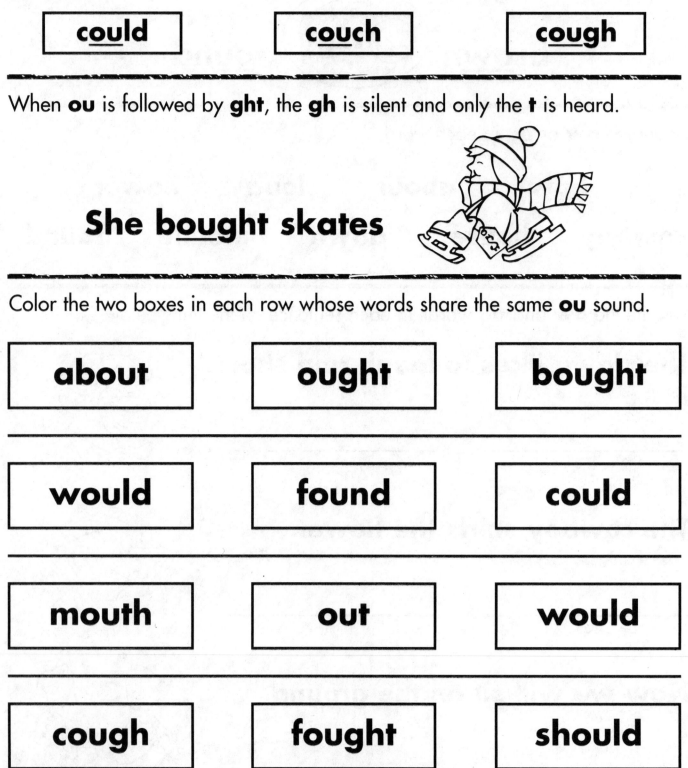

Color the two boxes in each row whose words share the same **ou** sound.

about	ought	bought
would	found	could
mouth	out	would
cough	fought	should

Recognizing multiple sounds of **ou**

Check out ch

The sound for **ch** is heard at the beginning of **<u>ch</u>air** and at the end of **bran<u>ch</u>**.

<u>ch</u>air   **bran<u>ch</u>**

Write **ch** to complete each word. Match each word with its picture.

_____eck

ben_____

_____est

tea_____er

_____ain

in_____

_____ief

_____ur_____

Phonics II

Showing Off sh

The sound for **sh** is heard at the beginning of <u>**sh**oe</u> and at the end of <u>fi**sh**</u>.

shoe

 **fish**

Write **sh** to complete each word. Match each word with its picture.

_____irt

di_____

fla_____

bu_____

_____apes

tra_____

_____op

_____ark

Recognizing the sound of the consonant digraph **sh**

Two Sounds of th

One sound for **th** is heard in the words **<u>th</u>e** and **mo<u>th</u>er**.

The other sound for **th** is heard in the words **<u>th</u>irty** and **tee<u>th</u>**.

mo<u>th</u>er  **tee<u>th</u>**

Read each word on the left aloud. If it has the same **th** sound as **mother**, circle the 👶. If it has the same **th** sound as **thirty**, circle the **30**.

thing		**30**
thin		**30**
there		**30**
then		**30**
thick		**30**
father		**30**

Phonics II

Recognizing the two sounds of the consonant digraph **th**: voiced and unvoiced

What's Up with wh?

The sound for **wh** is heard at the beginning of the word **wheel**.

Read each sentence. Draw a line to the missing **wh** word.

whale
What
wheat
Where
Which
while
white

The girl sat ___ she ate.

A ___ lives in the sea.

Some farmers grow ___.

Snow is ___.

___ did you say?

___ did my dog go?

___ toy do you want?

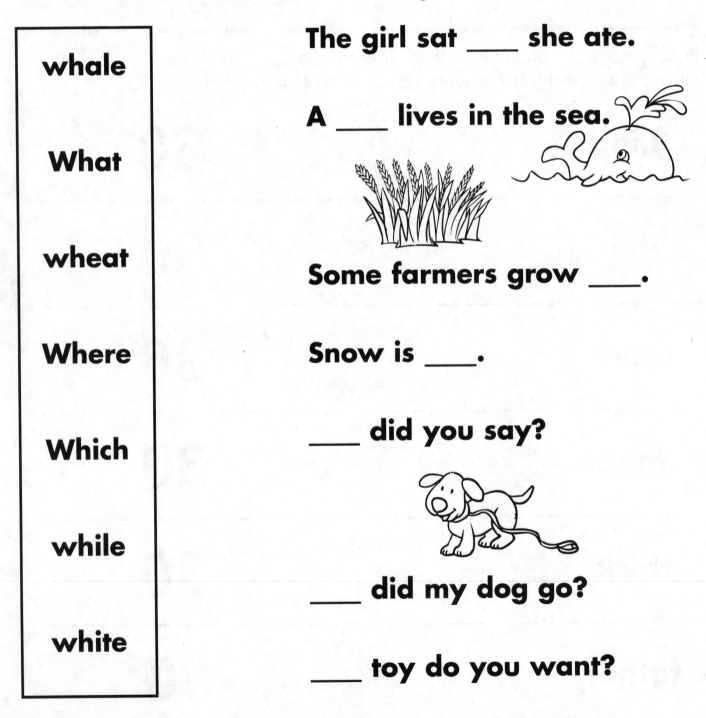

Completing short sentences; recognizing the sound of the consonant digraph **wh**

Using ng

The sound for **ng** is heard at the end of **king** and **bang**.

king   **bang**

Write **ng** to complete each word. Match each word with its picture.

wi_____

ri_____

swi_____

wro_____

fi_____er

si_____

What Do You See?

Read the word in each space. Color the picture using the code.

ch words = blue   **sh** words = green   **ng** words = pink

wh words = brown   **th** words = yellow

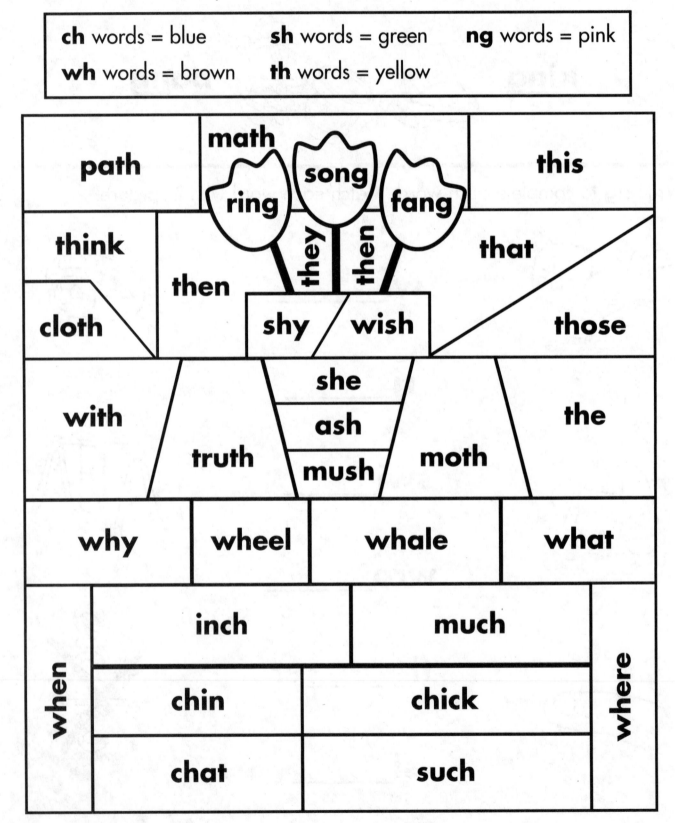

Reviewing the sounds of consonant digraphs

Answer Key

As the child completes the pages in this section, review his or her answers. When you take the time to correct the work and explain mistakes, you're showing your child that you feel learning is important.

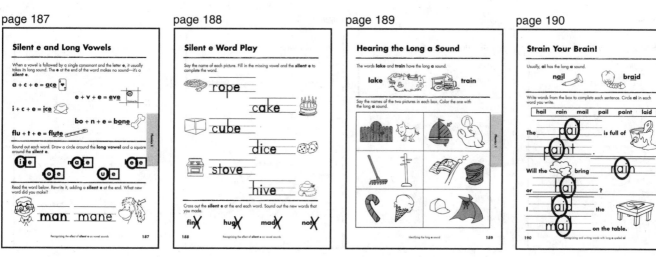

page 187

Silent e and Long Vowels

When a vowel is followed by a single consonant and the letter **e**, it usually takes its long sound. The **e** at the end of the word makes no sound—it's a **silent e**.

a + c + e = **ace**

e + v + e = **eve**

i + c + e = **ice**

bo + n + e = **bone**

flu + t + e = **flute**

Sound out each word. Draw a circle around the **long vowel** and a square around the **silent e**.

Read the word below. Rewrite it, adding a **silent e** at the end. What new word did you make?

man   mane

187

page 188

Silent e Word Play

Say the name of each picture. Fill in the missing vowel and the **silent e** to complete the word.

rope

cake

cube

dice

stove

hive

Cross out the **silent e** at the end each word. Sound out the new words that you made.

fin~~e~~   hug~~e~~   mad~~e~~   not~~e~~

188

page 189

Hearing the Long a Sound

The words **lake** and **train** have the long **a** sound.

lake   train

Say the names of the two pictures in each box. Color the one with the long **a** sound.

189

page 190

Strain Your Brain!

Usually, **ai** has the long **a** sound.

n**ai**l   br**ai**d

Write words from the box to complete each sentence. Circle **ai** in each word you write.

| hail | rain | mail | pail | paint | laid |

The ___p**ai**l___ is full of

___p**ai**nt___.

Will the ___ bring ___r**ai**n___

or ___h**ai**l___?

I ___ ___ the

___m**ai**l___ on the table.

190

page 191

Another Way to Make Long a

Usually, **ay** has the long **a** sound.

h**ay**   tr**ay**

Write words from the box to complete each sentence. Circle **ay** in each word you write.

| clay | pay | day | play | gray | stay |

Every ___d**ay**___ I

___pl**ay**___ with friends.

I ___st**ay**___ inside when

the clouds are ___gr**ay**___.

Did you ___p**ay**___

for the ___cl**ay**___?

191

page 192

Hearing the Long e Sound

The words **weed** and **meat** have the long **e** sound.

w**ee**d   m**ea**t

Say the names of the two pictures in each box. Color the one with the long **e** sound.

192

page 193

Neat!

Usually, **ea** has the long **e** sound.

l**ea**f   s**ea**l

Write words from the box to complete each sentence. Circle **ea** in each word you write.

| meal | eat | tea | team | leap | cream |

We will ___**ea**t___ our

___m**ea**l___ now.

Everyone on the ___t**ea**m___

can ___l**ea**p___ high.

I put ___cr**ea**m___

in my ___t**ea**___.

193

page 194

We Keep Up with e

When the only vowel in a word is one **e** at the end, that usually has a long sound.

be   he   she   me   we

Usually, **ee** has the long **e** sound.

kn**ee**   m**ee**t

Circle the word that completes each sentence.

Spring will ___ here soon.
be   he   me

Cars drive on the ___.
sleep   steep   **street**

How far can you ___?
see   seem   sheep

A ___ is on the flower.
feet   beef   **bee**

I ___ happy today.
fee   **feel**   free

194

page 195

Hearing the Long i Sound

The words **kite** and **light** have the long **i** sound.

kite   light

Say the names of the two pictures in each box. Color the one with the long **i** sound.

195

page 196

Like, Lie, Light—All Long i

Usually, **ie** has the long **i** sound.

p**ie**   t**ie**

Usually, **igh** has the long **i** sound.

n**igh**t   r**igh**t

Cross out the word in each box that does not have the long **i** sound.

tie	fight	die	~~cot~~
~~dug~~			light
lie	might	night	pie
	~~wag~~	~~dog~~	
tight	~~hit~~	bright	~~kit~~
nice		sigh	

196

page 197

Hearing the Long o Sound

The words **nose** and **coat** have the long **o** sound.

nose   coat

Say the names of the two pictures in each box. Color the one with the long **o** sound.

197

page 198

Partners with o

Usually, **oe** at the end of a word has the long **o** sound.

d**oe**   h**oe**

Usually, **oa** has the long **o** sound.

c**oa**st   fl**oa**t

Match each word with its picture.

toe
boat
coal
toast
soap
coat

198

Phonics II

page 199

Which Long o Word Fits?

When **o** is at the end of a word, it often takes its long sound.

"Ho, ho, ho!"

In many words, **ow** has the long **o** sound.

b**ow** sn**ow**

Circle the long **o** word that best completes each sentence.

We will _____ to the store.
| no | **go** | so |

A big, black _____ is on the roof.
| row | low | **crow** |

Did the wind _____ the tree down?
| mow | **blow** | throw |

I like to sleep in my _____ bed.
| **own** | blown | grown |

199

page 200

Hearing the Long u Sound

The words **mule** and **fruit** have the long **u** sound.

mule   fruit

Say the names of the two pictures in each box. Color the one with the long **u** sound.

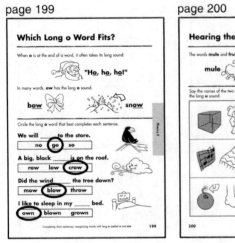

200

page 201

Partners with u

Usually, **ue** has the long **u** sound.

gl**ue**   T**ue**sday

In some words, **ui** has the long **u** sound.

fr**ui**t   j**ui**ce

Match each word with its picture.

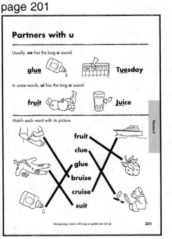

fruit
clue
glue
bruise
cruise
suit

201

page 202

Y as a Vowel

The letter **y** can be used as a vowel as well as a consonant. Sometimes it has the long **i** sound, as in **fly**.

fly

Sometimes it has the long **e** sound, as in **happy**.

happy

Say each word aloud. If it has the long **i** sound, write **i** on the line. If it has the long **e** sound, write **e**. Then color the pictures.

cry **i**   fry **i**

silly **e**   family **e**

city **e**   hydrant **i**

202

page 203

Are You Ready for ar?

Usually, **ar** has the vowel sound you hear in **barn**.

barn

Circle the correct name for each picture.

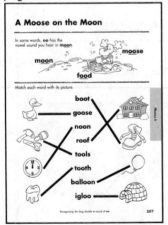

| aim | **arm** | pack | **park** | **star** | stay |
| make | **mark** | **cat** | cart | **party** | pantry |

Write **ar** to complete each word below. Then read the words aloud.

f**ar**   st**ar**t
h**ar**d   d**ar**k

203

page 204

Don't Forget or!

Usually, **or** has the vowel sound you hear in **fork**.

fork

Circle the correct name for each picture.

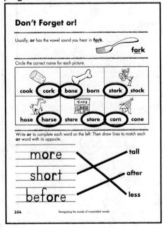

| cook | **cork** | bone | born | **stork** | stock |
| hose | **horse** | stare | **store** | **corn** | cone |

Write **or** to complete each word on the left. Then draw lines to match each **or** word with its opposite.

m**or**e   tall
sh**or**t   after
bef**or**e   less

204

page 205

The Early Bird Gets the Worm

The vowel sound is the same in each of the words below.

b**ir**d   w**or**m   t**ur**n   f**er**n   **ear**th

The **ar** in **backward** also has this vowel sound.

backw**ar**d

Write five different letter pairs that can have the same vowel sound that you hear in **earth**.

ir   or
ur   er   ar

Circle the words that have the same vowel sound that you hear in **earth**.

| **nurse** | **fur** | four | **forward** |
| **burn** | more | **girl** | **word** |

205

page 206

Different Letters, Same Sound

Usually, **aw** has the vowel sound you hear in the word **saw**.

saw

Often, **al** has the same sound.

c**al**l   t**al**k

Use the words in the box to write the name of each picture.

| salt | walk | ball | yawn | paw | hawk |

ball   walk
yawn   hawk

206

page 207

A Moose on the Moon

In some words, **oo** has the vowel sound you hear in **moon**.

moon   moose
food

Match each word with its picture.

boot
goose
noon
roof
tools
tooth
balloon
igloo

207

page 208

Let's Buy Some New Glue

Often, **ew** and **ue** have the same vowel sound as the **oo** in **moon**.

New Glue on Sale!
n**ew**   gl**ue**

Choose a word that best completes each sentence and write it on the line.

When will the tulips **bloom** ?
| blew | bloom | blue |

Ron **drew** a picture.
| drew | droop | due |

Mom put meat in the **stew** .
| clue | gloom | stew |

Anna **threw** the ball.
| true | threw | troop |

208

page 209

Looking at oo

In some words, **oo** has the vowel sound you hear in the word **look**.

look   hood
brook

Match each word with its picture.

book
cookie
foot
hood
hook
wood

Underline each word with the same vowel sound as **foot**.

| **stood** | **took** | tooth | **good** | boot | **look** |

209

page 210

Some Special Words

The words in the box below all have the same vowel sound as **look**.

| could | would | bull |
| put | should | full |

The **l** in the words **could**, **would**, and **should** is silent—it has no sound.

Circle the word that best completes each sentence.

The box is _____ of pens.
| **full** | pull |

The big _____ has horns.
| **bull** | could |

You _____ be kind to pets.
| **should** | would |

I _____ my bike away.
| pull | **put** |

210

page 211

Surprise Spellings

In some words, **ie** has the long **e** sound.

chief   field   bel**ie**ve   p**ie**ce

In a few words, **eigh** has the long **a** sound.

n**eigh**bor   **eigh**t   sl**eigh**   w**eigh**

Circle the word that best completes each sentence.

I live next door to my ___. **(neighbor)** chief

Look how much I ___! eight **(weigh)**

Flowers grow in that ___. **(field)** piece

Recognizing irregular spellings of the e and a long vowel sounds   211

page 212

The Joyful Noise of oi and oy!

Both **oi** and **oy** have the same vowel sound.

b**oy**   b**oi**l

Underline **oi** or **oy** in each word.

oil   ch**oi**ce   n**oi**se   p**oi**nt
J**oi**n   ann**oy**   t**oy**   J**oy**

Rewrite the **oi** and **oy** words in each sentence on the lines below.

The boy will boil a hot dog.
boy   **boil**

An oyster is not noisy.
oyster   **noisy**

Point to the cowboy.
Point   **cowboy**

212   *Recognizing the sounds of the diphthongs oi and oy*

page 213

And Now About ow and ou

Both **ow** and **ou** can have the same vowel sound.

br**ow**n   r**ou**nd

Underline **ow** or **ou** in each word.

h**ow**   ab**ou**t   l**ou**d   fl**ow**er
c**ow**boy   h**ou**se   d**ow**n   m**ou**th   f**ou**nd

Rewrite the **ow** and **ou** words in each sentence on the lines below.

The clown likes to laugh and shout.
clown   **shout**

The cowboy sniffs the flower.
cowboy   **flower**

Now we will sit on the ground.
Now   **ground**

Recognizing the sounds of the diphthongs ow and ou   213

page 214

Ought We to Trust ou?

There are different sounds for **ou**. Say each word below and listen for the **ou** sound.

could   couch   cough

When **ou** is followed by **ght**, the **gh** is silent and only the **t** is heard.

She bought skates

Color the two boxes in each row whose words share the same **ou** sound.

about	ought	bought
would	found	could
mouth	out	would
cough	fought	should

214   *Recognizing multiple sounds of ou*

page 215

Check out ch

The sound for **ch** is heard at the beginning of **chair** and at the end of **branch**.

chair   **branch**

Write **ch** to complete each word. Match each word with its picture.

check
ben**ch**
chest
tea**ch**er
chain
in**ch**
chief
chur**ch**

Recognizing the sound of the consonant digraph ch   215

page 216

Showing Off sh

The sound for **sh** is heard at the beginning of **shoe** and at the end of **fish**.

shoe   **fish**

Write **sh** to complete each word. Match each word with its picture.

shirt
di**sh**
fla**sh**
bu**sh**
shapes
tra**sh**
shop
shark

216   *Recognizing the sound of the consonant digraph sh*

page 217

Two Sounds of th

One sound for **th** is heard in the words **the** and **mother**.   The other sound for **th** is heard in the words **thirty** and **teeth**.

mother   **teeth**

Read each word on the left aloud. If it has the same **th** sound as **mother**, circle the picture. If it has the same **th** sound as **thirty**, circle the **30**.

thing		(30)
thin		(30)
there	(pic)	30
then	(pic)	30
thick		(30)
father	(pic)	30

Recognizing the two sounds of the consonant digraph th: voiced and unvoiced   217

page 218

What's Up with wh?

The sound for **wh** is heard at the beginning of the word **wheel**.

Read each sentence. Draw a line to the missing **wh** word.

whale   The girl sat ___ she ate.
What   A ___ lives in the sea.
wheat   Some farmers grow ___.
Where   Snow is ___.
Which   ___ did you say?
while   ___ did my dog go?
white   ___ toy do you want?

218   *Completing short sentences; recognizing the sound of the consonant digraph wh*

page 219

Using ng

The sound for **ng** is heard at the end of **king** and **bang**.

king   bang

Write **ng** to complete each word. Match each word with its picture.

wi**ng**
ri**ng**
swi**ng**
wro**ng**
fi**ng**er
si**ng**

Recognizing the sound of the consonant digraph ng   219

page 220

What Do You See?

Read the word in each space. Color the picture using the code.

ch words = blue   **sh** words = green   **ng** words = pink
wh words = brown   **th** words = yellow

pink pink pink
green yellow
yellow green
brown brown
brown blue brown

220   *Reviewing the sounds of consonant digraphs*

Phonics II

Answers   **223**

It Has a Name!

A word that names a person, place, or thing is called a **noun**.

mother
person

home
place

purse
thing

My **mother** went **home** to get her **purse**.

Use the **nouns** in the box to write the name of each picture. Then color the pictures.

girl	car	barn	hat

Recognizing nouns

Which Ones Are Nouns?

Nouns are words that name people, places, and things.

Circle all the **nouns** in the word box.

hen	**farmer**	**barn**	**if**
and	**green**	**sun**	**tree**

Draw a picture of one of the **nouns** from the box in the space below. Write the **noun** below the picture.

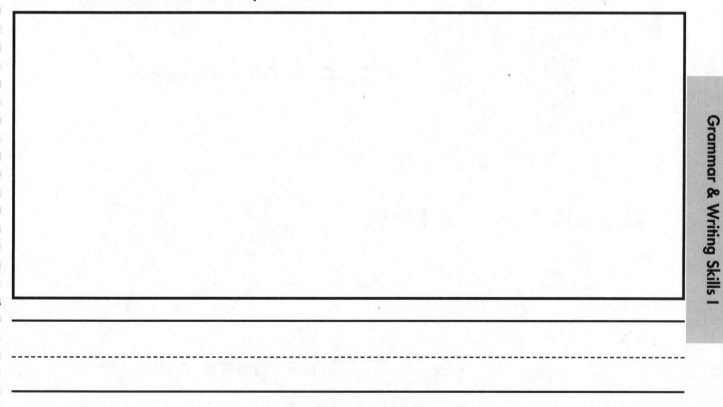

Grammar & Writing Skills I

Searching for Nouns

Circle all the **nouns** in each sentence.

The turtle lives in a pond.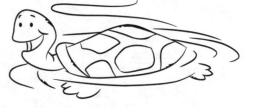

The monkey has a tail.

The giraffe eats leaves.

A zebra has stripes.

The pilot sees a bird.

 Ants make hills.

Identifying nouns in sentences

The First Day of School

Write a **noun** from the box to complete each sentence.

teacher	school	bell	pencil	desks

The _____ rings.

_____ has begun.

The _____ smiles.

The girls and boys sit at _____.

Ann writes with a _____.

How Many?

To make many **nouns** mean "more than one," add **s** at the end.
A **noun** that names "more than one" is a **plural noun**.

one bear   **three bears**

Look at the picture. Then read the questions and circle the answers.

1. Look for a cap. How many do you see?

| one cap | two caps | three caps |

2. Look for a rope. How many do you see?

| one rope | two ropes | three ropes |

3. Look for a mat. How many do you see?

| one mat | two mats | three mats |

4. Look for a ball. How many do you see?

| one ball | two balls | three balls |

Forming plurals of regular nouns by adding **s**

Animal or Animals

Read the word under each picture.
If it's a **noun**, write it on the **ANIMAL** list.
If it's a **plural noun**, write it on the **ANIMALS** list.

birds

pig

cats

lion

dogs

tiger

ANIMAL

ANIMALS

Not Just One

Ad **es** to a **noun** ending in **s**, **x**, **ch**, or **sh** to make it a **plural noun**.

one dress   **two dress<u>es</u>**   **one fox**   **two fox<u>es</u>**

Rewrite each **noun**, adding **es** at the end to make it **plural**.

match

_____

_____

bus

_____

_____

brush

_____

_____

box

_____

_____

Adding **-es** to form plurals of nouns ending in **s**, **x**, **ch**, and **sh**

One and More Than One

Read the **nouns** inside the ◇s. Circle the correct **plural** form of each one.

watch — watches / watchs

truck — truckes / trucks

broom — brooms / broomes

bug — buges / bugs

six — sixs / sixes

dish — dishes / dishs

glass — glasses / glasss

pail — pails / pailes

Watch Out for y

Sometimes **y** comes after a consonant at the end of a **noun**.
To make these nouns **plural**, change the **y** to **i** and add **es**.

one bunny   bunn~~y~~ **i** + es = bunnies   two bunnies

Rewrite each **noun** to make it **plural**.

candy

fly

baby

berry

kitty

lady

Forming plurals of nouns ending in **y** after a consonant

Making Plurals

Read the **nouns** inside the ◇s. Circle the correct **plural** form of each one.

daisy — daisies / daisys

cherry — cherries / cherryes

lunch — lunchs / lunches

fly — flies / flyes

fox — foxs / foxes

city — cityes / cities

chick — chickes / chicks

puppy — puppies / puppys

Noun Search

Read the **nouns** and their **plural** forms. Then find and circle them in the puzzle. The words may go across or down.

baby	ball	box	snake	fly
babies	balls	boxes	snakes	flies

a b a l l s b

b o x e s n o

a b a b y a a

b x s n a k e

i b o x f e f

e f l i e s l

s b a l l d y

Plural noun review

Special Plurals

Some **nouns** have a special **plural** form.

One	More Than One
man	men
woman	women
child	children
mouse	mice
foot	feet
tooth	teeth

Write the **plural** form of the **noun** in the box to complete each sentence.

I have two _____ . | foot |

Both _____ can swim. | child |

The _____ like the maze. | mouse |

Two _____ wrote the song. | man |

I brush my _____ . | tooth |

Three _____ baked pies. | woman |

Recognizing irregular plurals

More Special Plurals

A few **nouns** do not change in their **plural** form.

One	More Than One
deer	deer
fish	fish
moose	moose
scissors	scissors
sheep	sheep

Look at the picture clues. Write the missing **plural noun** in each sentence.

Many _____ live in the park.

Luis saw two _____ in the woods.

The _____ eat grass.

Feed the _____ before lunch.

Use _____ to cut paper.

Recognizing irregular plurals

What is a Verb?

A **verb** is a word that tells what a person or thing does.

run   spin

Match each picture with its **verb**.

march

sing

dance

clap

Circle the **verb** to complete each sentence.

The bell _____.

soft	rings

The cat _____.

purrs	top

Where is the Verb?

A **verb** is a word that tells what a person or thing does.

The sun **shines**.

Circle the **verb** in each sentence.

Ships sail on the sea.

She sits in the sun.

Waves roll in.

They play a game.

He throws a ball.

Recognizing verbs in sentences

Bears in Space

A **verb** usually ends in **s** when it tells about only one.
It usually does not end in **s** when it tells about more than one.

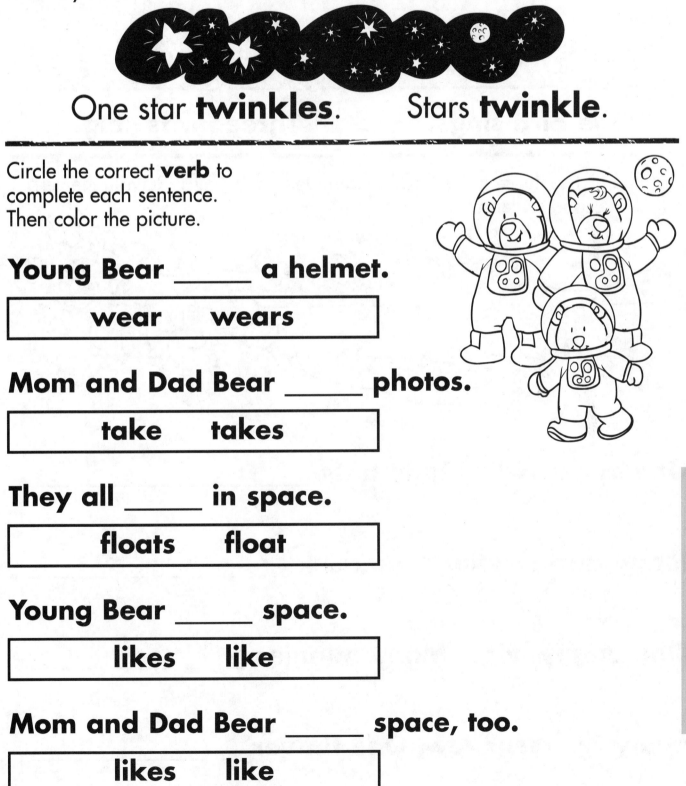

One star **twinkles**.   Stars **twinkle**.

Circle the correct **verb** to
complete each sentence.
Then color the picture.

Young Bear _____ **a helmet.**

| wear | wears |

Mom and Dad Bear _____ **photos.**

| take | takes |

They all _____ **in space.**

| floats | float |

Young Bear _____ **space.**

| likes | like |

Mom and Dad Bear _____ **space, too.**

| likes | like |

Pretty as a Picture

A **verb** ending in **s** usually tells about one person or thing.
A **verb** not ending in **s** usually tells about more than one.

One bird sings.   **Three birds sing.**

Read the first sentence in each row and underline the verb. Rewrite the verb to fit the second sentence.

One ant crawls. Many ants _____.

Many ducks swim. One duck _____.

One bunny hops. Many bunnies _____.

Many flowers grow. One flower _____.

Writing the correct verb form to agree in number with the subject

Which is Correct?

Fill in the ◯ by the sentence that uses the correct **verb**.

◯The children like art.
◯The children likes art.

◯A girl paint.
◯A girl paints.

◯A boy use clay.
◯A boy uses clay.

◯Two boys draw cars.
◯Two boys draws cars.

◯The teacher hangs up the art.
◯The teacher hang up the art.

◯They all works hard.
◯They all work hard.

Choosing the correct verb form to agree in number with the subject

Am, Are, and Is

Verbs may also tell what
a person or thing is.
We use the verbs **am**, **are**,
and **is** to do this.

Verb Chart	
I – – – – – – – – –	**am**
You – – – – – – – –	**are**
He, She, or It – – – –	**is**
We – – – – – – – –	**are**
They – – – – – – –	**are**

Use **am** with **I** when you
tell about yourself.

I **am** happy!

Use **is** with **he**, **she**, or **it**
when you tell about
another person or thing.

He **is** happy!

Use **are** with **you** or
when you tell about
more than one.

The dogs **are** happy!

Write **am**, **are**, or **is** to complete each sentence.

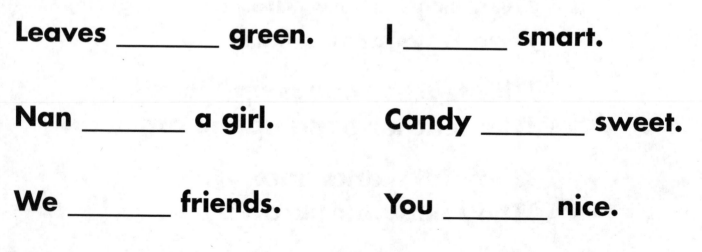

Leaves _____ green.   I _____ smart.

Nan _____ a girl.   Candy _____ sweet.

We _____ friends.   You _____ nice.

Using **am**, **are** and **is**: present tense forms of the verb **to be**

You Are Smart!

Fill in the ○ by the sentence that uses the correct **verb**.

○I am your friend.
○I is your friend.

○You is the winner!
○You are the winner!

○Brian is a good kicker.
○Brian are a good kicker.

○The puppy is tiny.
○The puppy are tiny.

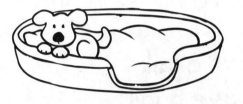

○We are sleepy.
○We is sleepy.

Using **am**, **are** and **is**: present tense forms of the verb **to be**

Has and Have

Verbs may also tell what a person or thing has.
We use the verbs **has** and **have** to do this.

Use **has** with **he**, **she**, or **it**.
Use **has** with a noun that names one.

He **has** a tail.
The squirrel **has** a tail.

Use **have** with **I**, **you**, **we**, or **they**.
Use **have** with a plural noun.

We **have** tails!

They **have** tails.
The squirrels **have** tails.

has	have
he, she, it	I, you, we, they
noun	plural noun

Fill in the ◯ by the sentence that uses the correct **verb**.

◯ A dog **has** a tail.
◯ A dog **have** a tail.

◯ I **has** a nose.
◯ I **have** a nose.

◯ We **have** gum.
◯ We **has** gum.

◯ Birds **has** wings.
◯ Birds **have** wings.

Using **has** and **have**: present tense forms of the verb **to have**

Have Fun!

Write **has** or **have** to complete each sentence.

_____

- -

The panda_____ **a baby.**

_____

- -

Nuts _____ **hard shells.**

_____

- -

He_____ **broken the law.**

_____

- -

The shaker _____ **salt in it.**

_____

- -

The crabs_____ **claws.**

Using **has** and **have**: present tense forms of the verb **to have**

Does and Do

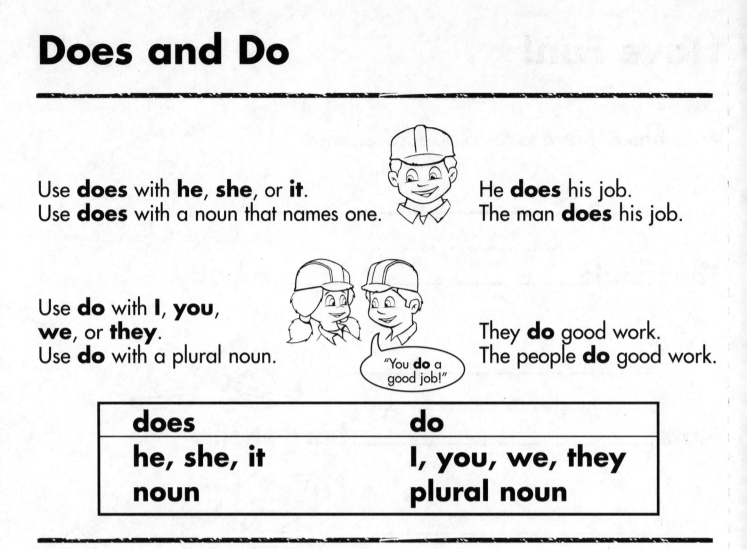

Use **does** with **he**, **she**, or **it**.
Use **does** with a noun that names one.

He **does** his job.
The man **does** his job.

Use **do** with **I**, **you**, **we**, or **they**.
Use **do** with a plural noun.

"You **do** a good job!"

They **do** good work.
The people **do** good work.

does	do
he, she, it	I, you, we, they
noun	plural noun

Write **does** or **do** to complete each sentence.

Cats _____ purr.

She _____ tricks.

I _____ my homework.

Tim _____ his chores.

Using **does** and **do**: present tense forms of the verb **to do**

Do Your Best!

Write **does** or **do** to complete each sentence.

This hat _____ not have stripes.

Fairies _____ magic.

Mom _____ like to read.

Clowns _____ funny tricks.

Ann _____ skate well.

Grammar & Writing Skills I

Let's Go Shopping!

Circle the **verb** that correctly completes each sentence.

Many people (**come** / **comes**) to the store.

He (**set** / **sets**) food on the shelf.

Dad (**chooses** / **choose**) a box.

The cart (**has** / **have**) wheels.

The clerk (**does** / **do**) her job.

Dad (**carries** / **carry**) the bag.

Present tense verb-subject agreement review

Let's Go to the Zoo!

Write a **noun** or **verb** from the box to complete each sentence.

| ape | bear | made | went | were |

_____ verb _____

We _____ to the zoo.

_____ noun _____

I waved to the _____.

_____ verb _____

The monkeys _____ me laugh.

_____ noun _____

The _____ was asleep.

_____ verb _____

The hippos _____ fat.

Completing sentences with nouns and verbs

Let's Go to the Movies!

Write a **noun** or **verb** from the box to complete each sentence.

box	buy	is	meet	seats

verb
_____

Rita and Tom_____at the door.

verb
_____

They_____tickets.

noun
_____

They buy a_____of popcorn.

noun
_____

They choose their_____.

verb
_____

The movie_____funny.

Completing sentences with nouns and verbs

Fish Story

Read the short story or
have someone read it to you.
Circle all the **nouns**.
Underline all the **verbs**.

Hal likes to fish in the brook. The water is clean. The water is cold. There are lots of fish in the water.

Hal feels a fish tug the line. Hal catches the fish. Then he puts it back into the clean, cold water. It is too small to keep.

Recognizing nouns and verbs in a short story

Pete and Pat

Read the short story or
have someone read it to you.
Circle each correct **noun** or **verb**.
Then color Pete and Pat.

Pete (has have) a dog. The dog (is am) tan.
Her name is Pat.

Pat (like likes) to run. Her (tail tails) wags
when she (run runs). Pat likes to chew
(bone bones). Pete (give gives) her a bone
every (day dry). Pat likes to (plays play). Pete
throws a (ball bull) to her. Pat likes that
(game gum).

Pat (love loves) Pete. Pete (loves love) Pat.
They are good (friends friend).

Completing a short story with nouns and verbs

Answer Key

As the child completes the pages in this section, review his or her answers. When you take the time to correct the work and explain mistakes, you're showing your child that you feel learning is important.

page 224

It Has a Name!

A word that names a person, place, or thing is called a **noun**.

mother (person)　home (place)　purse (thing)

My **mother** went **home** to get her **purse**.

Use the **nouns** in the box to write the name of each picture. Then color the pictures.

girl　car　barn　hat

car

hat

barn

girl

224　Recognizing nouns

page 225

Which Ones Are Nouns?

Nouns are words that name people, places, and things.

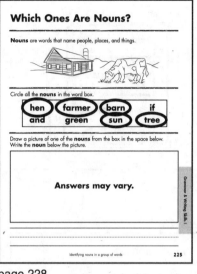

Circle all the **nouns** in the word box.

hen　farmer　barn　if
and　green　sun　tree

Draw a picture of one of the **nouns** from the box in the space below. Write the **noun** below the picture.

Answers may vary.

Identifying nouns in a group of words　225

page 226

Searching for Nouns

Circle all the **nouns** in each sentence.

The turtle lives in a pond.

The monkey has tail.

The giraffe eat leaves.

zebra as stripes.

The pilot sees a bird.

Ants make hills.

226　Identifying nouns in sentences

page 227

The First Day of School

Write a **noun** from the box to complete each sentence.

teacher　school　bell　pencil　desks

The bell rings.

School has begun.

The teacher smiles.

The girls and boys sit at desks.

Ann writes with a pencil.

Using nouns to complete sentences　227

page 228

How Many?

To make many **nouns** mean "more than one" add **s** at the end. A **noun** that names "more than one" is a **plural noun**.

one bear　　three bears

Look at the picture. Then read the questions and circle the answers.

1. Look for a cap. How many do you see?
   one cap　two caps　**three caps**

2. Look for a rope. How many do you see?
   one rope　two ropes　three ropes

3. Look for a mat. How many do you see?
   one mat　**two mats**　three mats

4. Look for a ball. How many do you see?
   one ball　**two balls**　three balls

228　Forming plurals of regular nouns by adding s

page 229

Animal or Animals

Read the word under each picture.
If it's a **noun**, write it on the **ANIMAL** list.
If it's a **plural noun**, write it on the **ANIMALS** list.

birds　　pig　　cats

lion　　dogs　　tiger

ANIMAL	ANIMALS
pig	birds
lion	cats
tiger	dogs

Recognizing plural nouns　229

page 230

Not Just One

Add **es** to a **noun** ending in **s**, **x**, **ch**, or **sh** to make it a **plural noun**.

one dress　two dresses　one fox　two foxes

Rewrite each **noun**, adding **es** at the end to make it **plural**.

match　matches

bus　buses

brush　brushes

box　boxes

230　Adding -es to form plurals of nouns ending in s, x, ch, and sh

page 231

One and More Than One

Read the **nouns** inside the ◇s. Circle the correct **plural** form of each one.

watch	**watches**	truck	truckes
	watchs		**trucks**
broom	**brooms**	bug	buges
	broomes		**bugs**
six	sixs	dish	**dishes**
	sixes		dishs
glass	**glasses**	pail	**pails**
	glasss		pailes

Recognizing the plural forms of nouns　231

page 232

Watch Out for y

Sometimes **y** comes after a consonant at the end of a **noun**. To make these nouns **plural**, change the **y** to **i** and add **es**.

one bunny　bunn*y* + es = bunnies　two bunnies

Rewrite each **noun** to make it **plural**.

candy　candies

fly　flies

baby　babies

berry　berries

kitty　kitties

lady　ladies

232　Forming plurals of nouns ending in y after a consonant

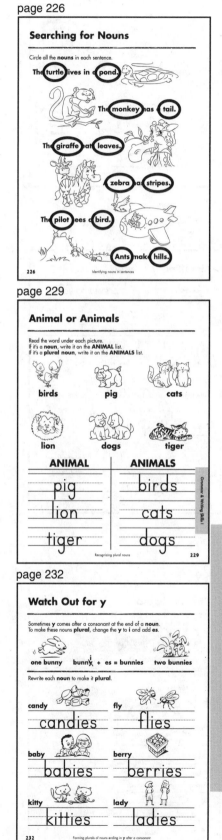

Answers

page 233

Making Plurals

Read the **nouns** inside the ◇s. Circle the correct **plural** form of each one.

- daisy → **daisies** / daisys
- cherry → **cherries** / cherryes
- lunch → lunchs / **lunches**
- fly → **flies** / flyes
- fox → foxs / **foxes**
- city → cityes / **cities**
- chick → chickes / **chicks**
- puppy → **puppies** / puppys

Recognizing the plural forms of nouns   233

page 234

Noun Search

Read the **nouns** and their **plural** forms. Then find and circle them in the puzzle. The words may go across or down.

| baby | ball | box | snake | fly |
| babies | balls | boxes | snakes | flies |

```
a  b  a  l  l  s  b
b  o  x  e  s  n  o
a  b  a  b  y  a  a
b  x  s  n  a  k  e
i  b  o  x  f  e  f
e  f  l  i  e  s  l
s  b  a  l  l  d  y
```

234   Plural noun review

page 235

Special Plurals

Some **nouns** have a special **plural** form.

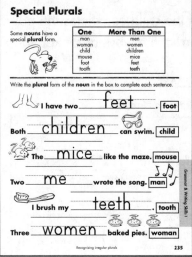

One	More Than One
man	men
woman	women
child	children
mouse	mice
foot	feet
tooth	teeth

Write the **plural** form of the **noun** in the box to complete each sentence.

I have two **feet**. [foot]

Both **children** can swim. [child]

The **mice** like the maze. [mouse]

Two **me** wrote the song. [man]

I brush my **teeth**. [tooth]

Three **women** baked pies. [woman]

Recognizing irregular plurals   235

page 236

More Special Plurals

A few **nouns** do not change in their **plural** form.

One	More Than One
deer	deer
fish	fish
moose	moose
scissors	scissors
sheep	sheep

Look at the picture clues. Write the missing **plural noun** in each sentence.

Many **deer** live in the park.

Luis saw two **moose** in the woods.

The **sheep** eat grass.

Feed the **fish** before lunch.

Use **scissors** to cut paper.

236   Recognizing irregular plurals

page 237

What is a Verb?

A **verb** is a word that tells what a person or thing does.

run   spin

Match each picture with its **verb**.

- march
- sing
- dance
- clap

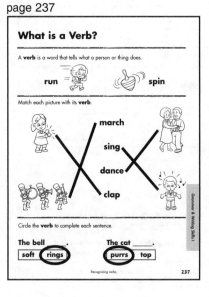

Circle the **verb** to complete each sentence.

The bell ____.   soft (**rings**)

The cat ____.   (**purrs**) top

Recognizing verbs   237

page 238

Where is the Verb?

A **verb** is a word that tells what a person or thing does.

The sun **shines**.

Circle the **verb** in each sentence.

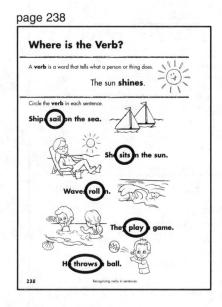

Ships (**sail**) on the sea.

She (**sits**) in the sun.

Waves (**roll**) in.

They (**play**) a game.

He (**throws**) a ball.

238   Recognizing verbs in sentences

page 239

Bears in Space

A **verb** usually ends in **s** when it tells about only one.
It usually does not end in **s** when it tells about more than one.

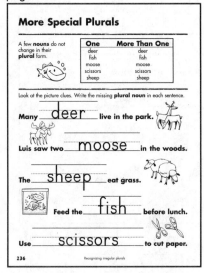

One star **twinkles**.   Stars **twinkle**.

Circle the correct **verb** to complete each sentence. Then color the picture.

Young Bear ____ a helmet.   wear (**wears**)

Mom and Dad Bear ____ photos.   (**take**) takes

They all ____ in space.   floats (**float**)

Young Bear ____ space.   (**likes**) like

Mom and Dad Bear ____ space, too.   likes (**like**)

Choosing the correct verb form to agree in number with the subject   239

page 240

Pretty as a Picture

A **verb** ending in **s** tells about one person or thing.
A **verb** not ending in **s** usually tells about more than one.

One bird sings.   Three birds sing.

Read the first sentence in each row and underline the verb. Rewrite the verb to fit the second sentence.

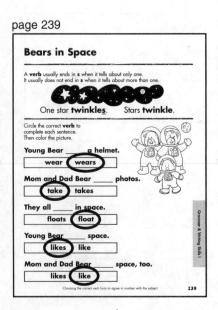

One ant <u>crawls</u>. Many ants **crawl**.

Many ducks <u>swim</u>. One duck **swims**.

One bunny <u>hops</u>. Many bunnies **hop**.

Many flowers <u>grow</u>. One flower **grows**.

240   Writing the correct verb form to agree in number with the subject

page 241

Which is Correct?

Fill in the ○ by the sentence that uses the correct **verb**.

- ● The children like art.
- ○ The children likes art.

- ○ A girl paint.
- ● A girl paints.

- ○ A boy use clay.
- ● A boy uses clay.

- ● Two boys draw cars.
- ○ Two boys draws cars.

- ● Teacher hangs up the art.
- ○ Teacher hang up the art.

- ○ They all works hard.
- ● They all work hard.

Choosing the correct verb form to agree in number with the subject   241

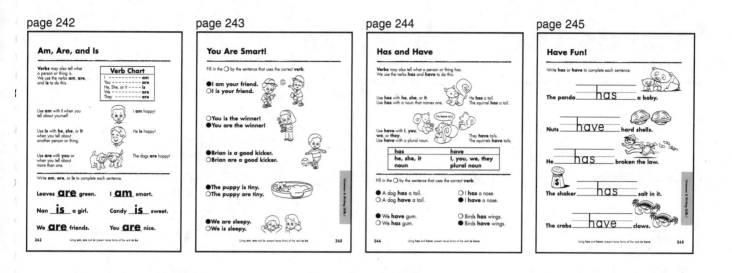

page 242

Am, Are, and Is

Verbs may also tell what a person or thing is. We use the verbs **am**, **are**, and **is** to do this.

Verb Chart

I	— — — — — —	am
You	— — — — — —	are
He, She, or It	— — — —	is
We	— — — — — —	are
They	— — — — — —	are

Use **am** with I when you tell about yourself.

I **am** happy!

Use **is** with **he, she, it** when you tell about another person or thing.

He **is** happy!

Use **are** with **you** or when you tell about more than one.

The dogs **are** happy!

Write **am**, **are**, or **is** to complete each sentence.

Leaves **are** green.　I **am** smart.

Nan **is** a girl.　Candy **is** sweet.

We **are** friends.　You **are** nice.

page 243

You Are Smart!

Fill in the ◯ by the sentence that uses the correct **verb**.

● I am your friend.
◯ I is your friend.

◯ You is the winner!
● You are the winner!

● Brian is a good kicker.
◯ Brian are a good kicker.

● The puppy is tiny.
◯ The puppy are tiny.

● We are sleepy.
◯ We is sleepy.

page 244

Has and Have

Verbs may also tell what a person or thing has. We use the verbs **has** and **have** to do this.

Use **has** with **he, she,** or **it**.
Use **has** with a noun that names one.

He **has** a tail.
The squirrel **has** a tail.

Use **have** with **I, you, we,** or **they**.
Use **have** with a plural noun.

They **have** tails.
The squirrels **have** tails.

has	have
he, she, it	I, you, we, they
noun	plural noun

Fill in the ◯ by the sentence that uses the correct **verb**.

● A dog has a tail.　◯ I has a nose.
◯ A dog have a tail.　● I have a nose.

● We have gum.　◯ Birds has wings.
◯ We has gum.　● Birds have wings.

page 245

Have Fun!

Write **has** or **have** to complete each sentence.

The panda **has** a baby.

Nuts **have** hard shells.

He **has** broken the law.

The shaker **has** salt in it.

The crabs **have** claws.

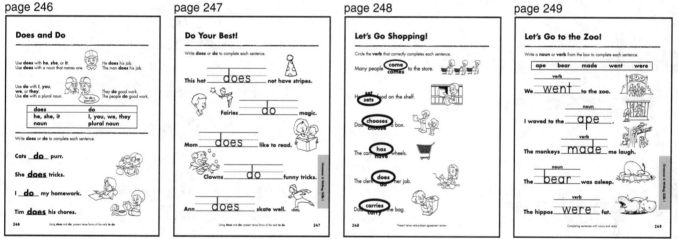

page 246

Does and Do

Use **does** with **he, she,** or **it**.
Use **does** with a noun that names one.

He **does** his job.
The man **does** his job.

Use **do** with **I, you, we,** or **they**.
Use **do** with a plural noun.

They **do** good work.
The people **do** good work.

does	do
he, she, it	I, you, we, they
noun	plural noun

Write **does** or **do** to complete each sentence.

Cats **do** purr.

She **does** tricks.

I **do** my homework.

Tim **does** his chores.

page 247

Do Your Best!

Write **does** or **do** to complete each sentence.

This hat **does** not have stripes.

Fairies **do** magic.

Mom **does** like to read.

Clowns **do** funny tricks.

Ann **does** skate well.

page 248

Let's Go Shopping!

Circle the **verb** that correctly completes each sentence.

Many people (come) to the store.

He (sets) food on the shelf.

Dad (chooses) a box.

The cart (has) wheels.

The clerk (does) her job.

Dad (carries) the bag.

page 249

Let's Go to the Zoo!

Write a **noun** or **verb** from the box to complete each sentence.

ape	bear	made	went	were

verb
We **went** to the zoo.

noun
I waved to the **ape**.

verb
The monkeys **made** me laugh.

noun
The **bear** was asleep.

verb
The hippos **were** fat.

page 250

Let's Go to the Movies!

Write a **noun** or **verb** from the box to complete each sentence.

box	buy	is	meet	seats

verb
Rita and Tom **meet** at the door.

verb
They **buy** tickets.

noun
They buy a **box** of popcorn.

noun
They choose their **seats**.

verb
The movie **is** funny.

page 251

Fish Story

Read the short story or have someone read it to you.
Circle all the **nouns**.
Underline all the **verbs**.

(Hal) likes to fish in the (brook.)
The (water) is clean. The (water) is cold. There are lots of (fish) in the (water.)

(Hal) feels a (fish) tug the (line.)
(Hal) catches the (fish.) Then (he) puts it back into the clean, cold (water.) (It) is too small to keep.

page 252

Pete and Pat

Read the short story or have someone read it to you.
Circle each correct **noun** or **verb**.
Then color Pete and Pat.

Pete (has) have) a dog. The (dog) (is) am) tan. Her name is Pat.

Pat (like (likes) to run. Her (tail) tails) wags when she (run (runs.) Pat likes to chew (bone (bones.) Pete (give (gives) her a bone every (day (day.) Pat likes to (play) play) Pete throws a (ball (ball) to her. Pat likes (game) gum).

Pat (love (loves) Pete. Pete (loves) love) Pat. They are good (friends) friend).

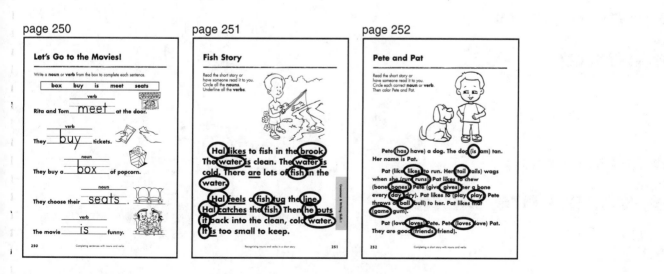

Words that Tell More

Some words tell more about nouns.
They are called **adjectives**.
Adjectives can answer these questions:

What kind?   How many?   What color?
fuzzy bears   **two** bears   **white** bears

Circle the **adjective** in each sentence.

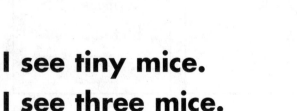

This is a pretty flower.
It has two leaves.

I see tiny mice.
I see three mice.

She has long hair.
She has big eyes.

The bus is big.
The wheels are black.

Recognizing adjectives

In the Summertime

Adjectives tell more about nouns.

Write an **adjective** from the box to complete each sentence.

| big | two | black | four |

A _____ bird sings.
What color?

There are _____ clouds.
How many?

A _____ dog takes a nap.
What kind?

I see _____ squirrels.
How many?

Adjective Search

Circle two **adjectives** in each sentence.

Two <image> swim under deep water.

Long <image>s play by the old ship.

Are those round <image>s in the open chest?

One clam sits on the smooth sand.

Tall <image>s grow in the cool sea.

Three happy <image>s play.

Identifying adjectives in sentences

Gardening

Circle the **adjectives** in the box.

four	pretty	pea	proud
rake	neat	two	are

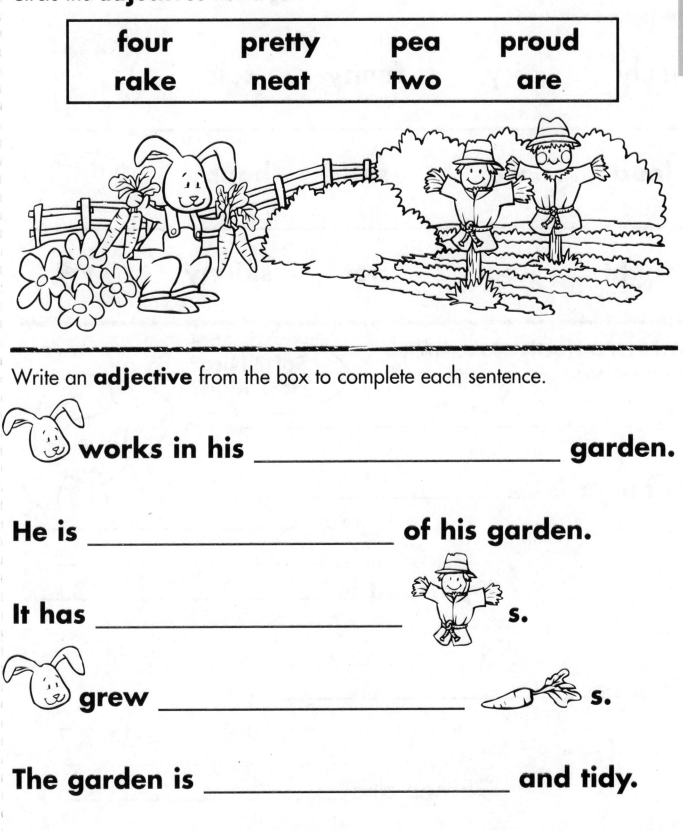

Write an **adjective** from the box to complete each sentence.

_____ works in his _____ garden.

He is _____ of his garden.

It has _____ s.

_____ grew _____ s.

The garden is _____ and tidy.

Adjective Time

Read the words in each row. Circle the two **adjectives** that tell about the picture.

silly	icy	funny	cold

loud	wet	soft	happy

bright	cool	hot	skinny

Write an **adjective** to complete each sentence.

Soft? Nice? Hot? Kind?

Summer is _____ .

My friend is _____ .

Pets are _____ .

Games are _____ .

Tell About a Toy

Write the name of a toy you like in the square.
Write an **adjective** that tells about the toy in each circle.

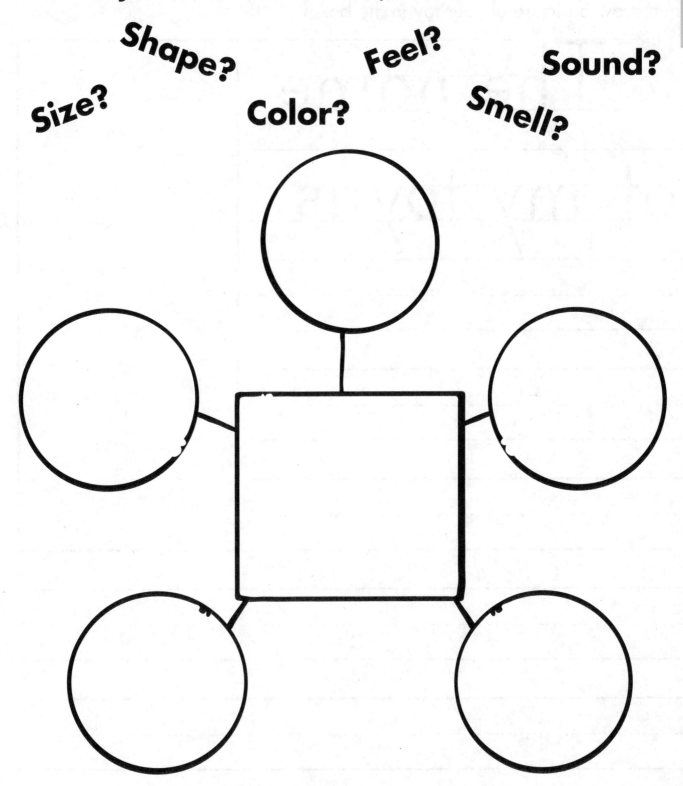

Size? Shape? Color? Feel? Smell? Sound?

Using a graphic organizer to plan a description

Write About a Toy

On page 261 you wrote **adjectives** that tell about your toy.
Use them to write sentences about your toy on the lines below.
Then draw a picture of your toy in the box.

The name
of my toy is

Telling it All

Some sentences tell something. They are called **statements**.
A **statement** begins with a capital letter and ends with a **period**.

capital letter

The wind is strong.

period

Circle the **statement** below.

Rain fell all day.

When will the rain stop?

Fill in the ○ by the **statement** that is written correctly.

○ **today is a cold day.**
○ **Today is a cold day.**

○ **The sky is blue.**
○ **the sky is blue.**

○ **The children made a snowman**
○ **The children made a snowman.**

Did You Ask Me?

Some sentences ask something. They are called **questions**.
A **question** begins with a capital letter and ends with a **question mark**.

capital letter   question mark

<u>W</u>ho is it<u>?</u>

Circle the **questions**.

Where is my shoe?

Will you come with me?

The cat is in the tree.

Rewrite each **question** correctly.

what is your name

_____

- -

_____

how old are you

_____

- -

_____

where do you live

_____

- -

_____

Jungle Questions

Color all the **questions marks** hidden in this picture red.
Then color the rest of the picture.

Visual discrimination; identifying question marks

Nice Ice

Every **statement** ends with a **period**.
Every **question** ends with a **question mark**.

Add a **period** or **question mark** to the end of each sentence.

The day is cold____

Did the lake freeze____

Bob has a new hat____

Who will win the race____

Can you ice skate____

The dog slips____

Reviewing punctuation usage with statements and questions

Wow!

A sentence that shows excitement is called an **exclamation**.
Every **exclamation** begins with a capital letter and ends with an
exclamation point.

capital letter

Watch out!

exclamation point

Circle the **exclamations** below.

I was scared!

What time is it?

I see the ice cream truck!

Ice Cream

Fill in the ○ by the **exclamation** that is written correctly.

○ **The soup is hot!**
○ **the soup is hot!**

○ **My toe hurts!**
○ **My toe hurts.**

○ **Look at the sunset!**
○ **look at the sunset!**

In the Lunch Room

Add a **period**, **question mark**, or **exclamation point** to the
end of each sentence.

Lisa likes milk_____

May I sit here_____

Sam likes fruit_____

I'm so hungry_____

Why is Sam so silly_____

Hurry and eat_____

Reviewing types of sentences: statements, questions, and exclamations

Please Write!

Read this letter. Look at the names of the different parts of the letter.

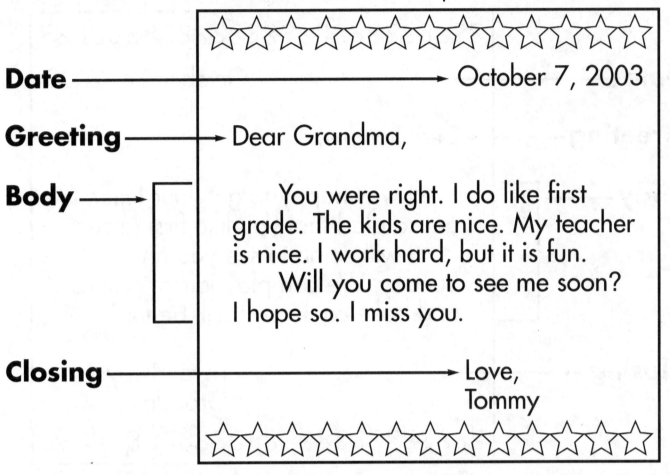

Date ⟶ October 7, 2003

Greeting ⟶ Dear Grandma,

Body ⟶ You were right. I do like first grade. The kids are nice. My teacher is nice. I work hard, but it is fun.
Will you come to see me soon? I hope so. I miss you.

Closing ⟶ Love,
Tommy

Circle the answer.

October 7, 2003	is the	body	date
Love,	is the	greeting	closing
I miss you.	is part of the	body	greeting
Dear Grandma,	is the	greeting	closing

Return Mail

Read this letter. Circle all the capital letters.

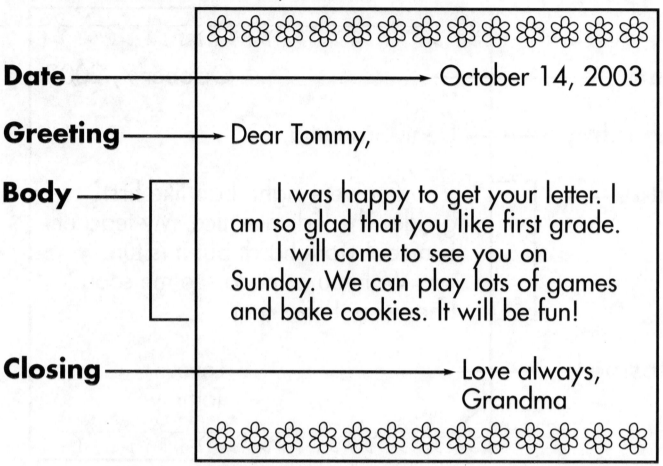

Date —————————→ October 14, 2003

Greeting ————→ Dear Tommy,

Body ——→
I was happy to get your letter. I am so glad that you like first grade. I will come to see you on Sunday. We can play lots of games and bake cookies. It will be fun!

Closing —————————→ Love always,
Grandma

Circle all the answers that are correct.

A capital letter is used at the beginning of:

the name of a day   **a person's name**

the name of the month   **every sentence**

the year   **the greeting**   **the closing**

Understanding capitalization usage in a letter

Friend to Friend

Read this letter and look for the **commas**.
Circle each **comma** that you find.

comma ———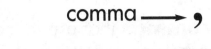

> July 11, 2003
>
> Dear Linda,
>
>   Last week my family went to the zoo. The animals I liked the best were the monkeys. Here's a picture of one. Do you like monkeys?
>
> Your friend,
> Ally

Circle the word that tells where each **comma** is.

The comma in the date comes after the ___.	month	day
The comma in the greeting comes after ___.	Dear	Linda
The comma in the closing comes after ___.	friend	Your

Letter Fix

Read this letter.
Cross out **commas** that are in the wrong places.
Write in **commas** that are missing.
Circle the letters that should be capital letters.

december, 2 2003

dear, lisa

   I am on a ski trip! my family and I drove to Ski-Happy Trails last week.

   I can ski down a big hill. i can ride a rope tow back to the top. it is fun!

                your friend
                Jane,

Reviewing punctuation and capitalization in a letter

Proper Nouns Use Capitals

A **proper noun** is the name of a specific person, place, or thing. Your name is a **proper noun**.

Every **proper noun** begins with a capital letter.

<u>U</u>nited <u>S</u>tates

<u>J</u>une

Underline the **proper noun** in each sentence that is not written correctly.

The train goes to boston.

maria ran home.

I was born on june 2, 1997.

This man lives in japan.

My cat's name is misty.

ken has a red bike.

Recognizing proper nouns and their use of capitalization

Start with a Capital

The first word in a sentence always begins with a capital letter.

This pig is fat.   **The store is open.**

Rewrite each sentence correctly.

cake is yummy.

_____

- -

_____

use a pen to write.

_____

- -

_____

bill digs a hole.

_____

- -

_____

the pin is sharp!

_____

- -

_____

my fish's name is Goldy.

_____

- -

_____

Using a capital letter at the beginning of a sentence

Titles Need Capitals

Read the title of this book. Color the capital letters red. Color the other letters yellow. Then color the rest of the book cover.

Book List

Read the list of books. Circle each capital letter.

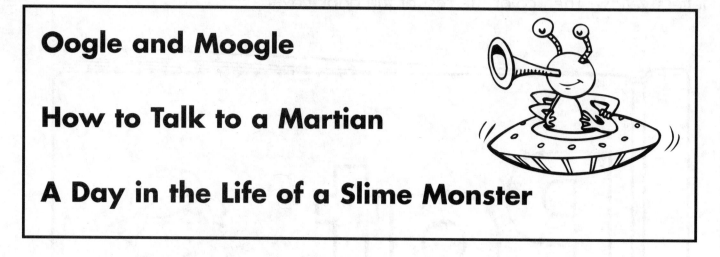

Oogle and Moogle

How to Talk to a Martian

A Day in the Life of a Slime Monster

Where are capital letters used in book titles? Circle every correct answer.

every word in the title

the first word in the title

the last word in the title

little words like of and the when they are not first or last

names of people and things

verbs

other important words, even when they are not first or last

Recognizing capitalization usage in book titles

Writing Book Titles

When you write about a book, always underline the title.

I read the book <u>Fred Goes to the Zoo</u>.

Think of a book you like. Write its title.
Remember to underline.

_____

- -

_____

Fill in the ◯ by each title that is written correctly.

◯ **<u>Cluck, Cluck, Scoot!</u>**
◯ **<u>cluck, cluck, Scoot!</u>**

◯ **The Very Long Day**
◯ **<u>The Very Long Day</u>**

◯ **<u>My Pal sal</u>**
◯ **<u>My Pal Sal</u>**

Capital Review

Rewrite each sentence correctly.

bob put on a mask.

I like the book A prince's Tale.

----

the baby horse is cute.

I want to visit alaska.

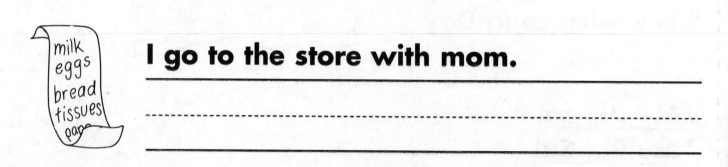

I go to the store with mom.

One Word from Two

A **compound word** is made up of two smaller words.

tug + boat = **tugboat**

Find and write two words in each **compound word**.

_____ + _____ = **sunshine**

_____ + _____ = **sailboat**

_____ + _____ = **seashell**

_____ + _____ = **starfish**

_____ + _____ = **swimsuit**

Putting Words Together

A **compound word** is made up of two smaller words.

black + bird = **blackbird**

Write a **compound word** by putting each pair of words together.

cook + book = _____

pan + cake = _____

blue + berry = _____

grape + fruit = _____

high + chair = _____

Forming compound words

Build-a-Word

Write a word from the box to finish each **compound word** below.
Then write the **compound word**.

boat	**brush**	**dog**
sand	**scare**	**fire**

_____ + **house** = _____

sail + _____ = _____

camp + _____ = _____

_____ + **box** = _____

_____ + **crow** = _____

tooth + _____ = _____

Compound Word Coloring

Use the code to color the spaces.

compound word = yellow	other word = blue

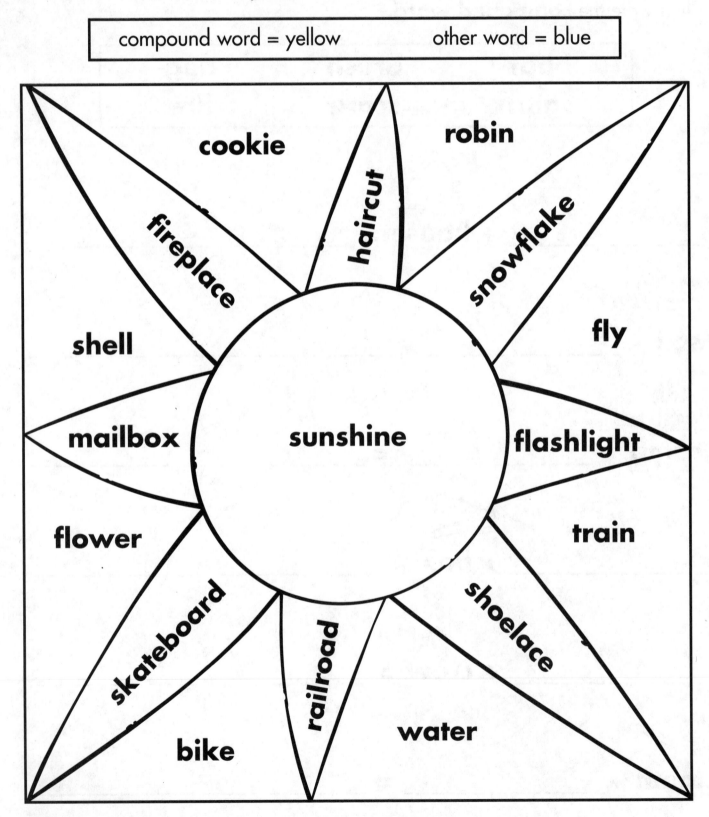

cookie

robin

haircut

fireplace

snowflake

shell

fly

mailbox

sunshine

flashlight

flower

train

skateboard

railroad

shoelace

bike

water

Reviewing compound words

Answer Key

As the child completes the pages in this section, review his or her answers. When you take the time to correct the work and explain mistakes, you're showing your child that you feel learning is important.

page 256

Words that Tell More

Some words tell more about nouns.
They are called **adjectives**.
Adjectives can answer these questions:

What kind?
fuzzy bears

How many?
two bears

What color?
white bears

Circle the **adjective** in each sentence.

This is a (pretty) flower.
It has (two) leaves.

I see (tiny) mice.
I see (three) mice.

She has (long) hair.
She has (big) eyes.

The bus is (big.)
The wheels are (black.)

256   Recognizing adjectives

page 257

In the Summertime

Adjectives tell more about nouns.

Write an **adjective** from the box to complete each sentence.

| big | two | black | four |

A **black** bird sings.
What color?

There are **four** clouds.
How many?

A **big** dog takes a nap.
What kind?

I see **two** squirrels.
How many?

Choosing adjectives to complete sentences   257

page 258

Adjective Search

Circle two **adjectives** in each sentence.

(Two) fish swim under (deep) water.

(Long) eels play by the (old) ship.

Are those (round) crabs in the (open) chest?

(One) clam sits on the (smooth) sand.

(Tall) plants grow in the (cool) sea.

(Three) (happy) seahorses play.

258   Identifying adjectives in sentences

page 259

Gardening

Circle the **adjectives** in the box.

(four) (pretty) pea (proud)
rake (neat) (two) are

Write an **adjective** from the box to complete each sentence.

works in his **pretty** garden.

He is **proud** of his garden.

It has **two** s.

grew **four** s.

The garden is **neat** and tidy.

Identifying and using adjectives   259

page 260

Adjective Time

Read the words in each row. Circle the two **adjectives** that tell about the picture.

silly   (icy)   funny   (cold)

loud   (wet)   (soft)   happy

(bright)   cool   (hot)   skinny

Write an **adjective** to complete each sentence.

Soft? Nice?
Hot? Kind?

Answers may vary.

Summer is _____.

My friend is _____.

Pets are _____.

Games are _____.

260   Adjective review

page 261

Tell About a Toy

Write the name of a toy you like in the square.
Write an **adjective** that tells about the toy in each circle.

Shape?   Feel?   Sound?

Size?   Color?   Smell?

Answers may vary.

Using a graphic organizer to plan a description   261

page 262

Write About a Toy

On page 261 you wrote **adjectives** that tell about your toy. Use them to write sentences about your toy on the lines below. Then draw a picture of your toy in the box.

The name
of my toy is

Answers may vary.

262   Writing a description

page 263

Telling it All

Some sentences tell something. They are called **statements**.
A **statement** begins with a capital letter and ends with a **period**.

capital letter

The wind is strong.

period

Circle the **statement** below.

(Rain fell all day.)
When will the rain stop?

Fill in the ○ by the **statement** that is written correctly.

○ today is a cold day.
● Today is a cold day.

● The sky is blue.
○ the sky is blue.

○ The children made a snowman
● The children made a snowman.

Recognizing statements and their usage of capital letters and periods   263

page 264

Did You Ask Me?

Some sentences ask something. They are called **questions**.
A **question** begins with a capital letter and ends with a **question mark**.

capital letter   question mark

Who is it?

Circle the **questions**.

(Where is my shoe?)
(Will you come with me?)
The cat is in the tree.

Rewrite each **question** correctly.

what is your name
What is your name?

how old are you
How old are you?

where do you live
Where do you live?

264   Recognizing questions and their usage of capital letters and question marks

page 265

Jungle Questions

Color all the **questions marks** hidden in this picture red.
Then color the rest of the picture.

Visual discrimination: identifying question marks · 265

---

page 266

Nice Ice

Every **statement** ends with a **period**.
Every **question** ends with a **question mark**.

Add a **period** or **question mark** to the end of each sentence.

The day is cold **.**

Did the lake freeze **?**

Bob has a new hat **.**

Who will win the race **?**

Can you ice skate **?**

The dog slips **.**

266 · Reviewing punctuation usage with statements and questions

---

page 267

Wow!

A sentence that shows excitement is called an **exclamation**.
Every **exclamation** begins with a capital letter and ends with an **exclamation point**.

capital letter

Watch out!

exclamation point

Circle the **exclamations** below.

(I was scared!)
What time is it?
(I see the ice cream truck!)

Ice Cream

Fill in the ○ by the **exclamation** that is written correctly.

● The soup is hot!
○ the soup is hot!

● My toe hurts!
○ My toe hurts.

● Look at the sunset!
○ look at the sunset!

Recognizing exclamations and their usage of capital letters and exclamation points · 267

---

page 268

In the Lunch Room

Add a **period**, **question mark**, or **exclamation point** to the end of each sentence.

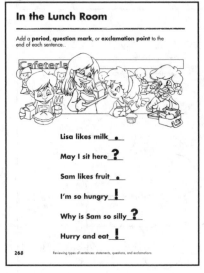

Cafeteria

Lisa likes milk **.**

May I sit here **?**

Sam likes fruit **.**

I'm so hungry **!**

Why is Sam so silly **?**

Hurry and eat **!**

268 · Reviewing types of sentences: statements, questions, and exclamations

---

page 269

Please Write!

Read this letter. Look at the names of the different parts of the letter.

Date — October 7, 2003

Greeting — Dear Grandma,

Body — You were right. I do like first grade. The kids are nice. My teacher is nice. I work hard, but it is fun. Will you come to see me soon? I hope so. I miss you.

Closing — Love, Tommy

Circle the answer.

October 7, 2003	is the	body	(date)
Love,	is the	greeting	(closing)
I miss you.	is part of the	(body)	greeting
Dear Grandma,	is the	(greeting)	closing

Understanding the parts of a letter · 269

---

page 270

Return Mail

Read this letter. Circle all the capital letters.

Date — (O)ctober 14, 2003

Greeting — (D)ear (T)ommy,

Body — (I) was happy to get your letter. (I) am so glad that you like first grade. (I) will come to see you on (S)unday. (W)e can play lots of games and bake cookies. (I)t will be fun!

Closing — (L)ove always, (G)randma

Circle all the answers that are correct.

A capital letter is used at the beginning of:

(the name of a day)   (a person's name)

(the name of the month)   (every sentence)

the year   (the greeting)   (the closing)

270 · Understanding capitalization usage in a letter

---

page 271

Friend to Friend

Read this letter and look for the **commas**.
Circle each **comma** that you find.

comma — **,**

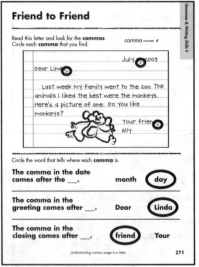

July 9**,** 2003

Dear Linda**,**

Last week my family went to the zoo. The animals I liked the best were the monkeys. Here's a picture of one. Do you like monkeys?

Your friend**,**
Ally

Circle the word that tells where each comma is.

The comma in the date comes after the ___.	month	(day)
The comma in the greeting comes after ___.	Dear	(Linda)
The comma in the closing comes after ___.	(friend)	Your

Understanding comma usage in a letter · 271

---

page 272

Letter Fix

Read this letter.
Cross out **commas** that are in the wrong places.
Write in **commas** that are missing.
Circle the letters that should be capital letters.

(d)ecember~~,~~ 2, 2003

(d)ear Lisa**,**

I am on a ski trip! (m)y family and I drove to Ski-Happy Trails last week.

I can ski down a big hill (i) can ride a rope tow back to the top. (i)t is fun!

(y)our friend**,**
Jane~~,~~

272 · Reviewing punctuation and capitalization in a letter

---

page 273

Proper Nouns Use Capitals

A **proper noun** is the name of a specific person, place, or thing.
Your name is a **proper noun**.

Every **proper noun** begins with a capital letter.

United States   June

Underline the **proper noun** in each sentence that is not written correctly.

The train goes to <u>boston</u>.

<u>maria</u> ran home.

I was born on <u>June</u> 2, 1997.

This man lives in <u>japan</u>.

My cat's name is <u>misty</u>.

<u>ken</u> has a red bike.

Recognizing proper nouns and their use of capitalization · 273

---

284   Answers

page 274

Start with a Capital

The first word in a sentence always begins with a capital letter.

__This__ pig is fat.   __The__ store is open.

Rewrite each sentence correctly.

cake is yummy.

Cake is yummy.

use a pen to write.

Use a pen to write.

bill digs a hole.

Bill digs a hole.

the pin is sharp!

The pin is sharp!

my fish's name is goldy.

My fish's name is Goldy.

page 275

Titles Need Capitals

Read the title of this book. Color the capital letters red. Color the other letters yellow. Then color the rest of the book cover.

Pat at Bat

COACH

page 276

Book List

Read the list of books. Circle each capital letter.

(O)gle and (M)oogle

(H)ow to (T)alk to a (M)artian

(A) (D)ay in the (L)ife of a (S)lime (M)onster

Where are capital letters used in book titles? Circle every correct answer.

every word in the title

(the first word in the title)

(the last word in the title)

little words like **of** and **the** when they are not first or last

(names of people and things)

(verbs)

(other important words, even when they are not first or last)

page 277

Writing Book Titles

When you write about a book, always underline the title.

I read the book Fred Goes to the Zoo.

Think of a book you like. Write its title.
Remember to underline.

_____ **Answers may vary.** _____

Fill in the ○ by each title that is written correctly.

● **Cluck, Cluck, Scoot!**
○ cluck, cluck, Scoot!

○ The Very Long Day
● **The Very Long Day**

○ My Pal sal
● **My Pal Sal**

page 278

Capital Review

Rewrite each sentence correctly.

bob put on a mask.

Bob put on a mask.

I like the book A prince's Tale.

I like the book __A Prince's Tale.__

the baby horse is cute.

The baby horse is cute.

I want to visit alaska.

I want to visit Alaska.

I go to the store with mom.

I go to the store with Mom.

page 279

One Word from Two

A **compound word** is made up of two smaller words.

tug + boat = **tugboat**

Find and write two words in each **compound word**.

__sun__ + __shine__ = sunshine

__sail__ + __boat__ = sailboat

__sea__ + __shell__ = seashell

__star__ + __fish__ = starfish

__swim__ + __suit__ = swimsuit

page 280

Putting Words Together

A **compound word** is made up of two smaller words.

black + bird = **blackbird**

Write a **compound word** by putting each pair of words together.

cook + book = **cookbook**

pan + cake = **pancake**

blue + berry = **blueberr**

grape + fruit = **grapefruit**

high + chair = **highchair**

page 281

Build-a-Word

Write a word from the box to finish each **compound word** below. Then write the **compound word**.

boat	brush	dog
sand	scare	fire

dog + house = **doghouse**

sail + **boat** = **sailboat**

camp + **fire** = **campfire**

sand + box = **sandbox**

scare + crow = **scarecrow**

tooth + **brush** = **toothbrush**

page 282

Compound Word Coloring

Use the code to color the spaces.

| compound word = yellow | other word = blue |

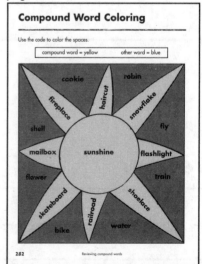

Answers

285

Under the Sea

Read each color word and then rewrite it. Use the number next to each color word to color the picture.

red   **1**

_____

- - - - - - - - - - - - - - - - - - -

_____

green   **2**

_____

- - - - - - - - - - - - - - - - - - -

_____

blue   **3**

_____

- - - - - - - - - - - - - - - - - - -

_____

yellow   **4**

_____

- - - - - - - - - - - - - - - - - - -

_____

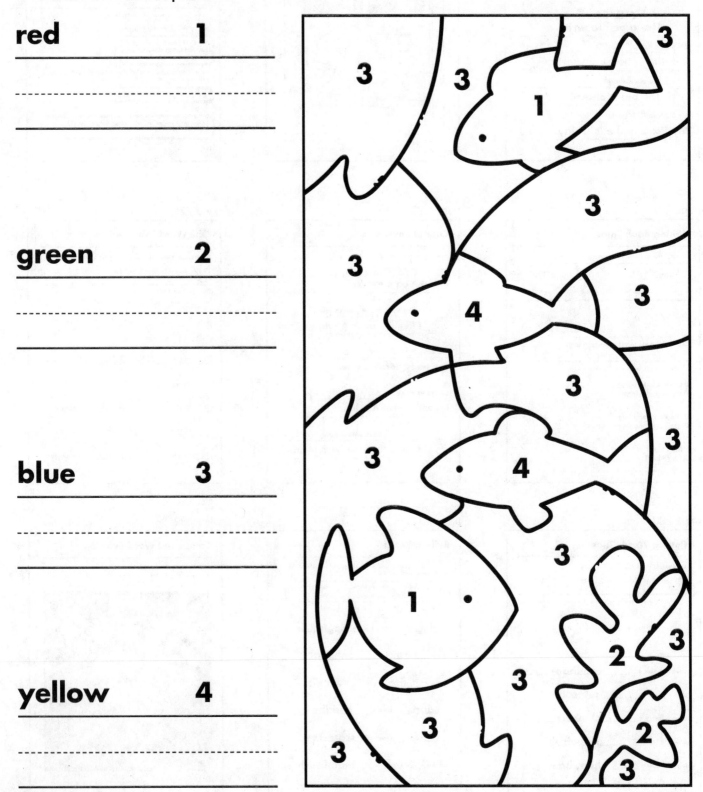

    Recognizing and writing color words

A Colorful House

Read each color word and then rewrite it. Use the number next to each color word to color the picture.

orange   **1**

brown   **2**

black   **3**

purple   **4**

Recognizing and writing color words

Words to Know—People

Read the word under each picture.

girl   boy   mother   father

Write the name of each picture.

Reading and writing commonly used nouns: people

Words to Know—Animals

Read the word under each picture.

cat   **dog**   **fish**   **bird**

Write one of the words above to complete each sentence.

_____

My _____ **chews bones.**

_____

My _____ **has a long tail.**

_____

My _____ **sings a song.**

_____

My _____ **swims in water.**

Words to Know—School Tools

Read the word under each picture.

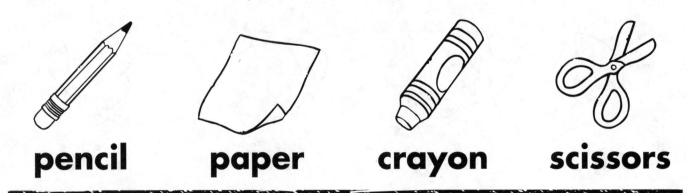

pencil **paper** **crayon** **scissors**

Write the name of each picture.

Reading and writing commonly used nouns: school supplies

Words to Know—Directions

Read the word under each picture.

cut   **color**   **write**   **draw**

1. What do we cut paper with? Draw its picture in Box 1.
2. Color the bird in Box 2.
3. Write **OK** in Box 3.
4. Draw a 🌷 in Box 4.

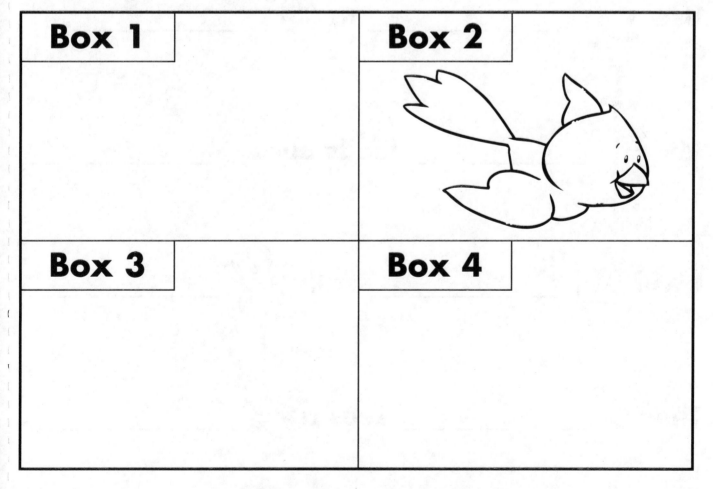

Box 1

Box 2

Box 3

Box 4

Words To Know Review

Write two words from the box to complete each sentence.

| mother | fish | bird | cut | scissors |
| boy | father | write | draw | pencil |

My _____ likes to _____ .

Use a _____ to _____ .

My _____ feeds our _____ .

I will _____ with _____ .

The _____ sees a _____ .

Reviewing commonly used nouns and verbs

Which House is Mine?

Each girl is saying something. The missing words are on her house. Write the correct words to complete the sentences.

My cat is _____ .

She has a pink _____ .

nose
cute

I _____ ice cream.

It is good with _____ .

cake
like

Dad will _____ home soon.

Then we will _____ .

play
be

Completing sentences with words involving long vowel sounds

Goldilocks and the Three Bears, Part 1

Fill in the missing words in the story and then read it aloud.

Mother Bear

Goldilocks

Father Bear

Baby Bear

The _____ **(had, hid)** a little

_____ **(in, on)** the woods.

One day _____ **(Mother, mixer)** Bear

said, "I will _____ **(fax, fix)** a ⌣ for you."

But the ⌣ was too _____ **(hit, hot)**. So the

_____ **(went, want)** for a walk.

A little _____ **(green, girl)** named Goldilocks

was _____ **(last, lost)** in the woods. Goldilocks

saw the 🏠 and went _____ **(in, on)**.

Reading a story and supplying missing words

Goldilocks and the Three Bears, Part 2

Goldilocks _____ **(sat, sot)** in Baby Bear's

. She was too _____ **(bag, big)**

for the and _____ **(at, it)** broke.

Goldilocks saw the that was _____

(sat, set) out to cool. She ate _____ **(all, ill)** of

Baby Bear's ! Then she laid _____

(down, duck) on Baby Bear's _____ **(bad, bed)**.

The came _____ **(back, buck)**.

They saw the and the . Baby Bear was

_____ **(sad, sod)**. His _____ **(dad, did)**

was _____ **(mud, mad)**.

Then the saw Goldilocks

_____ **(and, end)** she saw them. Goldilocks

jumped _____ **(up, us)** and ran away—

_____ **(fast, fist)**!

The _____ **(End, And)**!

Real or Not?

A story that tells about things that could really happen is called **realistic**. A story that tells about things that could not happen and are make-believe is called a **fantasy**.

Look at each picture. If it shows something happening that could be real, circle **R** for **realistic**. If it shows something happening that is only make-believe, circle **F** for **fantasy**. Then color the pictures.

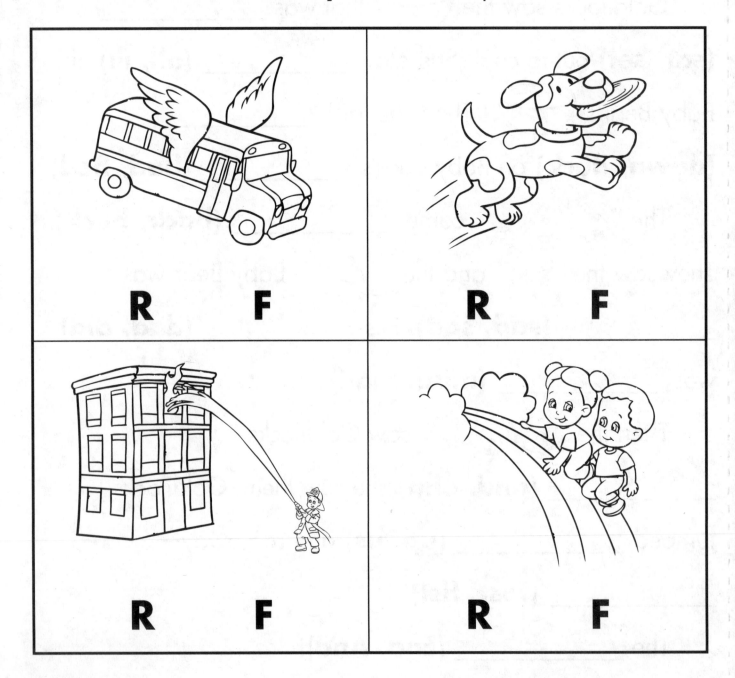

R   F   R   F

R   F   R   F

    Discriminating between reality and fantasy

Believe It or Not!

The picture below shows the beginning of a story. Color it.

Think about how you would finish the story and draw three more pictures to show what would happen next.

You can make your story **realistic** or you can make it a **fantasy**.

Which kind of story did you make? Circle one.

realistic   **fantasy**

Discriminating between reality and fantasy

Order Please!

The pictures in each row tell a story, but they are out of order.
Put them in order by numbering them **1**, **2**, and **3**. Then color the pictures.

Understanding story sequence

Out of Order

These pictures tell a story, but they are out of order. Number them from **1** to **6** to show the correct order. Then color the pictures and tell the story aloud.

A Walk in the Woods

Read the story.

   Dan took a walk in the woods. First he saw a bird. Then he saw a deer. Next he saw a bunny. Then Dan saw a skunk, and he ran away!

The pictures show the **events** in the story. The **events** are the things that happen in the story. Number the **events** in order from **1** to **4**. Then color the pictures.

Understanding story sequence

A Surprise Box

Read each sentence and draw a line to its matching picture. Then number the **events** in order from **1** to **4**.

☐ Kate finds a box.

☐ Kate puts the hat on.

☐ Kate opens the box.

☐ Kate sees a hat in the box.

That's the Idea!

The **main idea** of a story is its most important idea.

Each row of pictures tells a story. Underline the sentence that tells the **main idea** of each story.

The party was fun.

No one had fun at the party.

Jake wore a party hat.

The cake was big.

The kittens were white.

The kittens were small.

Sue gave away three kittens.

Sue kept three kittens.

Identifying the main idea of a story told in pictures

What Does Not Belong?

The pictures below tell more about a **main idea**. Cross out the picture that does not belong in each group.

Identifying pictures that do not relate to the main idea

What's the Main Idea?

The **main idea** is the most important idea.

Circle the **main idea** of each picture.

The giant is nice.

The giant eats a lot.

The clown is sad.

The clown is funny.

We have lots of fruit.

We have no fruit.

My friend moved away.

My friend has short hair.

Identifying main ideas

Choosing the Main Idea

Read each story. Circle the sentence that tells the **main idea**.

It is raining. Ann puts on boots. She puts on a raincoat. She puts on a hat. Now she is ready.

Ann dresses for a rainy day.

Ann takes a long time to dress.

The house is old. It needs new paint. The windows are broken. The door is loose. The roof has holes.

The house is old but nice.

The old house needs to be fixed.

Fun on the Farm

Look closely at the picture and then circle the answer to each question.

Which animal is asleep?

cow

cat

Where is the nest?

on a branch

in the barn

How many eggs are in the nest?

two

four

Where do flowers grow?

by the fence

by the barn

Where is the bird?

on the roof

in the air

What is by the fence?

dog

cow

Recalling picture details

A Beautiful Day

Look closely at the picture and then circle the answer to each question.

What is in the tree?

bird

cat

Who is on the slide?

girl

boy

What is the boy wearing?

a jacket

a hat

Who has a balloon?

boy

mother

Where is the bench?

by a tree

by a pond

Who is on the bench?

mother

girl

Story Memory

Read the story.

    Jim has three dogs. The names of the dogs are Tip, Jed and Bud.
    Tip likes meat. Jed likes bones. Bud likes to play ball.
    Jim gives Tip meat. He gives Jed a bone. He plays ball with Bud.
    The dogs love Jim. Jim loves his dogs.

Circle the answer to each question.

What does Bud like to do?

play ball	eat meat

What does Jim give Jed?

a bone	a ball

The names of the dogs are Jed, Bud and _____.

Jim	Tip

        Recalling details in a story

Details, Details

A **detail** is a fact that tells more about the **main idea**.

Look for **details** as you read this short story.

> **This is my cat, Tiger. He has soft fur. He has stripes. He has a long tail. He sleeps on my bed at night. He purrs in my ear to wake me up. He is a good friend.**

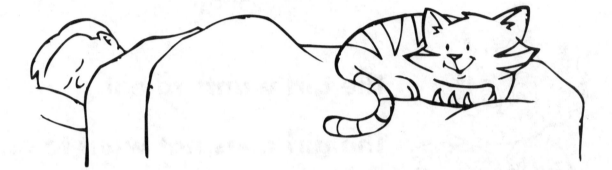

Circle the answers.

What is the name of the cat?	**Tiger** **Kitty**
What is his fur like?	**rough** **soft**
What is his tail like?	**long** **short**
Where does he sleep?	**on the bed** **in a box**

Using Picture Clues

Use the picture clues to guess what is happening. Circle the guess that fits the clues.

The boy won a race.

The boy lost a race.

The girl wants to eat.

The girl does not want to eat.

It is quiet.

There is a loud noise.

Sam ate some jelly.

Sam did not eat jelly.

Making inferences using visual clues

Picture Detective

Use the picture clues to guess what is happening. Circle the guess that fits the clues.

This girl likes carrots.

This girl does not like carrots.

Today is windy.

There is no wind today.

The bag is heavy.

The bag is light.

The team just lost the game.

The team just won the game.

Use Your Head

First look at the picture on the left of each row. Then look at the picture on the right. Circle the sentence that tells what most likely happened between the pictures.

The girl did not hit the ball.

The girl hit the ball into the window.

The sun came out.

It got colder.

The branch broke off.

The boy cut the branch off.

Drawing conclusions

A Day At School

Look at the picture and read about what is happening.

The boys and girls are at school.
Nell cuts paper. Ted colors with a crayon.
Ben writes with a pencil. Jill draws a fish.

Now that you have looked at the picture and read about it, circle all the answers you think are true.

The boys and girls work well in school.

The boys and girls do not work hard.

The boys and girls are sad.

The boys and girls are happy.

The teacher is proud of them.

The teacher is not proud of them.

What Comes Next?

It is fun to guess what will happen next in a story. To guess well, you need to think about all the clues.

These pictures tell part of a story. Use the picture clues to guess what will happen next.

Draw a picture of what you guessed.

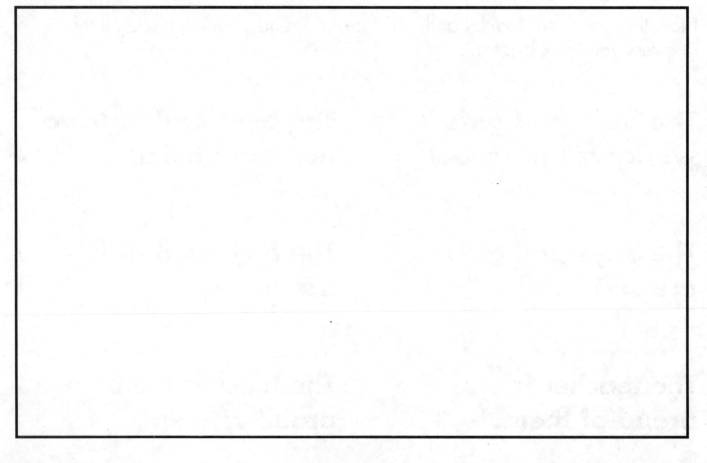

Predicting outcomes

What Will Happen Next?

Read this part of a story. Think about what might happen next.

The puppy has been told many times not to sit on the new chair. But one day he is home alone. He wants to take a nap. The chair looks so soft.

Draw a picture of what you think will happen next.

Write about what you think will happen next.

_____

- -

_____

_____

- -

_____

Why Did This Happen?

A **cause** is the reason why something happens.
An **effect** is what happens.

 **Cause:** ⟶ **Effect:**
Jenny gave her   The flower
flower water.   grew tall
and strong.

Draw a line to match each **cause** with its **effect**.

CAUSE   ## EFFECT

 **Bear was hungry.**   **He got a sunburn.**

Bear was tired.   **He ate a big meal.**

 **Bear sat in the sun.**   **He got lost.**

 **Bear went far away.**   **He went to bed.**

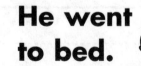

Understanding cause and effect

Be a Detective!

Look at the picture. Use the clues to discover **causes** and **effects**.

Draw a line between each **effect** and its **cause**.

EFFECT   ## CAUSE

The boy runs.   **She is sleepy.**

The girl is mad.   **He is getting a present.**

The baby yawns.   **She fell into the pond.**

The man smiles.   **He is being chased
                             by bees.**

Understanding cause and effect   **317**

Answer Key

As the child completes the pages in this section, review his or her answers. When you take the time to correct the work and explain mistakes, you're showing your child that you feel learning is important.

page 286

Under the Sea

Read each color word and then rewrite it. Use the number next to each color word to color the picture.

red   1
red

green   2
green

blue   3
blue

yellow   4
yellow

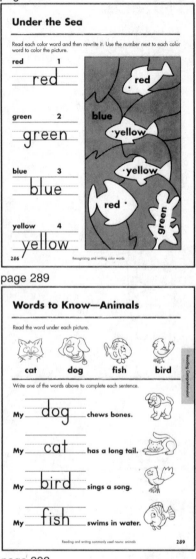

286   Recognizing and writing color words

page 287

A Colorful House

Read each color word and then rewrite it. Use the number next to each color word to color the picture.

orange   1
orange

brown   2
brown

black   3
black

purple   4
purple

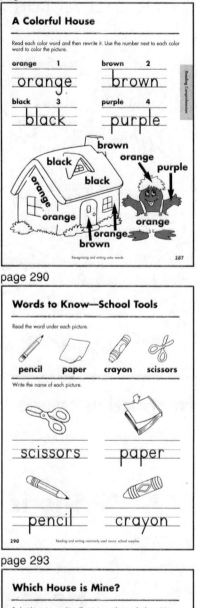

Recognizing and writing color words   287

page 288

Words to Know—People

Read the word under each picture.

girl   boy   mother   father

Write the name of each picture.

boy   *mother*

father   *girl*

288   Reading and writing commonly used nouns: people

page 289

Words to Know—Animals

Read the word under each picture.

cat   dog   fish   bird

Write one of the words above to complete each sentence.

My **dog** chews bones.

My **cat** has a long tail.

My **bird** sings a song.

My **fish** swims in water.

Reading and writing commonly used nouns: animals   289

page 290

Words to Know—School Tools

Read the word under each picture.

pencil   paper   crayon   scissors

Write the name of each picture.

scissors   *paper*

pencil   *crayon*

290   Reading and writing commonly used nouns: school supplies

page 291

Words to Know—Directions

Read the word under each picture.

cut   color   write   draw

1. What do we cut paper with? Draw its picture in Box 1.
2. Color the bird in Box 2.
3. Write **OK** in Box 3.
4. Draw a 🌸 in Box 4.

Box 1	Box 2
✂	🐦
Box 3	Box 4
OK	🌼

Reading and writing commonly used verbs in school activities   291

page 292

Words To Know Review

Write two words from the box to complete each sentence.

mother	fish	bird	cut	scissors
boy	father	write	draw	pencil

My **father** likes to **draw**.

Use a **pencil** to **write**.

My **mother** feeds our **fish**.

I will **cut** with **scissors**.

The **boy** sees a **bird**.

292   Reviewing commonly used nouns and verbs

page 293

Which House is Mine?

Each girl is saying something. The missing words are on her house. Write the correct words to complete the sentences.

My cat is **cute**.
She has a pink **nose**.
     nose / cute

I **like** ice cream.
It is good with **cake**.
     cake / like

Dad will **be** home soon.
Then we will **play**.
     play / be

Completing sentences with words involving long vowel sounds   293

page 294

Goldilocks and the Three Bears, Part 1

Fill in the missing words in the story and then read it aloud.

Mother Bear   Goldilocks
Father Bear   Baby Bear

The **had** (had, hid) a little
in (in, on) the woods.
One day **Mother** (Mother, mixer) Bear
said, "I will **fix** (fax, fix) a 🥣 for you."
But the was too **hot** (hit, hot). So the
went (went, want) for a walk.
A little **girl** (green, girl) named Goldilocks
was **lost** (last, lost) in the woods. Goldilocks
saw the 🏠 and went **in** (in, on).

294   Reading a story and supplying missing words

Goldilocks and the Three Bears, Part 2

Goldilocks **sat** (sat, sot) in Baby Bear's
. She was too **big** (bag, big)
for the and **it** (at, it) broke.
Goldilocks saw the that was **set**
(sat, **set**) out to cool. She ate **all** (all, ill) of
Baby Bear's ! Then she laid **down**
(down, duck) on Baby Bear's **bed** (bad, bed).
The came **back** (back, buck).
They saw the and the . Baby Bear was
sad (sad, sod). His **dad** (dad, did)
was **mad** (mud, mad).
Then the saw Goldilocks
and (and, end) she saw them. Goldilocks
jumped **up** (up, us) and ran away—
fast (fast, fist)!
The **End** (End, And)!

Reading a story and supplying missing words   295

Real or Not?

A story that tells about things that could really happen is called **realistic**.
A story that tells about things that could not happen and are make-believe is
called a **fantasy**.

Look at each picture. If it shows something happening that could be real,
circle **R** for **realistic**. If it shows something happening that is only
make-believe, circle **F** for **fantasy**. Then color the pictures.

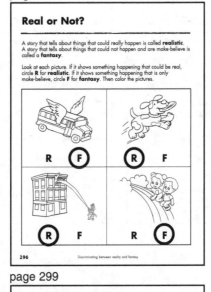

R (F)   (R) F

(R) F   R (F)

296   Discriminating between reality and fantasy

Believe It or Not!

The picture below shows the beginning of a story. Color it.

Think about how you would finish the story and draw three more pictures to
show what would happen next.

You can make your story **realistic** or you can make it a **fantasy**.

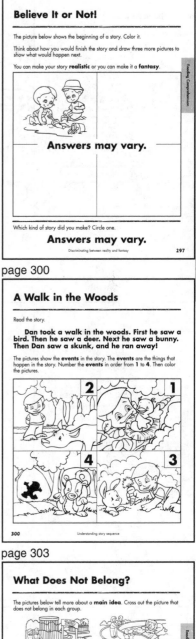

Answers may vary.

Which kind of story did you make? Circle one.

Answers may vary.

Discriminating between reality and fantasy   297

Reading Comprehension

Order Please!

The pictures in each row tell a story, but they are out of order.
Put them in order by numbering them **1**, **2**, and **3**. Then color the pictures.

298   Understanding story sequence

Out of Order

These pictures tell a story, but they are out of order. Number them from **1** to
6 to show the correct order. Then color the pictures and tell the story aloud.

Understanding story sequence   299

A Walk in the Woods

Read the story.

Dan took a walk in the woods. First he saw a
bird. Then he saw a deer. Next he saw a bunny.
Then Dan saw a skunk, and he ran away!

The pictures show the **events** in the story. The **events** are the things that
happen in the story. Number the **events** in order from **1** to **4**. Then color
the pictures.

300   Understanding story sequence

A Surprise Box

Read each sentence and draw a line to its matching picture. Then number
the **events** in order from **1** to **4**.

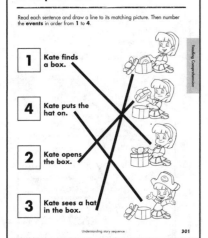

1 Kate finds a box.

4 Kate puts the hat on.

2 Kate opens the box.

3 Kate sees a hat in the box.

Understanding story sequence   301

That's the Idea!

The **main idea** of a story is its most important idea.

Each row of pictures tells a story. Underline the sentence that tells the
main idea of each story.

The party was fun.   Jake wore a party hat.

No one had fun at the party.   The cake was big.

The kittens were white.   <u>Sue gave away three kittens.</u>

The kittens were small.   Sue kept three kittens.

302   Identifying the main idea of a story told in pictures

What Does Not Belong?

The pictures below tell more about a **main idea**. Cross out the picture that
does not belong in each group.

Identifying pictures that do not relate to the main idea   303

Reading Comprehension

page 304

What's the Main Idea?

The **main idea** is the most important idea.

Circle the **main idea** of each picture.

The giant is nice.
The giant eats a lot.

The clown is sad.
The clown is funny.

We have lots of fruit.
We have no fruit.

My friend moved away.
My friend has short hair.

304   Identifying main ideas

page 305

Choosing the Main Idea

Read each story. Circle the sentence that tells the **main idea**.

It is raining. Ann puts on boots. She puts on a raincoat. She puts on a hat. Now she is ready.

Ann dresses for a rainy day.
Ann takes a long time to dress.

The house is old. It needs new paint. The windows are broken. The door is loose. The roof has holes.

The house is old but nice.
The old house needs to be fixed.

Identifying the main idea of a paragraph   305

page 306

Fun on the Farm

Look closely at the picture and then circle the answer to each question.

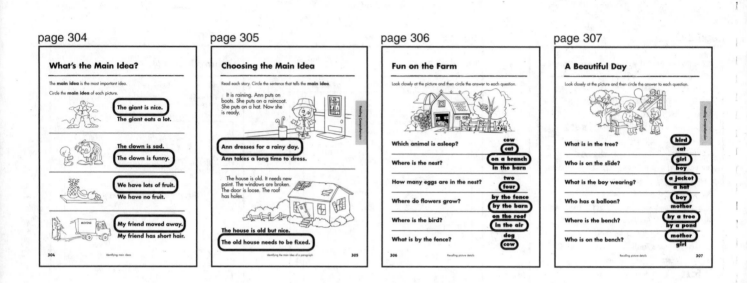

Which animal is asleep?   cow / **cat**

Where is the nest?   **on a branch** / in the barn

How many eggs are in the nest?   two / **four**

Where do flowers grow?   by the fence / **by the barn**

Where is the bird?   on the roof / **in the air**

What is by the fence?   dog / **cow**

306   Recalling picture details

page 307

A Beautiful Day

Look closely at the picture and then circle the answer to each question.

What is in the tree?   **bird** / cat

Who is on the slide?   **girl** / boy

What is the boy wearing?   **a jacket** / a hat

Who has a balloon?   **boy** / mother

Where is the bench?   **by a tree** / by a pond

Who is on the bench?   **mother** / girl

Recalling picture details   307

page 308

Story Memory

Read the story.

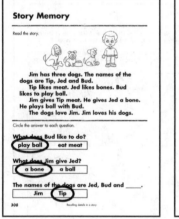

Jim has three dogs. The names of the dogs are Tip, Jed and Bud. Tip likes meat. Jed likes bones. Bud likes to play ball.
Jim gives Tip meat. He gives Jed a bone. He plays ball with Bud.
The dogs love Jim. Jim loves his dogs.

Circle the answer to each question.

What does Bud like to do?
play ball   eat meat

What does Jim give Jed?
a bone   a ball

The names of the dogs are Jed, Bud and _____.
Jim   **Tip**

308   Recalling details in a story

page 309

Details, Details

A **detail** is a fact that tells more about the **main idea**.

Look for **details** as you read this short story.

This is my cat, Tiger. He has soft fur. He has stripes. He has a long tail. He sleeps on my bed at night. He purrs in my ear to wake me up. He is a good friend.

Circle the answers.

What is the name of the cat?   **Tiger** / Kitty

What is his fur like?   rough / **soft**

What is his tail like?   **long** / short

Where does he sleep?   **on the bed** / in a box

Recognizing details in reading   309

page 310

Using Picture Clues

Use the picture clues to guess what is happening. Circle the guess that fits the clues.

The boy won a race.
The boy lost a race.

The girl wants to eat.
The girl does not want to eat.

It is quiet.
There is a loud noise.

Sam ate some Jelly.
Sam did not eat Jelly.

310   Making inferences using visual clues

page 311

Picture Detective

Use the picture clues to guess what is happening. Circle the guess that fits the clues.

This girl likes carrots.
This girl does not like carrots.

Today is windy.
There is no wind today.

The bag is heavy.
The bag is light.

The team just lost the game.
The team just won the game.

Making inferences using visual clues   311

page 314: Answers may vary.

page 315: Answers may vary.

page 312

Use Your Head

First look at the picture on the left of each row. Then look at the picture on the right. Circle the sentence that tells what most likely happened between the pictures.

The girl did not hit the ball.
The girl hit the ball into the window.

The sun came out.
It got colder.

The branch broke off.
The boy cut the branch off.

312   Drawing conclusions

page 313

A Day At School

Look at the picture and read about what is happening.

The boys and girls are at school. Nell cuts paper. Ted colors with a crayon. Ben writes with a pencil. Jill draws a fish.

Now that you have looked at the picture and read about it, circle all the answers you think are true.

The boys and girls work well in school.
The boys and girls do not work hard.

The boys and girls are sad.
The boys and girls are happy.

The teacher is proud of them.
The teacher is not proud of them.

Drawing conclusions   313

page 316

Why Did This Happen?

A **cause** is the reason why something happens. An **effect** is what happens.

Cause: Jenny gave her flower water. — Effect: The flower grew tall.

Draw a line to match each **cause** with its effect.

CAUSE	EFFECT
Bear was hungry.	He got a sunburn.
Bear was tired.	He ate a big meal.
Bear sat in the sun.	He got lost.
Bear went far away.	He went to bed.

316   Understanding cause and effect

page 317

Be a Detective!

Look at the picture. Use the clues to discover **causes** and **effects**.

Draw a line between each **effect** and its **cause**.

EFFECT	CAUSE
The boy runs.	She is sleepy.
The girl is mad.	He is getting a present.
The baby yawns.	She fell into the pond.
The man smiles.	He is being chased by bees.

Understanding cause and effect   317